WATERFALL
LOVER'S GUIDE
PACIFIC NORTHWEST

Well-written and superbly organized . . . This is a reference book that you will rely on to make any trip to the Pacific Northwest a treasure trove of finding new waterfalls . . . If you have any of Plumb's earlier editions, this one is worthwhile for the new falls it includes.

—Deseret Morning News

This trusty waterfall guide gets better each time it comes out . . . Plumb knows the Northwest's falling water better than anyone.

—Oregonian

A good resource for locating [waterfalls] throughout the Northwest.

—Bellingham Weekly

This book is an easy-to-use reference for anybody who is as crazy about waterfalls as Plumb.

—Idaho Falls Post Register

A useful and accurate guide.

—Salem Statesman-Journal

If you like your water a frothy white, you'll like *Waterfall Lover's Guide to the Pacific Northwest* . . . This book will help readers find the waterfalls and all of those things that spur them to seek that beauty in the first place.

—Bend Bulletin

An excellent, no-nonsense guide that includes waterfalls near and far.

—Klamath Falls Herald and News

WATERFALL LOVER'S GUIDE

PACIFIC NORTHWEST

Fourth Edition

GREGORY A. PLUMB

**Where to Find
Hundreds of
Spectacular
Waterfalls in
Washington,
Oregon, and
Idaho**

THE MOUNTAINEERS BOOKS

THIS BOOK IS DEDICATED TO ROBIN, COREY, SAVANAH, AND JARRETT.

THE MOUNTAINEERS BOOKS
*is the nonprofit publishing arm of The Mountaineers Club,
an organization founded in 1906 and dedicated to the exploration,
preservation, and enjoyment of outdoor and wilderness areas.*

1001 SW Klickitat Way, Suite 201, Seattle, WA 98134

First edition 1983. Second edition 1989. Third edition 1998. Fourth edition:
first printing 2005, second printing 2006, third printing 2007, fourth printing
2009

Manufactured in the United States of America

Edited by Paula Thurman
Maps by the author
Cover, book design, and layout by Mayumi Thompson
All photographs taken and prepared for publication by the author unless
otherwise noted.
Cover photograph: *Columbia Gorge* © James Martin
Frontispiece photograph: *Tunnel Falls, The Columbia Gorge*

Library of Congress Cataloging-in-Publication Data
Plumb, Gregory Alan, 1956-
  A waterfall lover's guide to the Pacific Northwest : where to find hundreds of
spectacular waterfalls in Washington, Oregon, and Idaho / by Gregory
Plumb.— 4th ed.
      p. cm.
  Includes bibliographical references and index.
  ISBN 0-89886-911-0
  1. Hiking—Northwest, Pacific—Guidebooks. 2. Waterfalls—Northwest,
Pacific. 3. Northwest, Pacific—Guidebooks. I. Title.
  GV199.42.N68P58 2004
  917.9504'44—dc22
                                                    2004027247
♻ Printed on recycled paper
ISBN 10: 0-89886-911-0
ISBN 13: 978-0-89886-911-8

CONTENTS

Bold indicates 5-star area

WATERFALLS QUICK-REFERENCE CHART

The numerals in the boxes on this chart represent the total number of falls within each region and falls area that include the features noted in the first row.

Region / Falls Area	Total Falls	★★★★★	★★★★	★★★	★★	★	Plunge	Horsetail	Fan	Punchbowl	Block	Tiered	Segmented	Cascades	Auto	Hike (Easy – Fairly Easy)	Hike (Moderate–Hard)	Backpack	Bushhack	Watercraft	4W Drive
NORTH CASCADES, WA	82	4	9	20	34	15	8	12	6	3	2	16	8	10	29	19	22	4	9	5	0
1 Snoqualmie	1	1					1								1						
2 North Bend	4		1		3			1	1			2		1	1		3				
3 Taylor River	3			2		1		1		1		1		1	1		3				
4 Snoqualmie Pass	3			1	1	1	1					1		1	1		2				
5 Stampede Pass	2		1	1			1	1								2					
6 Leavenworth	1				1			1				1			1						
7 Lake Wenatchee	2			1		1			1				1			2					
8 Stevens Pass	3				3	1							1	2	1	2			1		
9 Alpine Lakes	5		1			4						1		1		2	3				
10 Index	4		1	1	1	1		1				1		1	3		1	1			
11 Gold Bar	1	1													1						
12 Granite Falls	2			1	1	1								1	1		1		1		
13 Robe Valley	4			2	2	2			1			1			1	3	1				
14 Twin Falls Lake	1		1				1	1													
15 Boulder River	2			1	1	1		1							1	1					
16 Sauk River	2		1		1	1										1					
17 Suiattle River	3			1	1	1		1						1	1				2		
18 Sauk Valley	1				1							1							1		

Region / Falls Area	Total Falls	★★★★★	★★★★	★★★	★★	★	Plunge	Horsetail	Fan	Punchbowl	Block	Tiered	Segmented	Cascades	Auto	Hike (Easy - Fairly Easy)	Hike (Moderate-Hard)	Backpack	Bushwhack	Watercraft	4W Drive
19 Mount Baker	1			1			1								1						
20 Bellingham	2			1	1							1	1			2					
21 Maple Falls	1				1		1					1		1		1			1		
22 Nooksack River	3		1		2								1		2						
23 North Cascades Natl Pk	8		1	3	4		1		1			1	4	1	4	1	4	4			
24 Ross Lake	9			4	5		1	3				4			7	1				1	
25 Rainy Pass	1		1									1									
26 Methow Valley	2			1		1		1				1	1				1		1		
27 Winthrop	3			1	2			1	1			1		1	1		1		1		
28 Foggy Dew Creek	1				1																
29 Lake Chelan	4	1			2	1						1	1							4	
30 Entiat Valley	3			1	2			1	1		2				3	1					
OLYMPICS, WA	**33**	**0**	**3**	**5**	**14**	**11**	**0**	**8**	**1**	**4**	**1**	**6**	**2**	**1**	**9**	**11**	**7**	**2**	**2**	**3**	**0**
1 Orcas Island	4				1	3			1							4					
2 Elwha	2			1				2							1		1				
3 Mount Carrie	2				2			1				1			1		2				
4 Lake Crescent	1		1														1				
5 Soleduck	1			1																	
6 Beaver Creek	1			1												1			1		
7 Clallam Bay	5				1	4				1									1		
8 Olympic Coast	1				1			1					1				1			3	
9 Enchanted Valley	1		1									1				1		1			
10 Quilcene	1				1			1							1						

Location	Total
11 Dosewallips	2
12 Lake Cushman	1
13 Wynoochee Lake	2
14 Shelton	1
15 Kamilche	1
16 Olympia	4
17 Porter	2
18 Rainbow Falls State Park	1
MOUNT RAINIER, WA	**65**
1 Carbon River	6
2 Mowich Lake	1
3 Eatonville	3
4 Big Creek	2
5 Nisqually River	9
6 Paradise	6
7 Stevens Canyon	7
8 Upper Ohanapecosh	3
9 Chinook Creek	6
10 Cayuse Pass	2
11 Camp Sheppard	3
12 Rainier Valley	2
13 Naches	3
14 Rimrock Lake	4
15 Lower Ohahapecosh	5
16 Johnson Creek	1
17 Silverbrook	2
GIFFORD PINCHOT COUNTRY, WA	**62**
1 North Fork Cispus River	10
2 North Saint Helens	3
3 Kalama River Road	2

Region / Falls Area	Total Falls	★★★★★	★★★★	★★★	★★	★	Plunge	Horsetail	Fan	Punchbowl	Block	Tiered	Segmented	Cascades	Auto	Hike (Easy – Fairly Easy)	Hike (Moderate – Hard)	Backpack	Bushwhack	Watercraft	4W Drive
4 Lake Merwin	3				3		1	2							1	2			1	1	
5 Kalama Falls	1				1					1						1				1	
6 South Saint Helens	7		1	3	3		2					5				2	5		1		
7 Eagle Cliff	6		3	1	2		3				5	1				5					
8 Lewis River	8		1	2	5		1			1	1	1		1	2	2	4				
9 Chelatchie	8		1	1	4	2	1	1		2	2	1				1	8				
10 East Fork Lewis River	5	1		1	2										4						
11 Wind River Road	3	1					1		1			1	1			1	1		2		
12 Trout Lake	2		1													1			1		
13 Mount Adams	3			1	2			1				1	1		2		2				
14 Glenwood	1	1					1								1						
INLAND EMPIRE, WA	**30**	**1**	**4**	**5**	**12**	**8**	**1**	**3**	**3**	**2**	**3**	**6**	**1**	**2**	**16**	**8**	**3**	**0**	**4**	**3**	**0**
1 Spokane	4		1		3		1							1	1	3					
2 Spokane Indian Reservation	2														2						
3 Boundary Dam	1		1					1					1	1		1				1	
4 Park Rapids	1		1												1				1		
5 Colville	3			1	1	1			1			1			2	1					
6 Kettle Falls	2		1	1					1		1	1			2	1	2				
7 Northport	2								1	1											
8 Franklin D. Roosevelt Lake	2				1			2							1						
9 Sherman Creek	2							2				1			2				1	2	
10 Conconully	1																1		1		
11 St. Mary's	1											1							1		

	Total																					
12 Nespelem	3						1			1				1		2		2			1	2
13 Coulee City	2	1				1				1						2		1				2
14 Rock Creek Coulee	1		1				1			1						1		1				1
15 Palouse Canyon	3	1	1		1	1										3		1				3
COLUMBIA GORGE, WA/OR	**71**	**6**	**17**	**27**	**16**	**12**	**14**	**2**	**6**	**3**	**3**	**11**	**2**	**5**	**2**	**21**	**15**	**2**	**32**	**2**	**6**	**0**	**0**
1 Bridal Veil	5	1	2	2	1	2	1					2				2	1		2			2	
2 Multnomah Falls	9	1	1	2	4	2	1				1		1			3	3		7				
3 Oneonta Gorge	5	1	2	1		1	3						1	1		1	1		3	1			
4 Yeon State Park	2	1	1		1		1					1		1		1			1				
5 Tanner Creek	3	1		1	1			1				1				1	3						
6 Eagle Creek	14	2	2	4	5	3	1		2			2					1		12	2	2		
7 Cascade Locks	4		2		2	1	1								1		1		3				
8 Wyeth	1		1			1										1	1						
9 Starvation Creek State Park	4	1	1	2	2	2	2		1		1	1	1			3	2		1				
10 Hood River Valley	3		2	1	1	1		1	1			1				3							
11 Mosier	2		1		1				1							1	1						
12 The Dalles	2							1		1						2							
13 Husum	2		2	2						1			1			2						1	
14 Carson	2			2	2		1			1		1				2	1						
15 Rock Creek	2	1	1	1			1			1		1					1						
16 Beacon Rock	2		1	1	1							1		1		1			2				
17 Washougal River	6		2	5	1	1		1	1		2	2	2	2		5	2				1	1	
18 Camas	3			2	1			1	1					1		2	3		1		1	1	
NORTHERN COAST RANGE, OR	**19**	**2**	**4**	**8**	**5**	**1**	**1**	**4**	**0**	**2**	**3**	**3**	**0**	**3**	**7**	**7**	**3**	**0**	**3**	**0**	**2**	**0**	**0**
1 Scappoose	1		1	1	1										1	1							
2 Beaver Creek	2	1	1		1	1		1		1					1	1	1						
3 Olney	1	1	1				1									1							
4 Jewell	1			1		1	1									1	1						
5 Wilson River	5	1	1	2	2	2	1			1		1				2	2		1		1	1	

Region / Falls Area	Total Falls	★★★★★	★★★★	★★★	★★	★	Plunge	Horsetail	Fan	Punchbowl	Block	Tiered	Segmented	Cascades	Auto	Hike (Easy - Fairly Easy)	Hike (Moderate-Hard)	Backpack	Bushwhack	Watercraft	4W Drive
6 Tillamook	1		1			★						1				1					
7 Blaine	3			1	1							1	1		2		1				
8 Dolph	1			1	1		1		1										1		
9 Lincoln City	1		1																		
10 Cherry Grove	2			1	1								1				1				
11 Falls City	1										1				1						
SOUTHERN COAST RANGE, OR	**27**	**0**	**1**	**7**	**13**	**6**	**0**	**2**	**2**	**1**	**3**	**4**	**6**	**3**	**10**	**13**	**4**	**0**	**0**	**0**	**0**
1 Alsea	3				3				1	1				1	1	2					
2 Smith River	1		1								1				1						
3 Mapleton Ranger District	6			3	1	1			1			2	2		1	3	2		1		
4 Lorane	1										1					1					
5 Millicoma River	3			1	2			1					1	1		2					
6 East Fork Coquille River	3			2	2						1		1	1	3	1					
7 Powers	3			1	2	1		1			1	1	1		1	1	1				
8 The Wild Rogue	4			1	2	1						1				2	1				
9 Illinois River	3				1	2								1	1	2	1				
MIDDLE CASCADES, OR	**51**	**0**	**9**	**14**	**18**	**10**	**14**	**3**	**3**	**3**	**9**	**5**	**3**	**1**	**17**	**18**	**11**	**0**	**7**	**0**	**0**
1 Mount Hood Wilderness	1			1		1			1								1				
2 Zigzag River	3			1	2		1		1					1	2	1					
3 Bennett Pass	3			1				1	1						2	1					
4 Northeast Mount Hood	2		1		1		2										1				
5 Oregon City	1			1							1				1						

6 Eagle Creek	2												1			1	2					
7 Bagby Hot Springs	2							1		1	1		1			1	7	4		1		
8 Silver Falls State Park	11	2		4	4	1	6	1	1	1			1			1	7	4		1		1
9 Scotts Mills	3	1		1	1		1		2		1					1		2				
10 Mehama	3	1		1			2						1			1	2					
11 North Fork River	3	1		1	1		1			1						2	1					
12 Niagara Park	2				1	1				1						1				1		
13 Marion Forks	3	1		1	1													1		3		
14 McKenzie River	4	2		1	1				1		1					2	1	1				
15 Cascadia	3			1	1					1			1			1		1		1		
16 McDowell Creek Falls	5			2	2	1	1			2			2			1	3	1		1		
SOUTH CASCADES, OR	**78**	**2**	**6**	**21**	**35**	**14**	**5**	**5**	**14**	**7**	**6**	**7**	**14**	**7**	**6**	**16**	**26**	**33**	**0**	**3**	**0**	**2**
1 McKenzie Highway	5	1		2	2	1	1	1	2	1		1	1	1	1		5	4		1		
2 Cascade Lakes Highway	4			2	2	1		1		1	1		1		1	1				1		
3 Big Fall Creek	1																	1				
4 Erma Bell Lakes	1		1	1												1						
5 Salmon Creek	3			2	2	1			1		1	1	1	2	2		1	1				
6 Salt Creek	6	1	1	1	3		2		2	2						1	1	4				
7 Row River	10		4	6		3		5		1	3	2			2	3	4					1
8 Little River	8		4	3	1	1	2		2		2		1		1	1	6					
9 Cavitt Creek	2		1	1	1				1							1	1					
10 Idleyld Park	4		2	2	1								2	2	2	2						
11 Steamboat	4			2	2	1	1				1		2	1			1					
12 Toketee	2	1		1	1		1				1					2	1					
13 Northeast Umpqua	5	1		2	2	1	1		1		1	1	1		1	3	3	1				
14 South Umpqua	3			3	3						1	2			2	1						
15 Upper Rogue River	5			2	2		2	3		1		1		1	1	4		4				4
16 Natural Bridge	3			2	2	1	1				1		1	1		1	1	1		1		
17 Crater Lake National Park	2			1	1			1				1		1								
18 Mill Creek	5	2	2	2	1	1			1		1	1	1	2		4		1		1		1

Region / Falls Area	Total Falls	★★★★★	★★★★	★★★	★★	★	Plunge	Horsetail	Fan	Punchbowl	Block	Tiered	Segmented	Cascades	Auto	Hike (Easy - Fairly Easy)	Hike (Moderate-Hard)	Backpack	Bushwack	Watercraft	4W Drive
19 Sky Lakes Wilderness	3					✦			1			1					3				
20 Butte Falls	1			1	1	1								1		1					
21 Gold Bar	1				1	1					1					1					
COLUMBIA PLATEAU, OR	**24**	**1**	**2**	**10**	**8**	**3**	**1**	**2**	**1**	**2**	**2**	**5**	**3**	**4**	**9**	**9**	**6**	**0**	**2**	**0**	**0**
1 Tygh Valley	4		1	2	1							1	1		2	2	1				
2 Tumalo Creek	5		1	1	3	1	1	1		1		1	1		3	2			1		
3 Lava Butte Geological Area	3			2	1					1			1	2	1	2					
4 La Pine	2			1	1		1		1						1	1					
5 Newberry Crater	2	1		1								1	1			1	1				
6 Enterprise	4		1	1	1	1		1				1		2		2	2				
7 Wallowa Lake	2			2						1		1					2		1		
8 Ochoco	1				1						1				1	1					
9 Adel	1			1			2							1							
PANHANDLE, ID	**24**	**1**	**4**	**7**	**7**	**5**	**3**	**4**	**2**	**3**	**1**	**3**	**1**	**2**	**5**	**7**	**9**	**1**	**5**	**0**	**2**
1 Priest River	2		1	1	1	1		1		1					1	1	1		1		1
2 Priest Lake	2	1	1	1					1					1		1	1		1		1
3 Pend Oreille	3			2	1			1		1		1			1	2	1		1		
4 Colburn	1				1											1					
5 Pack River	1				1			1						1							
6 Bonners Ferry	2			1	1											1			1		
7 Moyie River	1	1	1	1								1	1		1						
8 Boundary Line	2		1	1	1			1						1			1		1		1
9 Mullan	2			1	1	1	2					1				2			1		

Location	Count
10 St. Joe River	1
11 Elk Creek	7
WILDERNESS AREAS, ID	**28**
1 Selway River	4
2 Lochsa River	4
3 Warm Springs Creek	1
4 Little Salmon River	4
5 Lost Valley	1
6 Garden Valley	2
7 South Fork Boise River	3
8 Sawtooths West	2
9 Baron Creek	3
10 Middle Fork Salmon River	1
11 Stanley Lake Creek	2
12 Sawtooths East	1
13 Ketchum	1
14 Leesburg	1
15 North Fork Salmon River	1
SNAKE RIVER PLAIN, ID	**28**
1 Jump Creek Canyon	1
2 Hagerman	4
3 Snake Plains Aquifer	3
4 Snake River Canyon West	3
5 Snake River Canyon East	4
6 Lava Hot Springs	3
7 City of Idaho Falls	1
8 Swan Valley	1
9 Henrys Fork	4
10 Yellowstone	4

Difficulty: Trails and bushwhacks are rated as follows:

| E | Easy | FH | Fairly Hard |

| FE | Fairly Easy | H | Hard |

| M | Moderate |

Ratings for individual hikes were determined primarily by considering trail length and overall steepness, as well as the condition of the trail surface and whether streams can be crossed via footbridges or must be forded by hopping rocks and/or wading. Unsigned or minimally signed trails are rated more difficult than those with clear signage.

Keep in mind these ratings are relative and will vary according to the abilities of each individual. If you are not sure of your physical condition, start with easier walks, then progress to more strenuous hikes. If you are not in good health, it would be wise to consult your doctor before embarking on trails that are not "easy" or "fairly easy".

Topographic Maps: The U.S. Geological Survey (USGS) has published a series of large-scale topographic maps of the entire United States. Each 1:24,000 scale map (1 map inch = 2000 feet on the ground) encompasses an area bounded within 7 ½ minutes of longitude and 7 ½ minutes of latitude, which corresponds to a little over 49 square miles at the northern extreme of the Pacific Northwest, increasing to nearly 55 ½ square miles at the southern end.

Accompanying each waterfall listed in this book is the name of the USGS 7 ½-minute map on which it can be found. Since these maps are periodically revised, the version (i.e., year published) used by the author is also reported. If a cataract is not labeled on the map, the annotation (nl) also appears. If it is not shown at all on the map, the annotation (ns) appears.

Most university libraries and libraries in major cities throughout the United States have a complete collection of these maps and can also provide instructions for purchasing them through the USGS. They also are now available in digital format.

THE COMPUTER COMPANION

The author has also written an online electronic supplement of this guidebook, entitled *The Computer Companion*. It offers waterfall enthusiasts a wealth of information not practical or possible to portray in hard copy, plus updates as changes occur to the accessibility to individual falls. Fingertip access is available for more than 1400 waterfalls in the Pacific Northwest. More than 500 digital color photographs are included, along with user-controlled pop-ups to annotated maps over a topographic background documenting the location of every cataract. Listings can also be generated alphabetically by waterfall name, chapter, USGS map, or county, with links back to each individual falls. *The Companion* is located at *www.mymaps.com/nwfalls/toc.htm*.

There is also a resource called the *Waterfalls WebRing,* a portal for wa-

terfall lovers worldwide. In the past its server location has changed periodically, so the best way to find it is through a search engine such as *google.com*
or *yahoo.com*.

A NOTE ABOUT SAFETY FROM THE MOUNTAINEERS

Safety is an important concern for all outdoor activities. No guidebook
can alert you to every hazard or anticipate the limitations of every reader.
Therefore, the descriptions of roads, trails, routes, and natural features
in this book are not representations that a particular place or excursion
will be safe for your party. When you visit any of the waterfalls described
in this book, you assume responsibility for your own safety. Under nor-
mal conditions, such excursions require the usual attention to traffic,
road and trail conditions, weather, terrain, the capabilities of your party,
and other factors. Keeping informed on current conditions and exercis-
ing common sense are the keys to a safe, enjoyable outing.

THE MAPS

To locate waterfalls, use each chapter1s regional map, along with the more detailed section maps which appear with individual falls' descriptions. A state highway map or a digital navigation system will also aid in route selection. A key to region and section map symbols is below, as is an overview map of the book1s chapter regions.

For the sake of consistency and to reduce map reading problems, each map has north oriented upward, or towards the top of the page. Confirm the accuracy of your odometer and make for allowances within 1/10 of a mile or more between distances. As a rough gauge of hiking times, an average person takes 30 minutes for a moderate hike of one mile.

As a further assistance to readers, 7-1/2-minute USGS topographic maps are listed for each waterfall, along with the year of publication.

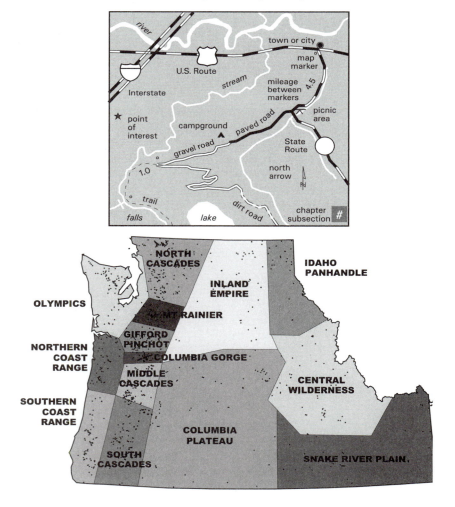

THE NORTH CASCADES, WASHINGTON

The Cascade Range extends from British Columbia through Washington and Oregon to northern California. A progression of spectacular volcanic peaks marks the range from north to south, with Mount Baker, Mount Rainier, and Mount Adams in Washington; Mount Hood, Three Sisters, and Mount McLoughlin in Oregon; and Mount Shasta in California. Since the Cascades encompass a large part of the Pacific Northwest and contain many waterfalls, the range has been divided into six chapters in this book.

The North Cascades extend from Interstate 90 to the Canadian border, dividing the Puget Sound area of Washington from the dry, eastern part of the state. This region features three large national forests, three wilderness areas, two national recreation areas, and North Cascades National Park. Of the 223 falls identified within the region, 84 are listed in this chapter.

Aside from two volcanoes, Mount Baker and Glacier Peak, most of the mountains of the North Cascades are older than those of the range's counterparts to the south. The North Cascades are a rugged and complex arrangement of various nonvolcanic materials, including large masses of granite. Other

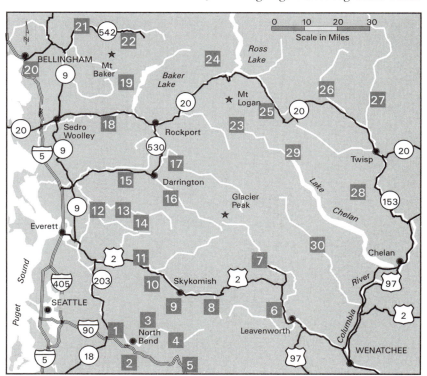

rock forms found in the area include gneiss and schists. These rock types vary from 50 million to 500 million years in age, but their arrangement in today's mountainous terrain is due to uplifting over the past 10 million years.

Intensive glaciation accounts for the region's pronounced relief. Four major periods of glacial activity occurred between 10,000 and 2 million years ago. The heads of glaciers eroded into the mountains, sharpening their peaks, and extended to lower elevations, deepening and widening valleys.

The abundance of waterfalls in the North Cascades is largely due to the glacial scouring of the range's bedrock surfaces. Many descents plummet into glacial troughs, or valleys. *Wallace Falls* and *Rainbow Falls* (the one near Lake Chelan) are stunning examples. Others, such as *Bridal Veil Falls, Gate Creek Falls,* and *Preston Falls*, skip and bounce off rock walls into the troughs.

Sometimes cataracts are associated with a rounded depression previously carved by the upper portion of a glacier. Water may pour into this cirque from ridge tops, or tumble from its outlet into a trough. The *Falls of Horseshoe Basin* and *Twin Falls* (at Twin Falls Lake) are examples.

Glaciers may erode unevenly when carving out their U-shaped troughs. The streams that presently occupy such valley floors are called *misfit streams,* and falls occur wherever there are sharp drops. Such descents are generally less dramatic than the types previously mentioned. Representative falls of this form include *Sunset Falls* and *Teepee Falls*.

---

1 SNOQUALMIE

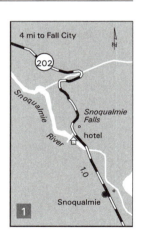

One should not be surprised, particularly in developed areas, to see hydroelectric facilities in association with waterfalls. A great amount of force is required to turn turbines for generating kilowatts of electricity. Because water can serve as that force, and its power is maximized where it is free-falling, falls sites can be desirable sources of energy. Water lines may be built into or beside the vertical escarpment and stream flow diverted to them. The scenic quality of the cataracts need not be lost, however, if enough water is allowed to continue its natural course. Such is the case, thankfully, for the following entry.

SNOQUALMIE FALLS ★★★★★

MAGNITUDE: 100 (h)   ELEVATION: 390 feet
WATERSHED: lg (d)   USGS MAP: Snoqualmie (1982)

This 268-foot plunge is one of Washington's most visited attractions. Puget Sound Power and Light Company preserves the integrity of the falls while

Snoqualmie Falls

diverting enough of the Snoqualmie River to provide power for 16,000 homes. This spectacle is located next to S.R. 202, 1 mile northwest of Snoqualmie and 4 miles southeast of Fall City. Look for signs and parking areas. There are several vantages of the cataract at the gorge rim adjacent to the lodge. Snoqualmie Falls River Trail, a steep 0.5-mile hike, offers views from the base of the falls.

2 NORTH BEND

Although the Snoqualmie River is best known for its namesake falls, additional descents occur several miles upstream from the main attraction. The construction of I-90 made these falls fairly difficult to reach. Since then, a trail system was built that has reopened this area and made accessible the following falls.

TWIN FALLS ★★★★

MAGNITUDE: 59   ELEVATION: 1020 feet
WATERSHED: lg (d)   USGS MAP: Chester Morse Lake (1989)

An exhilarating experience is to be gained from cliff-side viewing decks adjacent to this 135- to 150-foot plummet. Also known as Upper Snoqualmie Falls, this waterfall as well as the next two entries, is located within Twin Falls State Park, which is a day-use area.

Depart I-90 at Edgewick Road (Exit 34) and follow 468th Avenue Southeast for 0.7 mile. Turn left (east) at Southeast 159th Street and drive another 0.5 mile to the parking area at the end of the street. From the signed trailhead, hike 0.8 mile to the first, moderately distant, vantage of the cataract. Continue another 0.5 mile up the hillside, bearing left at the signed "Old Growth Fir Tree." Eventually you will reach an unsigned spur, to the right, consisting of a set of wooden stairs. Proceed down the steps, ending at the observation decks and the falls.

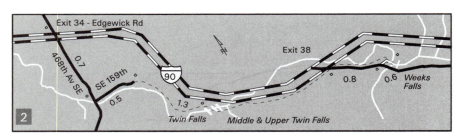

MIDDLE TWIN FALLS (U) ★★

MAGNITUDE: 41   ELEVATION: 1080 feet
WATERSHED: lg (d)   USGS MAP: Chester Morse Lake (1989 ns)

This pair of 10- to 15-foot punchbowls is located on the Snoqualmie River just upstream from Twin Falls (previously described). From the spur junction for Twin Falls, continue along the main trail for a moderately easy 0.1 mile to a wooden footbridge spanning the gorge. Looking upstream provides an excellent view of this entry.

UPPER TWIN FALLS (U) ★★

MAGNITUDE: 47   ELEVATION: 1090 feet
WATERSHED: lg (d)   USGS MAP: Chester
                       Morse Lake (1989 ns)

The Snoqualmie River plunges 20 to 30 feet before fanning out another 25 to 35 feet into a natural pool. From the footbridge below Middle Twin Falls (described earlier), hike another 0.1 mile up the steep trail to an open vista of this falls.

WEEKS FALLS ★★

MAGNITUDE: 37   ELEVATION: 1260 feet
WATERSHED: lg (d)   USGS MAP: Chester
                       Morse Lake (1989 ns)

This series of cascades descends 30 to 40 feet along the South Fork Snoqualmie River. It can be reached by hiking several additional miles beyond Twin Falls State Park (described earlier), but the easiest access is by vehicle.

Depart I-90 at the Forest Fire Training Center (Exit 38) and drive east for 0.8 mile to the obscurely signed entrance to Ollalie State Park. Continue 0.4 mile to an overlook of the falls. More cascades can be found by driving past the park entrance for 0.6 mile to a small hydroelectric facility. When leaving this area, eastbounders must first go west on I-90, then use Exit 34 as a U-turn.

3 TAYLOR RIVER

For decades, access to this area of the North Bend Ranger District in Mount Baker–Snoqualmie National Forest was deplorable. Road improvements have at last been made, so even passenger cars can now readily make

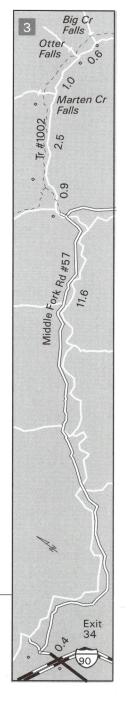

it up the Middle Fork Road without fear. This is definitely one place where funds from the National Forest Pass fee system have been put to good use.

Depart I-90 at Edgewick Road (Exit 34) and proceed northward. Go 0.4 mile, then turn right (east) onto Middle Fork Road #57. The way is signed as such 2.5 miles farther; the turnoff to the Middle Fork Trailhead is another 9.1 miles. Don't turn here; instead continue another 0.9 mile beyond this landmark to the end of the road at the start of Taylor River Trail #1002.

Marten Creek Falls (u) ★★★

MAGNITUDE: 25   ELEVATION: 1800 feet
WATERSHED: sm   USGS MAP: Snoqualmie Lake (1982 ns)

Embark upon Taylor River Trail #1002. After a junction at 0.3 mile, bear right along the river along a trail signed for Snoqualmie Lake. After another 2.2 miles of steady hiking, you will meet the first major tributary. The base of this 40- to 50-foot descent is barely visible from the trail, although the falls should certainly be audible. Walk 200 feet up the faint path next to the creek for a full view. The chemical action of hydrolysis has smoothed the granite streambed to such a degree that this place looks like it could be Bigfoot's waterslide! Its size makes it too risky for humans, though.

Otter Falls ★★★★★

MAGNITUDE: 80 (l)   ELEVATION: 1900
WATERSHED: sm   USGS MAP: Snoqualmie Lake (1982)

If Marten Creek Falls (described earlier) is a slide for Bigfoot, then this 700- to 800-foot gargantuan must be Paul Bunyon's. Continue another mile along Taylor River Trail #1002, passing by many side creeks. The one harboring the falls is actually a dry crossing because the stream has been diverted by a large 5-foot-diameter drainage pipe, visible just below the trail. Proceed along the trail a few hundred feet farther to an unsigned side path to the left. Follow this into the woods where the path quickly splits. Take the one that goes straight up the small hill, veering slightly to the right, toward the sound of the falls. The top of the cataract will soon be visible. In 0.1 mile tiny Lipsey Lake will be reached with full views of an awesome mountainside of water. It is best seen in late spring, as the creek usually dries up by the end of summer. Otter Falls is over 1000 feet high, but "only" three-fourths of it can be seen from a safe vantage.

Opposite: Otter Falls

BIG CREEK FALLS (U) ★★★

MAGNITUDE: 30   ELEVATION: 1800
WATERSHED: sm   USGS MAP: Snoqualmie Lake (1982 ns)

Although not as impressive as its prior two counterparts, this pretty cascade is worth the 0.6-mile hike beyond Otter Falls (described earlier). It is easy to find since the base of its 120- to 150-foot drop rushes down and under the only concrete footbridge along Taylor River Trail #1002. From here, it's 4.1 miles back to the trailhead.

---

4 SNOQUALMIE PASS

This area's main campground and one of its waterfalls have the unfavorable distinction of lying between the lanes of I-90! Actually it is not as bad as you may imagine, but the soft buzzing of the passing traffic does detract from the natural setting. Leave I-90 at Snoqualmie Pass Recreation Area (Exit 47 or 52) and follow Denny Creek Road #5800 for 2 to 3 miles to Road #5830, located 0.25 mile northeast of Denny Creek Camp. All of the following falls are located within North Bend Ranger District, Mount Baker–Snoqualmie National Forest.

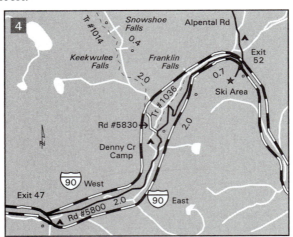

KEEKWULEE FALLS ★★

MAGNITUDE: 34 (l)   ELEVATION: 3330 feet
WATERSHED: sm   USGS MAP: Snoqualmie Pass (1989)

Water plunges 60 to 70 feet before tumbling another 15 feet along Denny Creek. Keekwulee is a Chinook word meaning "falling down." From Denny Creek

Camp, take Road #5830 for 0.25 mile to its end at the trailhead to Denny Creek Trail #1014. The trail goes underneath the interstate and crosses Denny Creek twice, the second time at 1.5 miles. The trail ascends fairly steeply 0.5 mile farther to a full view of the cataract.

If you continue another 0.4 mile, the roar of *Snowshoe Falls* ★ USGS Snoqualmie Pass (1989) will be heard. This 125- to 175-foot cataract along Denny Creek would deserve a higher scenic rating except the heavily timbered and dangerously steep slopes limit the viewpoints to obscured trailside glimpses. Both of these falls were named in 1916 by The Mountaineers.

FRANKLIN FALLS ★★★

MAGNITUDE: 59   ELEVATION: 2800 feet
WATERSHED: med   USGS MAP: Snoqualmie Pass (1989)

South Fork Snoqualmie River plummets 70 feet into a small pool. Drive about 2 miles northeast of Denny Creek Camp along Road #5800 to the historic Snoqualmie Pass Wagon Road. This route, now a footpath, leads to

Franklin Falls

the falls in less than 300 yards. Alternatively, one may take a moderately easy hike of about 1.5 miles along Franklin Falls Trail #1036 from Denny Creek Camp on Road #5830 (described earlier).

5 STAMPEDE PASS

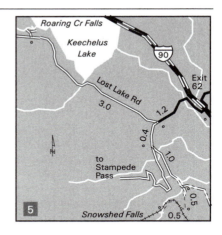

Although the next pair of falls is adjacent to private land holdings, both were accessible when last visited. Access the area by departing I-90 at Stampede Pass (Exit 62). Turn west and proceed for 1.2 miles to a junction where the right fork is signed for Lost Lake.

ROARING CREEK FALLS (U) ★★★

MAGNITUDE: 64 (h)   ELEVATION: 2500 feet
WATERSHED: med   USGS MAP: Stampede Pass (1989 nl)

Roaring Creek lives up to its name as it plunges 55 to 70 feet into a small gorge before draining into Keechelus Lake. At this junction (described earlier), proceed toward Lost Lake, driving 3 miles, then turn right onto Roaring Creek Court. If the street is gated, find an unobstructed place to park and walk down the street a few hundred feet. Look to the right for a sign blocking a road, stating "No Motor Vehicles." Turn here and walk a short 0.1 mile to its end. Turn left on a path into the woods, which almost immediately ends at the top of a 100-foot-high rock outcrop. Here find an airy, unprotected vista of the falls. Be careful.

SNOWSHED FALLS ★★★★

MAGNITUDE: 53   ELEVATION: 2900
WATERSHED: sm   USGS MAP: Stampede Pass (1989)

Take a different kind of hike to a different kind of waterfall. Instead of taking the turn to Lost Lake at the junction (described earlier), continue straight for another 0.4 mile. Bear left on the "low road" at the next junction. As the road deteriorates, continue going straight, avoiding the many spurs. After

Snowshed Falls

another mile, park at a wide spot in the open area. Start walking uphill along the road to the right. You will pass a gate preventing access to vehicles and then encounter a set of railroad tracks. The road parallels the tracks to its end 1 mile farther at the base of the 90- to 100-foot falls. They are named for the snowshed that not only protects trains from snow during the winter but also from spray from the cataract. At this point, the rail tunnel enters beneath Stampede Pass, emerging 2 miles farther on the opposite side. For safety's sake, do not enter the tunnel.

6 LEAVENWORTH

Downtown Leavenworth is a place of Old World character, where seasonal activities such as the Mai Fest, Autumn Leaf Festival, and Christmas Lighting can be enjoyed. The traditional storefronts and the surrounding alpine setting are reminiscent of the German province of Bavaria.

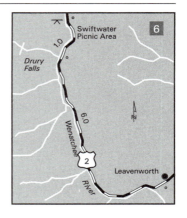

DRURY FALLS ★★

MAGNITUDE: 51 ELEVATION: 4120 feet
WATERSHED: sm USGS MAP: Winton (1989)

Fall Creek, located within Leavenworth Ranger District, Wenatchee National Forest, drops over 100 feet from the cliffs of Tumwater Canyon into the Wenatchee River. Only a moderately distant cross-river view of the cataract is possible. Drive 6 miles north of Leavenworth, or 1 mile south of Swiftwater Picnic Area, along U.S. 2 to an unsigned turnout.

7 LAKE WENATCHEE

Lake Wenatchee is a popular vacation area for family camping, with several campsites on the eastern shore. Drive 14 miles northwest of Leavenworth

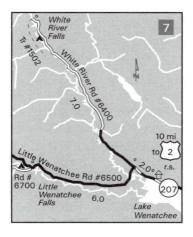

along U.S. 2 to S.R. 207, then 10 miles north to the ranger station for Lake Wenatchee Ranger District, Wenatchee National Forest. All the area's falls are located upstream from Lake Wenatchee.

WHITE RIVER FALLS ★★★

MAGNITUDE: 53 (h)   ELEVATION: 2200 feet
WATERSHED: lg   USGS MAP: Mount David (1989)

This forceful 60- to 100-foot cataract along the White River is situated next to a camp, but the best views require a modest hike. Drive to the end of White River Road #6400 and park. Follow Indian Creek Trail #1502 across the White River, then go downstream. In 1 mile, a spur trail to the left leads to good views of the falls. At White River Falls Campground, adults can also climb on chunks of bedrock for obstructed overviews of the descent. Be careful! This is definitely not a place for fooling around.

Also located in the vicinity is *Little Wenatchee Falls* (u) ★ USGS Mount Howard (1989 ns). Little Wenatchee River tumbles 20 to 30 feet over a series of rock steps. Turn off S.R. 207 onto Little Wenatchee River Road #6500. In 6 miles Road #6500 meets with Rainy Creek Road #6700. Park at the junction and backtrack about 150 feet to a primitive trail. The cascade is a short, easy walk away.

8 STEVENS PASS

Many waterfalls beckon from the roadside as you travel westward along U.S. 2 from the 4,061-foot elevation of Stevens Pass.

ALPINE FALLS ★★

MAGNITUDE: 17 (l)   ELEVATION: 1450 feet
WATERSHED: lg   USGS MAP: Scenic (1982)

Situated on land owned by the state of Washington, the South Fork Skykomish River tumbles 30 to 50 feet downward. Drive along U.S. 2 about 8.5 miles east of Skykomish or 1.5 miles west of Deception Falls (described later). Park at the unsigned turnout just past the bridge crossing the Tye

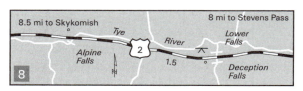

River. A very short trail leads to the top of this entry. Determined bushwhackers can find better views by hiking down the slope to the river from the far end of the parking turnout.

DECEPTION FALLS ★★

MAGNITUDE: 34 (h)   ELEVATION: 1850
WATERSHED: lg   USGS MAP: Scenic (1982)

This entry has been upgraded in its rating from previous editions due to the construction of a nice viewing deck. Take U.S. 2 to Deception Falls Picnic Area, located 8 miles west of Stevens Pass and 10 miles east of Skykomish. Walk over to the east (right) side of the parking area. A paved walkway leads 0.1 mile over a footbridge, then under the highway to a vantage of Deception Creek cascading 60 feet. Also known as Upper Falls.

LOWER FALLS ★★

MAGNITUDE: 26 (h)   ELEVATION: 1800
WATERSHED: lg   USGS MAP: Scenic (1982 ns)

From the west side of the footbridge (described earlier), walk down the loop trail 100 or so feet and look upstream to see Deception Creek tumbling 15 to 25 feet downward. The trail continues down to the Tye River where reportedly two more modest waterfalls occur.

9 ALPINE LAKES

"To cut or not to cut?" One criterion for designating an area as "wilderness" is that it is minimally impacted by humans. But what if an otherwise scenic viewpoint is obscured only by a couple of trees or some shrubs? Wearing my sightseer's "hat," I would argue if a trail is already impacting a location, let's enhance the wilderness experience by allowing the Forest Service to perform some selective cutting. Putting on my safety "hat," I would add that such minor alterations should reduce straying off the trail, reducing the risk of injury as well as lessening impact by hikers. Lastly, as I put on

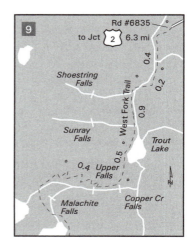

my geographer's "hat," I seriously doubt minimal cutting would have any statistically valid impact on the environment.

Why this discourse? I've surveyed many waterfalls where the best vantage is ever so slightly obscured. Several of them are not in wilderness areas, either. The following waterfall is within the Alpine Lakes Wilderness Area and serves as a classic example of the problem. It would otherwise possess a 5-star rating and be one of the very best of the Northwest.

MALACHITE FALLS ★★★★

MAGNITUDE: 80   ELEVATION: 3500 feet
WATERSHED: sm (g)   USGS MAP: Big Snow Mtn (1965 ns)

Drive U.S. 2 east from Skykomish for 1.8 miles or 0.5 mile east of Skykomish Ranger Station and turn right (south) onto Foss River Road #68. After an-

Malachite Falls

other 3.5 miles, turn left onto Forest Road #6835, signed for West Fork Camp. Proceed 1.9 miles to the trailhead at road's end.

Embark upon West Fork Trail. After a moderately easy 0.4 mile, reach a clearing with a distant vantage of one of the higher tiers of *Shoestring Falls* (u) ★ USGS Big Snow Mtn (ns). Continue another 0.2 mile, and cross a series of log footbridges, the last one spanning the West Fork. About 0.1 mile farther, a distant view can be gained of *Sunray Falls* (u) ★ USGS Big Snow Mtn (ns), also descending from the cliffs to your right. Observant hikers can briefly see both of these falls in tandem just before the log crossings.

Proceed up the moderate slopes to the outlet of Trout Lake, another 0.8 mile. The route now ascends moderately steeply for 0.5 mile to Copper Creek which roars 400 to 500 feet down a mountainside. The top of *Copper Creek Falls* (u) ★ USGS Big Snow Mtn (ns) can be seen by taking a side path all the way to the water and looking downstream. Back on the trail, glimpses of *Upper Copper Creek Falls* (u) ★ USGS Big Snow Mtn (ns) will be gained 0.2 mile upstream. The steep way now begins to switchback, time and again, progressively gaining better views of Malachite Falls. Unfortunately, vegetation hinders a completely clear vantage. The best trailside vista is around the sixth or seventh switchback in 1 mile from where Copper Creek is initially met. From the destination, it's 3 miles back to the trailhead.

10 INDEX

Although the following waterfalls are located near U.S. 2 and have been labeled for decades as points of interest on many state highway maps, most people never see them because there are no signs.

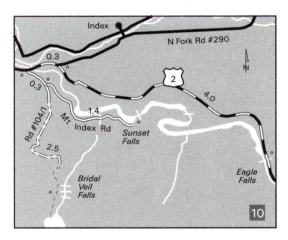

BRIDAL VEIL FALLS ★★

MAGNITUDE: 44 (l)   ELEVATION: 1800 feet
WATERSHED: sm   USGS MAP: Index (1989)

Water pours off Mount Index in four parts, each descending 100 to 200 feet along Bridal Veil Creek. The falls is also visible from the main highway, appearing as silvery white threads and is located within Skykomish Ranger District, Mount Baker–Snoqualmie National Forest.

Leave U.S. 2 at Mount Index Road, 0.3 mile past the turn for the hamlet of Index and immediately south of the bridge over the South Fork Skykomish River. After another 0.3 mile, turn right (south) on Road #104/1. Only high-clearance vehicles can follow the entire 1.5-mile length of the road. Most automobiles should park after 1 mile. A hiking trail begins at the road's end and ascends moderately to the first of the cataracts in 1 more mile.

SUNSET FALLS ★★★

MAGNITUDE: 37 (h)   ELEVATION: 620 feet
WATERSHED: lg   USGS MAP: Index (1989)

South Fork Skykomish River slides 60 to 100 feet in impressive fashion. Follow the directions to Bridal Veil Falls (described earlier), except continue toward the end of Mount Index Road, 1.4 miles past the junction with Road #104/1.

Nearby is *Canyon Falls* ★★★★ USGS Index (1989). Sadly, "No Trespassing" signs have been erected, making it inaccessible to the public. Cartographers will need to get their "white-out" and remove this falls as a point of interest from their maps.

Others: *Eagle Falls* ★ USGS Index (1989) has noisy frothing water that tumbles 25 to 40 feet along the South Fork Skykomish River. From Skykomish proceed west along U.S. 2 for about 9 miles and find the parking turnout closest to mile marker 39. A path immediately east of the marker quickly leads to the descent.

---

11 GOLD BAR

Wallace Falls State Park opened in 1977 to showcase and preserve one of the tallest single-drop cataracts in the Northwest.

WALLACE FALLS ★★★★★

MAGNITUDE: 88   ELEVATION: 1300 feet
WATERSHED: med   USGS MAP: Gold Bar (1989)

Wallace River curtains 260 feet in great splendor into a small natural pool, surrounded by bedrock and coniferous forest. Depart U.S. 2 at Gold Bar and follow the signs to the state park. Start hiking along Woody Trail, named after Frank Woody, a former state senator and lifelong outdoorsman. The way soon di-

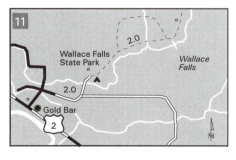

verges, the right fork ascending moderately, while the left goes up at a gentler rate. The trails converge after 1 mile on the steeper path or 2 miles on the gradual path. A short distance farther is a picnic area and a first view of the falls; another favorite viewpoint is 0.5 mile beyond.

The trail reportedly continues on to *Upper Wallace Falls* (u) USGS Gold Bar (1989 nl) and a vista of the Skykomish Valley.

---

12 GRANITE FALLS

The community of Granite Falls is named after these cascades, located north of town on the Mountain Loop Highway, which is an extension of S.R. 92.

GRANITE FALLS ★★

MAGNITUDE: 27   ELEVATION: 300 feet
WATERSHED: lg   USGS MAP: Granite Falls (1989)

Water froths along the South Fork Stillaguamish River in a series of descents totaling 30 to 40 feet. A 580-foot fishway connects the upper and lower levels of the river via a 240-foot tunnel, allowing salmon to bypass the cascades and proceed upstream to spawn. Drive 1.4 miles north of town on the Mountain Loop Highway. Just before a bridge crossing the river, find a parking area and a short trail that leads to the falls.

Others: *Explorer Falls* ★ USGS Lake Chaplain (1989 ns) occurs where an unnamed tributary of Woods Creek drops 50 to 70 feet from a cliff. Being secluded, the falls are perfect for taking an invigorating soapless shower, if you dare. Reach cottage-lined Lake Roesiger by driving 13 miles north from Monroe on Woods Creek Road. Alternatively, drive about 8 miles south from Granite Falls on Lake Roesiger Road, turning east on Monroe Camp Road. After 3.5 miles, park at an old gravel pit on the right side of the road. It has been reported the recently paved route may be closed to vehicles over the last mile. Once at the gravel pit, bushwhack upstream a few hundred feet to an open view of the waterfall. Refer to *The Computer Companion* online (described in the Introduction) to access a map to this entry.

---

13 ROBE VALLEY

Small waterfalls abound in this area, where creeks flow from Mount Pilchuck into the South Fork Stillaguamish River. They all occur either on state land or within Darrington Ranger District, Mount Baker–Snoqualmie National Forest. Follow the Mountain Loop Highway 10 miles northeast from Granite Falls to the Verlot Ranger Station and townsite. After the main road crosses

Opposite: Wallace Falls

junction with Road #4021. Drive to the next fork, in 1.5 miles, and turn left onto narrow Road #402/1016. After another 0.2-mile reach the signed trailhead.

TWIN FALLS ★★★★

MAGNITUDE: 81 (h)   ELEVATION: 2300 feet
WATERSHED: sm   USGS MAP: Mallardy Ridge (1989)

Wilson Creek pounds 125 feet into Twin Falls Lake, then tumbles another 400 feet from the lake's outlet as *Lower Twin Falls* (u) USGS Mallardy Ridge (1989 nl). Unfortunately, the only safe views of the lower falls are moderately distant and mostly obscured by the surrounding vegetation. An interpretive sign at the lake provides a geologic history of the area.

From the trailhead, begin a demanding, but rewarding journey along a path built by the state's Department of Natural Resources. The way begins in unassuming fashion, following an old dirt road for the first mile. When you reach a footpath signed for Ashland Lakes turn left. The way steepens a bit and after another mile, a spur goes left to Beaver Plant Lake. For the most direct way to the destination, stay to the right at this and all subsequent junctions. The trail becomes more difficult as wood planks, circular cedar crosscuts, and granite blocks are provided to negotiate the marshy terrain over the next mile past Upper and Lower Ashland Lakes. The route then steepens considerably along its last 1.5 miles to the falls.

15 BOULDER RIVER

The following entry occurs within Boulder River Wilderness, a part of Darrington Ranger District, Mount Baker–Snoqualmie National Forest. Access the area by taking S.R. 530 to French Creek Road #2010, located 8 miles west of Darrington, or 8 miles east of Oso. Proceed south on Road #2010 for 4.5 miles, where the gravel road now reportedly ends for vehicular traffic. Look for the trailhead to your right.

Verlot
4.7 mi

Ashland Lks Rd #4020

2.3

Rd #4021

1.5

0.2

trail

1.0

1.5

Ashland Lks Trail

0.5

Twin
Falls

Lower Twin
Falls

1.5

14

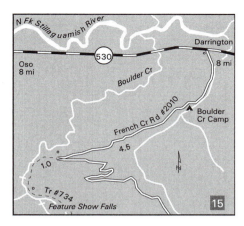

FEATURE SHOW FALLS ★★

MAGNITUDE: 23 (l)   ELEVATION: 1100 feet
WATERSHED: vsm   USGS MAP: Meadow Mtn (1989 nl)

Walk along the trail for 1 mile to a cross-river vista of Feature Show Falls, formed by an unnamed creek that curtains 80 feet over a cliff into Boulder Creek. This entry was erroneously identified as Boulder Falls, USGS Meadow Mtn (1989), in previous editions of this book. The latter cataract occurs a short distance downstream along Boulder Creek, but it cannot be seen from the trail and there is no developed access.

Others: At *Ryan Falls* ★ USGS Stimson Hill (1985 ns), water slides 50 to 75 feet down a hillside along an unnamed creek located on private property, with views restricted to the highway. Best viewed during late autumn, the falls is located just west of mile marker 28 on S.R. 530 about 7 miles northeast of Arlington, 1.1 miles west of the highway's crossing of the North Fork Stillaguamish River. Go online to *The Computer Companion* (described in the Introduction) to access a map to this entry.

16 SAUK RIVER

NORTH FORK FALLS ★★★★

MAGNITUDE: 57 (h)   ELEVATION: 1480 feet
WATERSHED: lg   USGS MAP: Sloan Peak (1982)

Water thunders 60 to 80 feet along the North Fork Sauk River. From Darrington, take Sauk River Road #20 south for 15.6 miles to North Fork

North Fork Falls

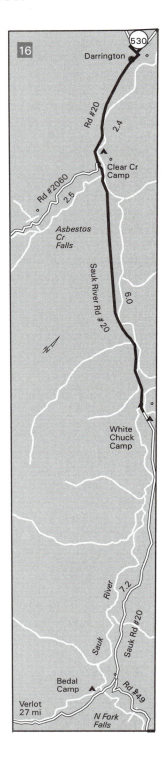

Road #49. Turn left and drive 1.2 miles to the sign for Trail #660. Hike 0.3 mile to an overlook above the falls, which is located within Darrington Ranger District, Mount Baker–Snoqualmie National Forest.

Asbestos Creek Falls (u) ★ USGS Helena Ridge (1989 ns) can be accessed by taking Sauk River Road #20 south from Darrington for 2.4 miles. Turn right onto Clear Creek Road #2060 and proceed another 2.5 miles to an unsigned turnout where Asbestos Creek flows beneath the gravel road. Scramble a few hundred feet up the drainage to a view of the stream splashing 35 to 45 feet steeply down the mountainside.

17 SUIATTLE RIVER

The following three falls increase in stature as one progresses up the drainage basin of the Suiattle River. Reach Suiattle River Road #26 via S.R. 530 by driving 6.5 miles north of Darrington or 12 miles south of Rockport. Look for the turn 0.2 mile east of the highway's crossing of the Sauk River.

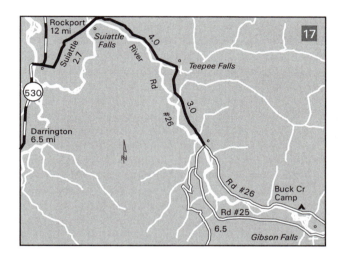

TEEPEE FALLS ★★

MAGNITUDE: 34   ELEVATION: 1000 feet
WATERSHED: med   USGS MAP: Prairie Mtn (1982)

Peer straight down from a bridge spanning the chasm of Big Creek into this series of 50- to 60-foot cascading waters. Proceed along Road #26 for 6.7 miles to reach this entry.

Bushwhackers can also find *Suiattle Falls* (u) ★ USGS Darrington (1982 nl) along the way. This double cascade occurs on an unnamed creek, dropping a total of 70 to 100 feet from Suiattle Mountain on undeveloped state land. Drive 2.7 miles along Suiattle River Road to an unsigned turnout on the right side of the road, past a culvert for the small creek. Walk to the drainage and scramble upstream 100 feet to a vantage of the cataract.

Gibson Falls ★★★

MAGNITUDE: 44   ELEVATION: 1600 feet
WATERSHED: sm   USGS MAP: Huckleberry Mtn (1982)

A narrow veil of water glistens 25 to 35 feet in a dimly lit recess of an un-named stream, which is located within Darrington Ranger District, Mount Baker–Snoqualmie National Forest. Continue 3 miles past Teepee Falls (de-scribed earlier) along Road #26 and turn right onto Road #25. Go 6.5 miles along this gravel route to an unsigned turnout. (Watch for a dip in the cul-vert over signed Circle Creek: the turnout is 0.1 mile past this point.) Follow the creek upstream for 200 feet to the base of the falls.

18 SAUK VALLEY

Teenagers and nimble adults will enjoy this waterfall. Depart S.R. 20 on Sauk Valley Road, located 1 mile west of Concrete. Proceed south, then after cross-ing the Skagit River, bear right (west). Look for a creek crossing 8 miles from the state highway. Park at the unsigned area located immediately west of the bridge.

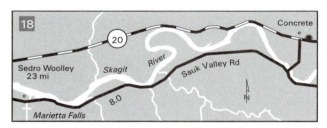

Marietta Falls ★★★

MAGNITUDE: 53   ELEVATION: 400 feet
WATERSHED: med   USGS MAP: Hamilton (1989)

O'Toole Creek, also called Marietta Creek, tumbles a total of 100 to 125 feet with a plunge at the end of its final descent. This falls is probably on private property. The trail begins as a well-worn 0.3-mile path. It will require fording the creek once or twice and climbing over a small rock outcrop near the base of the falls.

19 MOUNT BAKER

Mount Baker is one of the dominant features of the North Cascades. This gla-cier-covered volcano rises thousands of feet above the surrounding mountains.

Meltwaters from its northeast-facing glaciers feed numerous waterfalls.

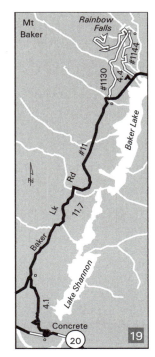

Rainbow Falls ★★★

MAGNITUDE: 70
ELEVATION: 1700 feet
WATERSHED: med (g)
USGS MAP: Shuksan Arm (1989)

Rainbow Creek pours 150 feet into a gorge. Most of the cataract is visible from a moderately distant overlook across the canyon; the bottom portion is hidden by vegetation and the canyon escarpment. The waterfall occurs within Mount Baker Wilderness, in Mount Baker Ranger District, Mount Baker–Snoqualmie National Forest.

At Concrete, turn north off the North Cascades Highway (S.R. 20), onto Baker Lake Road #11. (Eastbounders can take a shortcut to Road #11 by using the signed turnoff 6 miles west of Concrete.) After 16 or 18.5 miles, depending upon the route taken, turn left on Road #1130. There are views of Mount Baker and Mount Shuksan before the turn. Follow Road #1130 for 4.4 miles to the signed parking lot for the falls. The viewpoint is only a few steps away.

20 BELLINGHAM

The following waterfalls provide a natural refuge from the urbanization of the Bellingham area.

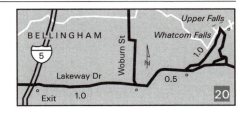

Whatcom Falls ★★★

MAGNITUDE: 58   ELEVATION: 300 feet
WATERSHED: lg   USGS MAP: Bellingham North (1994 ns)

One tier of the falls on Whatcom Creek pours 10 to 15 feet before the main display tumbles 25 to 30 feet over water-sculpted sandstone. Depart I-5 at the Lakeway Exit. Proceed 1.5 miles east along Lakeway Drive, then turn left onto Silver Beach Road at the sign marked for Whatcom Falls Park. Continue 1 more mile to the parking area, which is 50 feet from the descent.

Upper Whatcom Falls (u) ★★

MAGNITUDE: 43   USGS MAP: Bellingham North (1994 ns)

Erroneously listed as Lower Whatcom Falls in the previous edition, this 35- to 45-foot display can be found 0.2 mile up the trail along the creek at the outlet for Lake Whatcom. A minor 3- to 5-foot block waterfall will also be seen at the halfway point.

21 Maple Falls

Maple Falls ★★

MAGNITUDE: 6   ELEVATION: 550 feet
WATERSHED: med   USGS MAP: Maple Falls (1994 ns)

Yes, Virginia, there is a Maple Falls at Maple Falls. But only a modest one. Once in town, turn north onto a road signed for Silver Lake and find a place to park. Look for an unsigned trail behind the general store and walk about 0.1 mile down to Maple Creek and its 10- to 15-foot set of cascades. A bit farther eastward the trail follows an old railroad grade.

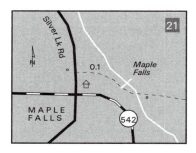

22 Nooksack River

As you near Washington's boundary with British Columbia you can explore some wild and woolly cataracts.

Nooksack Falls ★★★★

MAGNITUDE: 97 (h)   ELEVATION: 2600 feet
WATERSHED: lg (g)   USGS MAP: Bearpaw Mtn (1989)

This 170-foot waterfall explodes over a sheer escarpment along the Nooksack River. The landowner, Puget Sound Power and Light, has reconstructed an observation platform, with a view of almost the entire cataract. Drive 34 miles east of Bellingham along S.R. 542 to the hamlet of

Glacier and continue 7 miles east to Wells Creek Road #33. Turn right and drive 0.5 mile. Do not cross the bridge over the river or you will pass the access to the parking area.

In previous editions, *Lower Wells Creek Falls* (u) ★★ USGS Bearpaw Mtn (1989 ns) was described as descending 80 to 100 feet adjacent to Nooksack Falls. When last visited this falls could not be found. Puzzling indeed.

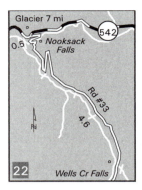

Nooksack Falls

WELLS CREEK FALLS (U) ★★

MAGNITUDE: 97 (h)   ELEVATION: 2600 feet
WATERSHED: med (g)   USGS MAP: Mount Baker (1989 nl)

The roadside view of this beautiful 80- to 100-foot plunge, located within
Mount Baker Ranger District, Mount Baker–Snoqualmie National Forest, is somewhat distant and obscured. From Nooksack Falls (described
earlier) continue 4.6 miles farther on Wells Creek Road #33 to an unsigned turnout, with a view of Mount Baker along the way. Better vantages of the falls require walking and scrambling along the creek, so plan
on getting wet.

23 NORTH CASCADES NATIONAL PARK

While the majority of national parks within the continental United States have
developed routes for motorized travel, North Cascades National Park remains
overwhelmingly wilderness in character. The only mainland road that pen-
etrates well into the park is the Cascade River Road. It begins in the town of
Marblemount where S.R. 20 bends northward and the highway junction is
signed "Road to Trails for Cascade Pass and Stehekin." Turn here at the bridge
crossing the Skagit River.

Speaking of Stehekin, hikers and backpackers often access the last four
waterfalls in this section from that outpost. Take the Lake Chelan Boat
Company's *Lady of the Lake* from Chelan (or splurge by flying one-way or
round-trip on a seaplane) to Stehekin and the Stehekin River Road. A shuttle
service transports hikers and backpackers to various campsites and trailheads
along the road. Go all the way to the end of the road at Cottonwood Camp.
Refer to the Lake Chelan section (described later) for information on additional waterfalls in the Stehekin area.

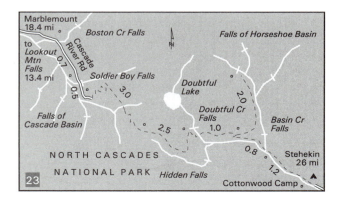

LOOKOUT MOUNTAIN FALLS (U) ★★

MAGNITUDE: 36   ELEVATION: 800 feet
WATERSHED: sm   USGS MAP: Big Devil Peak (1989 ns)

On the way into North Cascades National Park, it's hard to miss this roadside cataract. Drive 5 miles down the Cascade River Road to a wide spot adjacent to this 25- to 35-foot drop along an unnamed stream. Also unofficially known as *Mystery Falls,* its rating decreases with low discharge as summer progresses.

SOLDIER BOY FALLS (U) ★★

MAGNITUDE: 41   ELEVATION: 2400 feet
WATERSHED: sm   USGS MAP: Cascade Pass (1963 ns)

For close-up views of Soldier Boy Creek veiling 20 to 30 feet down near the road, resume driving past Lookout Mountain Falls (described earlier), passing Mineral Park West Campground in 7.4 miles and reaching the signed entrance to North Cascades National Park in another 2.2 miles. Beyond this point the Cascade River Road usually opens in mid-June. Proceed 4.5 miles to an unsigned turnout to view this falls.

FALLS OF CASCADE BASIN (U) ★★★

MAGNITUDE: 61   ELEVATION: 4800 feet
WATERSHED: sm (g)   USGS MAP: Cascade Pass (1963 ns)

Unless there's a low overcast, a multitude of cascades and small falls can be seen descending down the sides of the glacial valley along the last several miles of the Cascade River Road. Only the most significant ones are described here. Drive to the end of the road, 0.5 mile beyond Soldier Boy Falls (described earlier). Look across the valley to your right for a moderately distant view of several cataracts streaming and plunging 200 to 400 feet upon the ruggedly sculpted terrain of Johannesburg Mountain, Cascade Peak, and The Triplets.

BOSTON CREEK FALLS (U) ★★★

MAGNITUDE: 68   ELEVATION: 4300 feet
WATERSHED: sm (g)   USGS MAP: Cascade Pass (193 ns)

This moderately distant descent of 200 to 300 feet is most readily found departing the area, hence its placement after the Falls of Cascade Basin (described

earlier). From road's end, drive 1.2 miles eastward and look way up the mountains on your side of the glacial valley. If you wish to linger, park at an unsigned turnout located a short distance farther at the crossing of Boston Creek.

Hidden Falls (u) ★★★

MAGNITUDE: 61   ELEVATION: 4630 feet
WATERSHED: sm (g)   USGS MAP: Cascade Pass (1963 ns)

Ribbons of water descend steeply 260 to 300 feet from the meltwaters of Yawning Glacier. From the end of Cascade River Road (described earlier), embark upon Cascade Pass Trail. The route begins steeply as it ascends 3 miles to the pass. Proceed down the other side to the crossing of Doubtful Creek, 2.5 miles away. Enjoy cross-valley views of the cataract tumbling down an unnamed stream, with Pelton Peak providing a backdrop. Hikers from the opposite direction, marching westward from Cottonwood Camp (described earlier), will have a 3-mile journey to vantages at the creek crossing.

Doubtful Creek Falls (u) ★★

MAGNITUDE: 40   ELEVATION: 4470 feet
WATERSHED: vsm   USGS MAP: Cascade Pass (1963 ns)

The outlet of Doubtful Lake pours down a mountainside in a series of 20- to 50-foot cataracts. After admiring Hidden Falls from near the crossing of Doubtful Creek (described earlier), look upstream to see the upper tier of the waterfall directly above the ford, downstream to see the lower tier. Be careful when negotiating the ford.

Falls of Horseshoe Basin (u) ★★★★

MAGNITUDE: 63   ELEVATION: 6070 feet
WATERSHED: vsm (g)   USGS MAP: Cascade Pass (1963 ns)

An entire series of waterfalls pours off the surrounding mountain ridges into Horseshoe Basin. Nineteen falls can be seen in a single view! The basin is a good example of a cirque, a bowl-shaped depression eroded by the upper portion of a former alpine glacier.

From Doubtful Creek (described earlier), hike 1 mile east to a fork in

Opposite: Boston Creek Falls

the trail. Westbounders will continue 0.8 mile past Basin Creek Falls (described later). Turn north and follow switchbacks steeply upward, meeting Basin Creek in 0.5 mile. The basin and falls are 1.5 miles farther. Hope that there is a breeze to keep the black flies from biting you!

Basin Creek Falls (u) ★★

MAGNITUDE: 82   ELEVATION: 3430 feet
WATERSHED: sm (g)   USGS MAP: Cascade Pass (1963 ns)

This 125- to 175-foot drop from Basin Creek would deserve a higher scenic rating, except only a distant view is possible. From the junction with the spur for Horseshoe Basin (described earlier), proceed eastward along Cascade Pass Trail. Hike 0.8 mile to the Basin Creek swinging bridge. The best vantage of the cataract is 50 yards downstream from the footbridge. From here, it is 1.2 miles eastward to Cottonwood Camp, then to Stehekin via a shuttle bus.

---

24 Ross Lake

North Cascades National Park is bisected by Ross Lake National Recreation Area and its three reservoirs: Gorge Lake, Diablo Lake, and Ross Lake. Reach this rugged portion of Washington via the North Cascades Highway (S.R. 20), which is normally open from June through October.

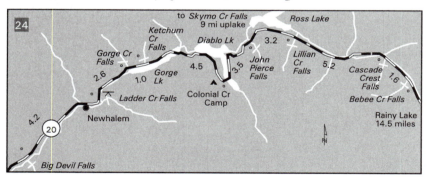

Big Devil Falls (u) ★★

MAGNITUDE: 78   ELEVATION: 900 feet
WATERSHED: sm   USGS MAP: Big Devil Peak (1989 ns)

This waterfall is tempting in that, despite the distant roadside vantage, one can tell it is of great stature. Drive along S.R. 20 to an unsigned turnout equivalent to mile marker 115.7, located 9.5 miles east of Marblemount and 4.2 miles west of the junction for the National Park Vistors Center in Newhalem. This 120- to 150-foot display deserves a higher rating, if only closer views were available.

LADDER CREEK FALLS ★★★

MAGNITUDE: 58   ELEVATION: 1410 feet
WATERSHED: med (g)   USGS MAP: Diablo Dam (1963)

This series of falls is unique because Seattle City Light illuminates them at night with colored lights. The major set of four descents totals 80 to 120 feet. Take S.R. 20 to the eastern side of Newhalem and park near the Gorge Powerhouse. Walk across the footbridge spanning the Skagit River and follow the trail through a landscaped rock garden, which contains many miniature cataracts. Viewing decks of the main display are 0.1 mile away.

GORGE CREEK FALLS ★★★

MAGNITUDE: 66
ELEVATION: 1660 feet
WATERSHED: sm
USGS MAP: Diablo Dam (1963 ns)

Ladder Creek Falls

Early summer is the best time for waterfall hunting along the North Cascades Highway. The smaller streams have yet to dry up and most of them harbor falls. The following entries all flow off escarpments adjacent to the highway. At Gorge Creek, water streams down 120 to 150 feet in three sections. Two smaller falls can also be seen adjacent to the featured attraction. From the Gorge Powerhouse (described earlier), take S.R. 20 east 2.6 miles to a parking area on the near (west) side of Gorge Creek Bridge. There are moderately distant views from the bridge walkway.

KETCHUM CREEK FALLS ★★

MAGNITUDE: 24 (l)   ELEVATION: 2280 feet
WATERSHED: vsm   USGS MAP: Diablo Dam (1963 ns)

This cataract descends 80 to 100 feet along Ketchum Creek. Drive 1 mile east from Gorge Creek Falls (described earlier). Park at the unsigned turnout on the far (east) side of the creek.

JOHN PIERCE FALLS ★★★

MAGNITUDE: 49   ELEVATION: 2200 feet
WATERSHED: sm   USGS MAP: Ross Dam (1963)

Water slides 40 to 50 feet toward Diablo Lake. Although the drainage extends 400 to 450 feet farther down, it is usually dry, its runoff absorbed by the rocky substrate. Also called *Pierce Falls* and *Horsetail Falls*.

Drive east on S.R. 20 for 3.5 miles from Colonial Creek Camp, or west for 0.5 mile past the junction for Ross Dam, to an unsigned turnout on the northeast side of the highway.

SKYMO CREEK FALLS ★★

MAGNITUDE: 41   ELEVATION: 1700 feet
WATERSHED: med   USGS MAP: Pumpkin Mtn (1969 ns)

Skymo Creek rushes 40 to 60 feet into Ross Lake about halfway up the reservoir. To reach Ross Dam and Ross Lake Resort, take a tugboat from Diablo Lake or hike 1 mile along Ross Lake Trail signed at the North Cascades Highway (S.R. 20) about 0.5 mile east of John Pierce Falls (described earlier). Rent a boat at the resort. Unfortunately, there are reportedly no launching facilities for private craft. The cataract is located on the west shore of the lake across from aptly named Tenmile Island.

LILLIAN CREEK FALLS (U) ★★

MAGNITUDE: 50   ELEVATION: 2100 feet
WATERSHED: sm   USGS MAP: Ross Dam (1963 ns)

Each tier of this cataract is 20 to 25 feet high. It is located just off of the highway 2.7 miles east of S.R. 20's junction to Ross Lake Trail and Resort. Park at the wide unsigned turnout on the mountain side of the highway next to the stream.

CASCADE CREST FALLS (U) ★★

MAGNITUDE: 38   ELEVATION: 2100 feet
WATERSHED: sm   USGS MAP: Carter Mountain (1973 ns)

This is another tiered falls, where an unnamed stream plunges 10 to 15 feet before cascading another 20 to 25 feet downward. Drive 5.2 miles southeast of Lillian Creek Falls (described earlier), 0.3 mile east of Canyon Creek Trailhead. Park at the unsigned turnout on the Granite Creek side of S.R. 20. Walk across the road to the tributary and a close-up view of its descent. (This falls is named by the author after a nearby trail.) This and the next entry are actually located in a part of Mount Baker–Snoqualmie National Forest administered by Okanogan National Forest.

Bebee Creek Falls (u) ★★★

MAGNITUDE: 48 (h)   ELEVATION: 2200 feet
WATERSHED: sm   USGS MAP: Carter Mountain (1973 ns)

Water pours 45 to 60 feet into a tiny gorge at an unusual 110-degree angle. Find the "driveway" sort of turnout next to Bebee Creek, located 1.6 miles southeast of Cascade Crest Falls (described earlier), 0.2 mile northwest of where East Creek Trailhead is signed at S.R. 20. Also unofficially known as Emerald Pool Falls, it's located just south of mile marker 143.

---

25 RAINY PASS

Sure the author is biased toward waterfalls, but it has always been confounding why some scenic falls have been excluded from maps and literature describing particular areas. Such has been the case at Rainy Pass, home to one of the highest magnitude cataracts in the Pacific Northwest. Not until its understated mention in the latest edition of the official map of

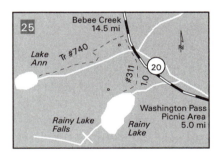

Okanogan National Forest did I know the falls even existed. Boy, I'm glad I found out.

Rainy Lake Falls (u) ★★★★

MAGNITUDE: 112   ELEVATION: 5500 feet
WATERSHED: vsm (g)   USGS MAP: McAlester Mtn (1977 ns)

A pair of horsetails each drop 200 to 300 feet, where they can be seen being fed by the meltwaters of Lyall Glacier. Drive to the signed parking area for Rainy Lake, located 14.5 miles southeast of Bebee Creek Falls (described earlier) and

Rainy Lake Falls

5 miles west of Washington Pass Picnic Area along S.R. 20. There are actually two trails; take Trail #311, the one to the left, which proceeds southward (not Trail #740 to Lake Ann). The way is flat and paved all the way to its end at Rainy Lake in 1 mile. This locale is a grandiose example of a cirque, a bowl-like depression carved into the mountains toward the upper end of a glacier. Lyall Glacier is the remnant of what several thousands of years ago was a much more extensive glacier. Rainy Lake is geomorphically known as a tarn, a lake occupying a cirque. The vista at this place is truly awe-inspiring, though the cataract itself is a fair distance away. Those with an inflatable raft, or similar such watercraft, can paddle across the lake for a 5-star vantage.

26 METHOW VALLEY

The town of Mazama represents the eastern outpost for travel along the North Cascades Highway (S.R. 20). For westbound travelers, it has the last facilities for 75 miles. The two falls located in this area are both within Okanogan National Forest, as are the entries within the succeeding Winthrop and Foggy Dew Creek sections of this chapter.

CEDAR FALLS ★★★

MAGNITUDE: 39   ELEVATION: 3670 feet
WATERSHED: med   USGS MAP: Mazama (1991)

Cedar Creek has cut deeply into granite bedrock to form this series of 20- to 30-foot cataracts. Drive 4.2 miles west of Mazama along S.R. 20 and turn left (south) on Sandy Butte–Cedar Creek Road #200. Follow this gravel route for 0.5 mile and park near the marked Cedar Creek Trail #476, leading to the right. The trail ascends moderately for 1.7 miles before reaching the falls.

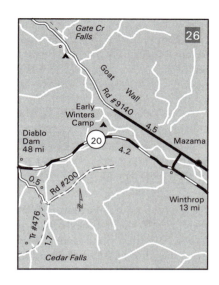

Those who like climbing rocks can seek out *Gate Creek Falls* (u) ★ USGS McLeod Mtn (1991 nl). This 100-foot drop skips down a portion of the Goat Wall, a glaciated cliff rising 2000 feet above the floor of the Methow Valley. Drive to an informal campsite located along West Fork Methow Road #9140, 4.5 miles north of S.R. 20. Find the creek on the far side of the camp and climb a rigorous 0.3 mile upstream along a steep talus (rocky) slope.

---

27 WINTHROP

The town of Winthrop has certainly created a niche in Washington tourism. Here is one of the few places in the state that harkens of the Old West. Virtually the entire commercial district possesses a frontier-style façade that successfully eludes looking hokey. The place has the staples of a Northwest tourist town: shopping, eating, and to the author's delight, a brewpub. Not to mention waterfalls that led me here in the first place. All three falls occur up the watershed of the Chewuch River.

BOULDER CREEK FALLS (U) ★★

MAGNITUDE: 30   ELEVATION: 2300 feet
WATERSHED: lg   USGS MAP: Lewis Butte (1991 nl)

Tannic acids natural to the area create the rust-colored tint of Boulder Creek and the 10- to 15-foot drop of its segmented punchbowls. Drive a short distance west of Winthrop, turning north off S.R. 20 onto Chewuch Road #51, located across from the Methow Valley Visitors Center. Go 5.6 miles and turn right onto an unsigned paved road. Proceed 0.2 mile and turn left at Forest Road #37. After another 1.8 miles, park along a wide

0.2 mile, looking to the right of the trail to see *Cavern Falls* ★ USGS Mount Constitution (1994), where water steeply tumbles 20 to 40 feet into a recess in the canyon. Lastly, *Hidden Falls* ★ USGS Mount Constitution (1994) will be met in another 0.3 mile. This 15- to 20-foot drop is "hidden" only if you are not observant. Cross the creek twice beyond Cavern Falls. The second crossing is above the top of the falls, 0.6 mile from the trailhead.

2 ELWHA

Olympic National Park is best known for its lush rain-forest valleys and snow-topped mountains, but its soothing cataracts also deserve attention. The waterfalls of seven of this chapter's sections are located within the park.

MADISON CREEK FALLS (U) ★★

MAGNITUDE: 47
ELEVATION: 540 feet
WATERSHED: sm
USGS MAP: Elwha (1985 ns)

This unpublicized 40- to 50-foot descent is just off one of the main roads into the park. Take U.S. 101 west from Port Angeles for 8 miles and turn left onto Olympic Hot Springs Road. Drive 2 miles to the park boundary and stop at the turn-out on the left side of the road. A short walk into a wooded tract brings this entry into view.

WOLF CREEK FALLS (U) ★★★

MAGNITUDE: 41 ELEVATION: 850 feet USGS
WATERSHED: sm MAP: Hurricane Hill (1976 nl)

This is actually a double-tiered falls, but only the 30- to 40-foot lower section is clearly visible. The 50- to 70-foot upper portion is hidden by the shape of the gorge. Drive 2 miles beyond the park boundary on Olympic Hot Springs Road (described earlier); just past the ranger station turn left onto a gravel road. After another 4 miles, park along the turnout at the marked trailhead for Lake Mills. Follow the steep trail to its end in 0.4 mile. Walk around the ridge to the right to Wolf Creek. The base of the cataract is easily reached by heading upstream less than 100 feet.

3 MOUNT CARRIE

The trail system for the following falls is reached by
staying on paved Olympic
Hot Springs Road (de-
scribed earlier) to its end.
The north shore of Lake
Mills is 2 miles past the
ranger station, with Boulder Creek Campground
and Trailhead 5.5 miles
farther.

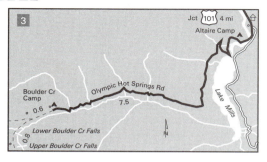

LOWER BOULDER CREEK FALLS ★★

MAGNITUDE: 48   ELEVATION: 2650 feet
WATERSHED: sm   USGS MAP: Mount Carrie (1950 nl)

Water froths 25 to 35 feet downward
into the upper reaches of Boulder
Creek Gorge. Just beyond the campsites of Boulder Creek Campground,
begin hiking along Boulder Creek
Trail. Bear left at the fork in 0.6 mile,
hiking along South Fork Boulder
Creek. The way ascends moderately
over the next 0.6 mile before inter-
secting with a short spur path that
soon leads to the falls.

UPPER BOULDER CREEK FALLS ★★

MAGNITUDE: 56
ELEVATION: 3030 feet
WATERSHED: sm
USGS MAP: Mount Carrie (1950 nl)

Boulder Creek tumbles 15 to 25 feet
before taking a 75- to 100-foot
plunge. A full view of the upper portion can be had at the end of the trail,

Lower Boulder Creek Falls

but only the top of the main display is safely visible. Take the Boulder Creek Trail 0.2 mile beyond Lower Boulder Creek Falls (described earlier) to a second marked spur trail. This short path quickly leads to a viewpoint between the descents.

4 LAKE CRESCENT

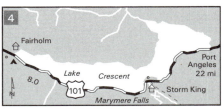

Lake Crescent is in the northwestern corner of Olympic National Park's inland section as is one of the most scenic falls of the region. Drive along U.S. 101, either 22 miles west from Port Angeles or 8 miles east from Fairholm, to Storm King Visitor Center and Ranger Station. The following entry is a short hike away.

MARYMERE FALLS ★★★★

MAGNITUDE: 62
WATERSHED: sm

ELEVATION: 1030 feet
USGS MAP: Lake Crescent (1985)

Falls Creek plunges and horsetails 90 feet over a rock wall. At Storm King Visitor Center, embark upon Falls Nature Trail, which leads to the cataract in 0.8 mile. Take a self-guided tour or accompany a scheduled group.

5 SOLEDUCK

For years, many of the names in this valley have been given as "Soleduck," an English variant of the Native American phrase *Sol Duc,* meaning "magic waters." The Geographic Names Information System, a database maintained by the U.S. Geological Survey, now uses the original spelling for the names of natural features but has retained the variant for cultural places.

Marymere Falls

Sol Duc Falls ★★★

MAGNITUDE: 58   ELEVATION: 2190 feet
WATERSHED: med   USGS MAP: Bogachiel Peak (1950)

The waters of the Sol Duc River rush 40 to 60 feet downward at a right angle to create this falls, which is also spelled Soleduck Falls (u). Drive west from Fairholm for 1.8 miles on U.S. 101 to Soleduck Road, which leads to Sol Duc Hot Springs in 12 miles. The road ends at Soleduck Trailhead 1.5 miles farther. Hike 1 mile beyond the trailhead, then turn right (south) at the first junction. The falls can be seen from the footbridge crossing the river.

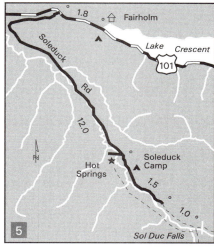

Sol Duc Falls

6 BEAVER CREEK

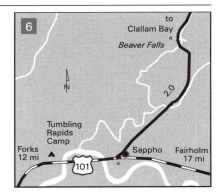

The falls in this and the next section are located outside Olympic National Park, but were accessible to the public when last surveyed.

BEAVER FALLS ★★★

MAGNITUDE: 34 (l)
ELEVATION: 600 feet
WATERSHED: med
USGS MAP: Lake Pleasant (1984)

Beaver Creek tumbles 30 to 40 feet in three sections across an 80-foot-wide rock escarpment. Turn off U.S. 101 at Sappho, 12 miles north of Forks and 17 miles west of Fairholm. Follow the northbound secondary road for 2 miles to an unsigned turnout 0.1 mile past Beaver Creek bridge. A short, unimproved path leads to the cataract.

7 CLALLAM BAY

Passing motorists probably miss the following cataracts as they admire the Clallam Bay portion of the Strait of Juan de Fuca, the passage connecting Puget Sound with the Pacific Ocean.

HOKO FALLS ★★

MAGNITUDE: 28 (h)   ELEVATION: 210 feet
WATERSHED: lg   USGS MAP: Hoko Falls (1984)

The normally calm waters of the Hoko River rush 5 to 10 feet at a narrow reach where erosion-resistant rock constricts the stream. Follow S.R. 112 to the seaside village of Clallam Bay. Continue on S.R. 112 for 4.1 miles, then turn left (south) toward Ozette Lake. Proceed 6.3 miles to a bridge over the Hoko River, parking on the far side. Fishermen's paths lead down to a view near the base of the falls.

Also in the vicinity is *Falls Creek Falls* (u) ★ USGS Clallam Bay (1984 nl). A low stream flow reduces the scenic quality of its 20- to 25-foot tumble along Falls Creek. Follow S.R. 112 to the seaside village of Clallam Bay. Continue

Hoko Falls

1.6 miles west to the hamlet of Sekiu, parking at an unsigned turnout on the north (right) side of the road. Walk down a jeep trail a short distance, passing beneath the highway and progressing to the base of the falls.

Others: One of the most rugged sections of the Washington coast is Cape Flattery, where the Strait of Juan de Fuca meets the Pacific Ocean. While most visitors take to the sea for fishing excursions, the scenic beauty of the cape's coast, accented by several minor waterfalls, also merits an afternoon boat ride. Charter or launch your own craft at Neah Bay, located about 5 miles east of the cape. Early summer is the best time of the year to view the falls, as stream discharge is usually adequate and the weather conditions most often favorable for boating. Go online to *The Computer Companion* (described in the Introduction) to access a map to the following three entries. In addition, obtain a large-scale nautical map at Neah Bay if you are navigating your own boat.

Beach Creek trickles 30 to 40 feet directly into the Strait of Juan de Fuca to create *Beach Creek Falls* (u) ★ USGS Cape Flattery (1984 nl). Proceed 3.6 miles west of Neah Bay to a small cove and its small cataract.

Titacoclos Falls ★ USGS Cape Flattery (1984) features a 100- to 120-foot drop and tends to be seasonal, seldom flowing from mid- to late summer. This falls deserves a higher rating during peak periods. Look for it about 0.4 mile west of Beach Creek Falls.

At *Flattery Creek Falls* (u) ★ USGS Cape Flattery (1984 nl), water slides 45 to 60 feet into a crevasse at the head of Hole-in-the-Wall Cove. This falls is accessible only by small-craft boaters experienced in navigating rocky embayments. Proceed 1 mile past Titacoclos Falls to Cape Flattery and enter Hole-in-the-Wall. After dropping anchor, walk up the drainage a short distance to view this previously unnamed cataract. An ankle-deep wade may be required part of the way. Intriguing ruins of early twentieth-century buildings can also be seen in the cove.

8 OLYMPIC COAST

For safe access to the following waterfall, hikers or backpackers must be aware of tide conditions. Some of the beaches are inundated by the Pacific at high tide. Appropriate information for coastal hiking, such as tide tables, can be obtained at the Mora or Kalaloch Ranger Stations of Olympic National Park.

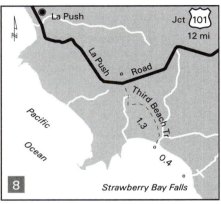

STRAWBERRY BAY FALLS (U) ★★

MAGNITUDE: 29 (l)   ELEVATION: 80 feet
WATERSHED: vsm   USGS MAP: Toleak Point (1982 nl)

An unnamed creek pours 100 to 120 feet into the surf. Five miles north of Forks turn left off U.S. 101, heading toward La Push and the Pacific Coast. After 8 miles, turn left (south), staying on La Push Road, and continue 4 miles to Third Beach Trailhead. Hike 1.3 miles to the ocean, then 0.4 mile south to the nearest beach-side view of the falls. Closer vantages are possible from wave-cut rocks, but for safety's sake walking on the rocks must be restricted to time periods when the tide is receding.

9 ENCHANTED VALLEY

This entry is for all the waterfall enthusiasts who also like to backpack. Marvel at the Enchanted Valley, located in the southern part of Olympic National Park. The most popular trailhead for accessing the valley, Graves Creek, is 23 miles east of Quinault, off U.S. 101, near the ranger station.

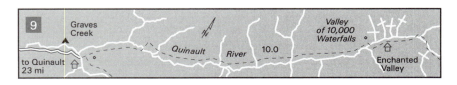

Valley of 10,000 Waterfalls (u) ★★★★

MAGNITUDE: not calculable   ELEVATION: 3400 to 4200 feet
WATERSHED: sm (g)   USGS MAP: Chimney Peak (1990 nl
and ns)

Many visitors and long-time residents of the Olympic Peninsula prefer the name Valley of 10,000 Waterfalls to the more common Enchanted Valley. Although the number of falls may be exaggerated in the name, you would be hard-pressed to keep track of the scores of waterfalls that can be seen during a single day's journey in this valley. Practically every tributary encountered along Enchanted Valley Trail breaks into a waterfall as it enters the glacially carved valley of the Quinault River. Varied vegetation completes the serene scenery of the gorge. Secure a back-country permit at the Graves Creek or Dosewallips Ranger Stations. Most of the falls are within 0.3 mile of the Enchanted Valley Ranger Station, which is 10 miles from the trailhead and is open during the summer if you need information or assistance.

A cataract in the Valley of 10,000 Waterfalls

10 QUILCENE

The following waterfall is located within Olympic National Forest in the vicinity of Quilcene Ranger Station.

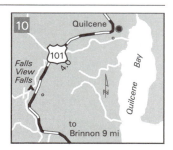

Falls View Falls (u) ★★

MAGNITUDE: 26 (l)
ELEVATION: 280 feet
WATERSHED: vsm
USGS MAP: Mount Walker (1985 ns)

An unnamed creek drops 80 to 120 feet into the Big Quilcene River. The flow is greatest during the wet season from autumn to spring. It may disappear entirely during droughts. The cataract is also known as Campground Falls (u).

Turn off U.S. 101 at Falls View Camp, 4 miles south of Quilcene and 9 miles north of Brinnon. A short trail at the south end of the campground leads to a fenced vista high above the canyon floor.

11 DOSEWALLIPS

Kudos to a local resident for pointing out this otherwise obscure yet entertaining spectacle. Although it is likely situated on private land, it was accessible when last visited and is currently listed as a recreation opportunity in material authored by Olympic National Forest.

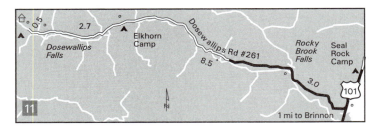

ROCKY BROOK FALLS (U) ★★★★

MAGNITUDE: 71   ELEVATION: 500 feet
WATERSHED: med   USGS MAP: Brinnon (1985 ns)

Water thunders 100 to 125 feet over a massive scarp. If you also plan on taking a day trip to Dosewallips Falls (described next), save this one for last. Drive 1 mile north of Brinnon on U.S. 101, then turn left (west) at Road #261, signed Dosewallips Recreation Area. Proceed west for 3 miles and park at the unsigned turnout on the west side of the bridge crossing Rocky Brook. A well-worn trail quickly leads to the base of the falls.

DOSEWALLIPS FALLS ★★★

MAGNITUDE: 53   ELEVATION: 1400 feet
WATERSHED: lg   USGS MAP: The Brothers (1985 nl)

Water pours 100 to 125 feet over and around boulders along the Dosewallips River. This scenic cascade is located within Olympic National Park. Continue driving 11.2 miles westward past Rocky Brook bridge (described earlier) along Dosewallips Road (#261). A signed turnout will be seen near the base of the cataract, 0.7 mile beyond the park boundary.

12 LAKE CUSHMAN

CUSHMAN FALLS ★★

MAGNITUDE: 44   ELEVATION: 850 feet
WATERSHED: sm   USGS MAP: Lightning Peak (1990 nl)

An unnamed creek slides 25 to 35 feet, nearly spraying onto the road. This falls is located on a strip of private property adjacent to Olympic National Park. Depart U.S. 101 at the hamlet of Hoodsport; the turnoff is signed Olympic National Park–Staircase Area. Lake Cushman State Park is in 7.2 miles. In another 2 miles turn left onto Road #24 toward the Staircase Area and reach the waterfall in 2.4 miles.

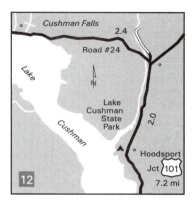

13 WYNOOCHEE LAKE

The south-central portion of Olympic National Forest, being remote from travelers' facilities, is one of the lesser-frequented areas of the Olympic Peninsula. The most reliable access to the following pair of cataracts is from the south. Depart U.S. 12 at Devonshire Road, 1.5 miles west of Montesano. After 0.1 mile, turn left (north) on Wynoochee Road #22 and drive 34 miles to Wynoochee Dam.

WYNOOCHEE FALLS ★★

MAGNITUDE: 44   ELEVATION: 1010 feet
WATERSHED: med   USGS MAP: Wynoochee Lake (1990 nl)

This pretty double punchbowl tumbles 25 to 35 feet along the Wynoochee River. At Wynoochee Dam turn north onto Road #2270. In 6 miles pass the turnoff to Noname Falls (described below). Proceed 1.2 miles farther and turn left onto Road #260 into an old national forest campground. Proceed to the north end of the camp, then walk along any of the several footpaths, all of which lead to the falls in 50 to 100 yards.

Along the way, waterfall collectors can find *Noname Falls* (u) ★ USGS Wynoochee Lake (1990 ns). An unnamed creek drops 40 to 60 feet in two major steps. Since no labeled features occur in the immediate vicinity, I have "no name" for the falls. Six miles north of Wynoochee Dam, bear right at a fork and proceed 1 more mile to a roadside view of this entry.

14 SHELTON

GOLDSBOROUGH CREEK FALLS (U) ★★

MAGNITUDE: 37   ELEVATION: 130 feet
WATERSHED: lg (d)   USGS MAP: Shelton (1981 nl)

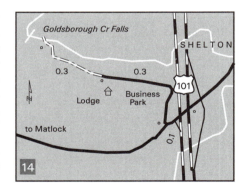

Goldsborough Creek once poured 8 to 12 feet over a small dam. With the removal of the dam, the descent has been reduced to a series of foot-high fish ladders. The property is owned by Simpson Timber, which allowed access, but no fishing, when this entry was field-truthed.

Depart the divided highway of U.S. 101 on the south side of Shelton at the Matlock Exit. Drive west for just 0.1 mile, then turn right at the sign for Golds-borough Business Park. Proceed 0.3 mile, stopping just before the parking lot for Sentry Park Pavalion-Lodge. Walk down the dirt road 0.3 mile to the falls, avoiding the side roads.

15 KAMILCHE

KENNEDY FALLS ★★

MAGNITUDE: 38   ELEVATION: 240 feet
WATERSHED: med   USGS MAP: Kamilche Valley (1981)

Kennedy Creek drops to an emerald-tinted gorge in two major tiers. The upper

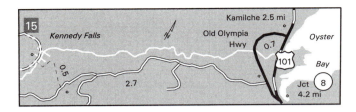

portion of this small but pleasant waterfall tumbles 5 to 10 feet into a pool. A short distance downstream, the creek pours 20 to 30 feet into the narrow gorge.

Turn off U.S. 101 onto Old Olympia Highway 2.5 miles south of the Kamilche/S.R. 108 Exit and 4.2 miles northwest of the junction of U.S. 101 and S.R. 8. Drive 0.7 mile to the dirt road south of Kennedy Creek. Turn west and stay on the main route for 2.7 miles, bearing right (toward the creek) at all major forks. Park along the side of the road at its junction with an un-signed jeep trail and hike for 0.5 mile to the creek. The best views of the falls are from the north side of the valley. Walk a short distance upstream to a fairly easy ford above the upper descent, then progress downstream to a clear, unguarded vista. This site is most likely on private land.

16 OLYMPIA

Four cataracts highlight a leisurely 30-minute stroll through the landscaped setting of Tumwater Falls Park, which is located on the grounds of the Miller Brewery (formerly the Olympia and Pabst Breweries). Depart I-5 at Exit 103. Visitor parking is one block east of the freeway. After visiting the falls, take a tour of the brewery and enjoy a complimentary glass of beer or soda in the hospitality room.

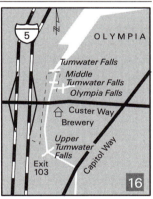

TUMWATER FALLS ★★★

MAGNITUDE: 41
WATERSHED: lg (d)

ELEVATION: 60 feet
USGS MAP: Tumwater (1994 nl)

This 40-foot waterfall has become famous over the years by having its like-ness shown on the labels of the brewery's Olympia brands. First called Puget Sound Falls by European settlers in 1829, it was renamed Shutes River Falls in 1841. In 1845 Michael Troutman Simmons led a party of American settlers to the vicinity. He coined the name Tumwater based on a Chinook word. The Chinook called running water *tumtum* because they thought its sound was like the throb of a heart.

Tumwater Falls

From the parking lot, walk downstream 0.2 mile to a vista overlooking the falls. A footbridge crosses above the descent. Before hiking, you may wish to see *Upper Tumwater Falls* (u) ★ USGS Tum-water (1994 nl). The form of this 10- to 20-foot drop along the Deschutes River has been modified to harness water power, reducing its scenic value. It is located near the picnic area adjacent to the visitor parking area for the brewery.

OLYMPIA FALLS (U) ★★

MAGNITUDE: 46
ELEVATION: 100 feet
WATERSHED: sm (?)
USGS MAP: Tumwater (1994 ns)

Purified water is returned to the Deschutes River from the brewery in a nice display descending a total of 40 to 60 feet. Cross the river at Tumwater Falls (described earlier) and walk upstream a short distance; the trail passes between the upper and lower portions of this waterfall.

Walk a short distance downstream to see *Middle Tumwater Falls* (u) ★ USGS Tumwater (1994 ns). Water tumbles 15 to 25 feet along the Deschutes River, whose name is French for "River of the Falls."

17 PORTER

PORTER FALLS ★★

MAGNITUDE: 32   ELEVATION: 400 feet
WATERSHED: med   USGS MAP: Malone (1986 nl)

This largest in a series of small cataracts along West Fork Porter Creek drops 8 to 12 feet just above the stream's confluence with North Fork Porter Creek.

It is located within Capitol State Forest. Leave U.S. 12 at the hamlet of Porter on unsigned Porter Creek Road. Drive 2.7 miles, where the road turns into a graveled surface. Continue another 0.5 mile to the Porter Creek entrance to Capitol State Forest. Stay on this road, now called B-Line, for another 0.6 mile to a generic trail sign immediately before the entrance to Porter Creek Camp. Park here, where

Porter Falls

an interpretive sign describes the logging railroad that played a large role in the history of the area. The 0.5-mile trail parallels North Fork for 0.3 mile before ending at the falls.

Others: The Mima Prairie consists of the rolling terrain within the Black Hills, most of which is managed by the Washington Department of Natural Resources as Capitol State Forest. The most interesting features in this area occur on the eastern fringe of the forest at Mima Mounds, a small prairie composed of numerous small hummocks. It is theorized that these 5- to 10-foot-high "pimpled mounds" were formed thousands of years ago by rodent activity and/or processes related to glaciation. *Mima Falls* ★ USGS Littlerock (1986), tumbling 20- to 25-feet along Mima Creek, can be found in the vicinity.

Depart S.R. 121 at the village of Littlerock on 128th Avenue/Littlerock Road, signed for Mima Mounds. Continue 0.8 mile to a T intersection and turn left on Mima Road. (Turning right will take you to the Mima Mounds interpretive area.) Go 1.3 miles and turn right onto Bordeaux Road. Proceed 0.7 mile, then turn right on Marksman Road; reach the entrance to Mima Falls camp, signed Mima Falls Trailhead, in 0.9 mile. Drive 0.3 mile to a small parking area.

Mima Porter Trail #8 starts here and follows gentle terrain most of the way; the trick is making the correct turns at its various junctions. The first junction, signed for a variety of destinations, is met in 0.4 mile. Continue straight rather than bearing right. The path crosses a dirt road in another 0.2 mile. Look for a sign stating "Mima Falls 1.7 miles." In 1.2 miles after passing the sign, bear left at another trail junction and continue for 0.5 mile to the falls. A wooden bench above the cataract offers the best vantage. Its scenic rating may increase during periods of peak discharge.

Go online to *The Computer Companion* (described in the Introduction) to access a map to this entry.

18 RAINBOW FALLS STATE PARK

RAINBOW FALLS ★★

MAGNITUDE: 24 (h)   ELEVATION: 400 feet
WATERSHED: lg   USGS MAP: Rainbow Falls (1986)

A large pool at the base of this 5- to 10-foot waterfall along the Chehalis River serves as a popular swimming hole. Drive to Rainbow Falls State Park, which is adjacent to S.R. 6, about 3 miles east of Doty and 12 miles west of Adna. Views of the falls

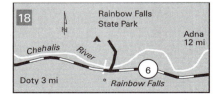

can be had from the bridge over the river at the park entrance. Within the park, interpretive trails guide the visitor through stands of virgin timber.

MOUNT RAINIER REGION, WASHINGTON

The region within and surrounding Mount Rainier National Park is among the most scenic in North America. While the mountain itself, called *Takhoma* by the Yakama Indians, is the centerpiece of the area, many other attractions await discovery. Of the 159 waterfalls known to occur within the area, 66 are mentioned in this chapter.

This is a land of fire and ice. The oldest rocks predate Mount Rainier itself. Between 30 million and 60 million years ago, the region was part of a large, low-lying coastal zone scattered with terrestrial and subterranean volcanoes, which deposited thick accumulations of lava over a wide area. Ten million to 30 million years later, continued volcanic activity forced molten material, magma, toward the surface of the earth. Most of this magma cooled before it could pour from the volcanoes' vents as lava. It solidified to become bedrock, which was later thrust to the surface by internal earth forces or exposed by erosion.

Because of this complex history, the landscape along the periphery of Mount Rainier comprises many different types of rocks that streams erode at unequal rates. *Silver Falls* occurs where the Ohanapecosh River intersects resistant vertical layers of basalt before continuing its course along relatively weak volcanic breccia, which was formed when lava intermingled with sandstone and siltstone. At *Lower Stevens Falls,* magma was injected into an older

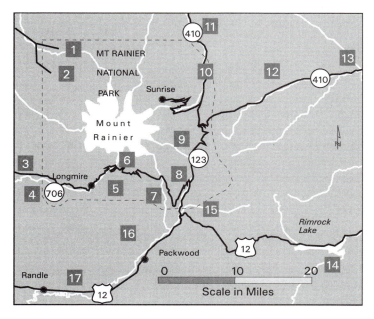

rock complex and the resulting bedrock proved to be more resistant than the neighboring material.

Mount Rainier formed some 1 million to 5 million years ago and is composed of interlayered andesitic lava and volcanic ash from repeated eruptions. One large lava flow blocks the northward course of Maple Creek, diverting the stream eastward. Coincidentally, a vertical break in the local topography, called a fault, is positioned along the redefined route of the stream. *Maple Falls* presently plummets down this fault.

The abundance of waterfalls in the region is due not only to the processes described above but also to the large-scale landscape modifications achieved by glaciers. A total of twenty-seven named glaciers surround Mount Rainier today; 10,000 years ago these awesome phenomena, the earth's greatest erosive agents, extended to much lower elevations.

A topographic feature called a *step* is common to the higher valleys of this area. It occurs where an alpine glacier gouges its valley floor unevenly. *Clear Creek Falls* and *Sylvia Falls* lie along breaks probably formed in this manner. Waterfalls that drop from hanging valleys are also common around Mount Rainier. Hanging valleys formed when small, tributary glaciers could not erode their valleys as deeply as the large, main glaciers. Therefore, the floor of a smaller glacial valley will be high above that of a main glacial valley where the two meet. *Comet Falls* and *Spray Falls* are dramatic examples of this type.

1 CARBON RIVER

Vacationers visiting the region for the first time usually overlook this northwestern portion of Mount Rainier National Park, favoring instead better-known locations like Sunrise and Paradise. Local residents call it "Our Own Little Corner of the Mountain." But wherever you are from, you will be welcomed. Drive to the city of Buckley on S.R. 410, then go south along S.R. 165 through the historic mining towns of Wilkeson and Carbonado. The road forks about 3 miles south of Carbonado. Bear left and follow the highway along the Carbon River for another 9 miles to the park entrance, where the road turns to gravel.

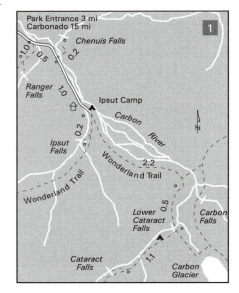

Ranger Falls ★★★★

MAGNITUDE: 70   ELEVATION: 2800 feet
WATERSHED: sm   USGS MAP: Mowich Lake (1971)

This entry tumbles a total of 100 to 125 feet along Ranger Creek. The form is eye-catching because the lower portion splits into twin falls. Proceed for 3 miles beyond the park entrance to Green Lake Trailhead. The trail ascends moderately for about 1 mile to a marked spur leading to the falls.

Chenuis Falls ★★

MAGNITUDE: 17 (l)   ELEVATION: 2180 feet
WATERSHED: med   USGS MAP: Mowich Lake (1971)

Water slides 70 to 100 feet across rock layers along Chenuis Creek. Drive 0.5 mile past Green Lake Trailhead (described earlier) to a parking turnout adjacent to the Carbon River. The falls is only 0.2 mile away. A log bridge provides access across the river.

Ipsut Falls ★★★

MAGNITUDE: 38   ELEVATION: 2600 feet
WATERSHED: sm   USGS MAP: Mowich Lake (1971)

This double falls along Ipsut Creek totals 40 to 60 feet. Please do not stray from the trail as the creek is the source of water for the campground. Drive just past Ipsut Camp to the trailhead at the end of the park road. Bear right (south) and hike along the Wonderland Trail a little way past the trailhead, to a signed spur trail leading 0.2 mile to the falls.

Carbon Falls (u) ★★

MAGNITUDE: 50   ELEVATION: 3300 feet
WATERSHED: vsm   USGS MAP: Mowich Lake (1971 nl)

The only view of a tributary creek tumbling toward the Carbon River is from across the valley. This waterfall is best viewed during the afternoon, if it is not overcast. Its rating decreases during the low-water periods of late summer.

Hike 2.2 miles from the Ipsut Camp trailhead along the Wonderland Trail. Soon after you leave the forested area and catch sight of the slopes across the river, the waterfall comes into view: first the lower falls, then the upper portion.

CATARACT FALLS ★★★

MAGNITUDE: 63   ELEVATION: 4020 feet
WATERSHED: sm   USGS MAP: Mowich Lake (1971)

Cataract Creek drops a total of 50 to 75 feet. In 1988, a major blowdown of trees blocked access to the spur trails and the descent. Before embarking, check with a ranger on the current status of the route.

Proceed 0.5 mile along the Wonderland Trail past the viewing area for Carbon Falls (described earlier), 2.7 miles from the trailhead. Pass *Lower Cataract Falls* (u) ★ USGS Mowich Lake (1971 ns), a 50- to 75-foot tumble along Cataract Creek, and at the trail junction follow the right (west) fork. The left fork goes to the toe of Carbon Glacier, which extends to a lower elevation than any other glacier in the continental United States. Expect a rough journey along the right fork, which reportedly is no longer maintained. After 1.1 miles, find the short spur trail quickly leading to the falls. From here it is 3.8 miles back to the trailhead.

2 MOWICH LAKE

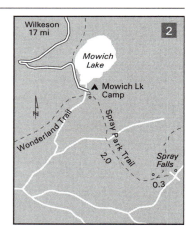

Drive to the city of Buckley via S.R. 410 and turn south on S.R. 165 toward Wilkeson and Carbonado. Three miles past Carbonado, turn right on the gravel extension of S.R. 165. This road, which has imposing views of Mount Rainier, ends at Mowich Lake, just inside the boundary of Mount Rainier National Park, in 16 miles.

SPRAY FALLS ★★★★★

MAGNITUDE: 98   ELEVATION: 5100 feet
WATERSHED: sm (g)   USGS MAP: Mowich Lake (1971)

This enormous display descends 300 to 350 feet along Spray Creek and is 50 to 80 feet wide. It is fed mostly from meltwaters of snowfields in Spray Park. Reach the falls by taking a substantial but not overly difficult hike of 2.3 miles. Embark upon the Wonderland Trail at the southeast end of Mowich Lake and proceed for 0.4 mile. Turn left onto Spray Park Trail and follow it for

1.6 miles. Finally, turn right at Spray Falls Trail. You
an exciting view of the spectacle 0.3 mile farther.

---

3 EATONVILLE

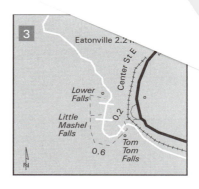

Confound it! Here we have three sepa-
rate waterfalls all accessible via the Falls
Trail within Charles Lathrop Pack Ex-
perimental Forest, owned by the University of Washington's College of Forest
Resources. The problem is finding a
trailhead. We drove into the forest entrance off of S.R. 7, but the road to the
waterfalls was gated. Strike one. Tried
hiking down a path off S.R. 161 starting
at the end of a day-use area, but it died out.
Strike two. Finally resorted to bush-
whacking. Success! But leave the children at home, as steep cliffs and a maze
of unsigned paths make this a somewhat challenging trek.

Drive to Eatonville, located west of Mount Rainier National Park on S.R.
161, about 3 miles northeast of S.R. 7. From downtown, take Center Street
beginning eastward before curving southwest for 2.2 miles to a very large unsigned turnout on the right side of the road. Park toward the far end. Find a
well-worn path and follow it down the hill to a set of railroad tracks. Cross the
tracks and continue along the path to the creek. (Walking on the trestle is discouraged; it is both dangerous and illegal.) Proceed downstream to a concrete
slab above the uppermost falls. All this is covered in about 0.2 mile.

TOM TOM FALLS ★★

MAGNITUDE: 28   ELEVATION: 1080 feet
WATERSHED: lg   USGS MAP: Eatonville (1990 ns)

Little Mashel River slides steeply 25 to 30 feet over a rock escarpment. From
the point described in the introduction above, make your way down the least
steep part of the escarpment, which is situated to your left, to airy views from
the base of the cataract. In the last edition, this entry was erroneously thought
to be Little Mashel Falls.

LITTLE MASHEL FALLS ★★★

MAGNITUDE: 48   ELEVATION: 1040 feet
WATERSHED: lg   USGS MAP: Eatonville (1990)

Little Mashel Falls

From the base of Tom Tom Falls (described earlier), find the trail heading in the downstream direction. After 0.1 mile, a spur path will be encountered that hopefully will still be marked with a blue blaze. Follow it steeply down for 0.2 mile to an excellent vista of a narrow fan descending 50 to 70 feet.

Lower Little Mashel Falls (u) ★★

MAGNITUDE: 59   ELEVATION: 980 feet
WATERSHED: lg   USGS MAP: Eatonville (1990 ns)

The river splits and time and again it plunges and curtains 20 to 40 feet in four strands. From the main trail at the junction for Little Mashel Falls (described earlier), continue in the downstream direction for another 0.1 mile, turning once again at a blue-blazed spur and following these blazes 0.4 mile moderately steeply down to a partially obstructed vantage. From here, it is 0.8 mile back to your vehicle.

---

4   Big Creek

Located southeast of Mount Rainier National Park, this drainage area reportedly harbors several waterfalls. Thus far, however, Cora Falls is the only one found to be readily accessible.

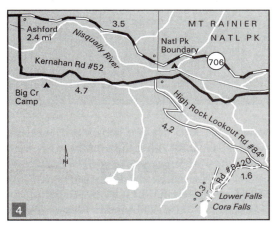

Cora Falls (u) ★★

MAGNITUDE: 43 (l)   ELEVATION: 3640
WATERSHED: vsm   USGS MAP: Sawtooth Ridge (1989 ns)

Depart S.R. 706 onto Kernahan Road #52, whose junction is located 2.4 miles east of Ashford. Proceed 4.7 miles, then turn right on High Rock

Van Trump Creek crashes 60 to 90 feet in tiered fashion. Do not give up hiking at Middle Van Trump Falls (described earlier). This double drop is only 0.2 mile farther, and you are less than 100 yards away from the best of them all.

COMET FALLS ★★★★★

MAGNITUDE: 106 (h)   ELEVATION: 5100 feet
WATERSHED: sm (g)   USGS MAP: Mt. Rainier West (1971)

Comet Falls

This spectacular 320-foot plunge is a classic example of a waterfall descending from a hanging valley, an escarpment that occurs where a tributary glacier did not erode as deeply as its larger relative.

The viewpoint for this descent is just beyond Van Trump Falls (described earlier), 1.6 miles from the trailhead. If you haven't had enough aerobic exercise by now, Comet Falls Trail continues steeply for another mile toward the top of the cataract.

CHRISTINE FALLS ★★★

MAGNITUDE: 57
ELEVATION: 3680 feet
WATERSHED: sm (g)
USGS MAP: Mt. Rainier West
(1971)

The stone masonry of the highway bridge forms a picturesque frame for this 40- to 60-foot drop along the lower reaches of Van Trump Creek. Drive along S.R. 706 eastward past Comet Falls Trailhead for 0.2 mile to the turnout on the east side of the bridge. Stairs lead quickly down to a view of this entry.

Christine Falls

TATO FALLS ★★

MAGNITUDE: 45   ELEVATION: 4280 feet
WATERSHED: sm (g)   USGS MAP: Mt. Rainier West (1971)

Only a moderately distant view is available of this 40- to 60-foot display as it drops along an unnamed tributary of the Nisqually River. Park at an old gravel spur road 0.5 mile east of Van Trump Creek bridge on S.R. 706. Walk along the gravel spur 0.3 mile to its end. Look upvalley and to the left for the falls. Surrounding vegetation obscures closer views.

Nearby, the best views of *Nahunta Falls* ★ USGS Mt. Rainier West (1971) can be gained by driving 0.4 mile south of the gravel spur. A cross-canyon view is afforded of an unnamed tributary steeply cascading 150 to 175 feet into the Nisqually River. It reduces to a trickle during low discharge periods of late summer.

---

6 PARADISE

At 5800 feet of elevation, Paradise is the highest point to which you can drive on Mount Rainier's southern face. Travel 15 miles east from the Nisqually entrance or 24 miles west from the Stevens Canyon entrance along the park's extension of S.R. 706. The contemporary-looking Visitors' Center and the traditionally rustic Paradise Inn are located about 1.5 miles off the main road and are accessible via the Paradise Loop Road.

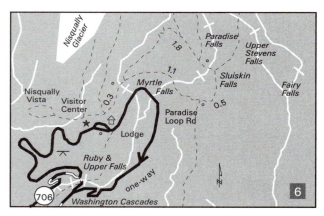

RUBY FALLS ★★

MAGNITUDE: 48 (h)   ELEVATION: 4780
WATERSHED: sm (g)   USGS MAP: Mt Rainier East (1971 ns)

Before departing the main highway, park at the unsigned turnout at the road junction to Paradise and admire several modest descents along the Paradise River. The first is *Upper Ruby Falls* (u) ★ Mt. Rainier East (1971 ns); gain a close-up view from the upstream side of the bridge. The top of Ruby Falls can be seen from the downstream side. Walk a couple of hundred feet down the trail for the best view. Only 0.1 mile down the trail is *Washington Cascades* ★★ Mt .Rainier East (1971 ns). Remnants of snowdrifts prevented the author from visiting it.

MYRTLE FALLS ★★★

MAGNITUDE: 34 (l)   ELEVATION: 5560 feet
WATERSHED: sm (g)   USGS MAP: Mt. Rainier East (1971 ns)

This entry provides one of the signature views of Mount Rainier, as Edith Creek tumbles 60 to 80 feet in the foreground. Find the Skyline Trail, which begins next to Paradise Inn. Walk an easy 0.3 mile to a stairway, descending to the overlook for a superb view.

SLUISKIN FALLS ★★★

MAGNITUDE: 40 (l)   ELEVATION: 5920 feet
WATERSHED: sm (g)   USGS MAP: Mt. Rainier East (1971)

A distant view of this 300-foot slide along the Paradise River is available from the 360-degree observation floor of the Visitors' Center. For a closer vantage, go just past Myrtle Falls (described earlier) and take the southern loop of the Skyline Trail to its junction with Lakes Trail, 1.4 miles from the trailhead. Bear left at the trail junction. Proceed another 0.5 mile, passing in succession the Paradise Glacier Trailhead, the Stevens-Van Trump historic monument, and a footbridge crossing the Paradise River. Proceed a few hundred yards farther to a view of the top portion of the falls. Short side spurs from the trail provide full views. Children and nervous adults should stay on the main trail, since the spurs end abruptly at cliffs. Either return the way you came or continue on for 2.1 miles to complete the northern portion of the loop. The falls was named for an Indian guide who aided Hazard Stevens and P. B. Van Trump in the first recorded climb of Mount Rainier in 1870.

Waterfall collectors can also add *Paradise Falls* (u) ★ USGS Mt. Rainier East (1971 nl) to their checklist of cataracts visited. From the footbridge near Sluiskin Falls, look upstream to a moderately distant view of this 30- to 50-foot descent near the headwaters of Paradise River.

---

7 STEVENS CANYON

It is no exaggeration to say that the National Park Service's eastward extension of S.R. 706 is one of the most scenic roads ever engineered. The Stevens Canyon stretch is not as convoluted as other sections of the route, but its construction was just as daring an undertaking. The view across the canyon from the Wonderland Trail confirms that judgment. The fine line of the highway can be seen cut into the side of Stevens Ridge over 400 feet above the canyon floor.

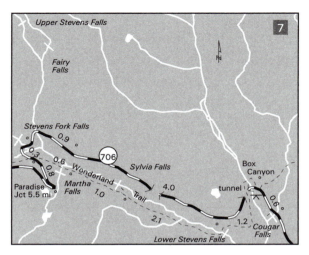

Stevens Fork Falls (u) ★★

MAGNITUDE: 36   ELEVATION: 4030 feet
WATERSHED: vsm   USGS MAP: Mt Rainier East (1971 ns)

Gain a roadside view of an unnamed tributary pouring 20 to 25 feet on its way to Stevens Creek. Drive to an unsigned turnout 6.6 miles east of Paradise junction; 0.9 mile west of the viewpoint for Martha Falls (described later). Additionally, you can see *Fairy Falls* ★ USGS Mt. Rainier East (1971), one of the highest recorded perennial waterfalls in North America. Too bad it is not highly regarded because there are no close views. It consists of two silvery white threads plummeting 700 feet from Stevens Basin as two large horsetails. Park at the turnout for The Bench, located 1.1 miles south of this entry. Look up the valley toward and to the right (east) of where you see Mount Rainier. Also look just to the left and you will see *Upper Stevens Falls* (u) ★ USGS Mt. Rainier East (1971 nl), where Stevens Creek drops 200 to 300 feet in the distance. Fairy Falls can also be viewed from Skyline Trail (refer to the Myrtle Falls map in the previous chapter section).

Martha Falls ★★★★

MAGNITUDE: 80   ELEVATION: 3680 feet
WATERSHED: sm   USGS MAP: Mt. Rainier East (1971)

Water spills 126 to 150 feet along Unicorn Creek. It can be viewed at a moderate distance from the highway or close-up from the trailside. Sightseers in cars can drive along S.R. 706 to the Martha Falls wayside, located 2 miles northeast of The Bench and 4 miles west of Box Canyon. Hikers can access the Wonderland Trail where it intersects the highway 0.8 mile north of The Bench or 0.3 mile south of Stevens Fork Falls (described earlier). Embark upon the trailhead on the east side of the road, where the path winds moderately down 0.6 mile to a footbridge overlooking the falls.

Sylvia Falls ★★★

MAGNITUDE: 38 (l)   ELEVATION: 3080 feet
WATERSHED: med (g)   USGS MAP: Mt. Rainier East (1971)

Stevens Creek tumbles 80 to 100 feet over a rock step within Stevens Canyon. Continue along the Wonderland Trail past Martha Falls (described earlier) for an additional mile. Look for an unsigned, but well-worn, spur trail that quickly leads to a vantage of the descent.

Lower Stevens Falls (u) ★★

MAGNITUDE: 23   ELEVATION: 2580 feet
WATERSHED: med (g)   USGS MAP: Mt. Rainier East (1971 nl)

Water cascades 30 to 40 feet over granite bedrock along Stevens Creek. Hike 1.2 miles south from Box Canyon on the Wonderland Trail, or continue 2.1 miles past Sylvia Falls (described earlier) for a total of 3.7 miles from the westward trailhead, to the footbridge above the falls.

Cougar Falls ★★★

MAGNITUDE: 65   ELEVATION: 2800 feet
WATERSHED: med   USGS MAP: Mt. Rainier East (1971)

This impressive 100- to 125-foot plunge shoots through a tight gorge. It is recommended for adults only. Drive southeast from Box Canyon along S.R. 706 for 0.6 mile to the unsigned turnout immediately northwest of the Nickel Creek bridge. Walk down the primitive trail to good direct views of the falls in 0.1 mile. Stay away from the bare rock surfaces near the creek. There are no guardrails along the precipitous rim, which slopes sharply into the steep canyon!

8 Upper Ohanapecosh

This popular area near the southeast entrance of Mount Rainier National Park boasts hot springs and a stand of forest giants in addition to waterfalls.

Walk a short distance from Ohanapecosh Campground to the natural setting of the hot springs. Feel dwarfed by the Grove of the Patriarchs between the Stevens Canyon entrance and Olallie Creek.

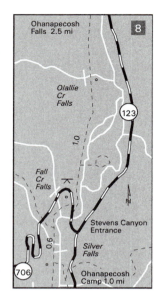

SILVER FALLS ★★★

MAGNITUDE: 55 (h)
ELEVATION: 2000 feet
WATERSHED: lg
USGS MAP: Chinook Pass (1987)

Rushing water thunders 30 to 40 feet into a pool. Limit your views to those available from the trail and designated vantages. While the falls do not look dangerous, the tumultuous river has claimed the lives of many who failed to heed the posted warnings.

From the Stevens Canyon entrance drive 0.3 mile south along S.R. 123 to the East Side Trailhead on the right (west) side of the road. A short trail leads down to the bottom of the gorge and the falls along the Ohanapecosh River. A pair of trails from Ohanapecosh Campground also provides a leisurely 1-mile stroll to the falls. There are three smaller descents immediately upstream and one downstream from the main falls.

FALL CREEK FALLS (u) ★★

MAGNITUDE: 24 (l)   ELEVATION: 2280 feet
WATERSHED: vsm   USGS MAP: Chinook Pass (1987 ns)

Fall Creek drops 30 to 50 feet, nearly spraying onto the highway before flowing beneath it. It deserves a lower rating during the low-water periods of late summer. A car-window glimpse of this entry can be gained from S.R. 706 just 0.2 mile from the Stevens Canyon entrance. If you wish to linger, stop at the parking area near the entrance and walk up the road.

Nearby, waterfall seekers can find *Olallie Creek Falls* (u) ★ USGS Chinook Pass (1987 nl), a modest 30- to 50-foot cascade. Hike north along the East Side Trail from the parking area near the Stevens Canyon entrance or from Silver Falls (described earlier). One mile north of the highway the East Side Trail crosses Olallie Creek, with the cataract visible upstream from the footbridge.

9 CHINOOK CREEK

This pleasant collection of water-falls lies along a sparsely used but easily accessible trail system within Mount Rainier National Park. Drive to the Owyhigh Lakes Trailhead next to S.R. 123, located 6.5 miles north of the Stevens Canyon entrance and 4.9 miles south of Cayuse Pass. Alternatively, hikers can continue north past Olallie Creek (refer to the previous section) along the East Side Trail.

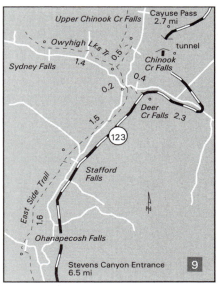

DEER CREEK FALLS (U) ★★★

MAGNITUDE: 45
ELEVATION: 3000 feet
WATERSHED: med
USGS MAP: Chinook Pass (1987 nl)

Deer Creek cascades steeply 60 to 80 feet on the way to its confluence with Chinook Creek. Wind down Owyhigh Lakes Trail, reaching Deer Creek in 0.2 mile. Look back upstream into the small gorge to see the falls.

CHINOOK CREEK FALLS (U) ★★

MAGNITUDE: 54   ELEVATION: 3120 feet
WATERSHED: med   USGS MAP: Chinook Pass (1987 nl)

This series of steep cascades totaling 75 to 100 feet descends from Chinook Creek. Views will be partially obstructed by trees in the foreground. From Deer Creek Falls (described earlier), continue hiking a short distance farther to the East Side Trail. Turn right at the junction and proceed 0.2 mile, passing the junction with Owyhigh Lakes Trail. Go 0.5 mile farther, where the falls are visible just before the trail switchbacks uphill.

SYDNEY FALLS ★★★★

MAGNITUDE: 65   ELEVATION: 3520 feet
WATERSHED: sm   USGS MAP: Chinook Pass (1987 nl)

Sydney Falls

Kotsuck Creek zigzags 125 to 150 feet over a bulbous escarpment. The best views, however, require a short bushwhack not recommended for children. From its junction with the East Side Trail (described earlier), ascend moderately along Owyhigh Lakes Trail. An uninspiring view at the top of the falls will be reached in 1.4 miles. For a better vista, retrace your steps down the trail, then carefully make your way through the woods to the canyon rim facing the falls. It was unofficially called Kotsuck Creek Falls in prior editions of this guidebook.

STAFFORD FALLS ★★★

MAGNITUDE: 48
ELEVATION: 2700 feet
WATERSHED: lg
USGS MAP: Chinook Pass (1987)

Water plummets 30 to 40 feet into a large pool along Chinook Creek. Follow the East Side Trail south from its junction with the Deer Creek access (described earlier). An easy 1.5 miles later, an unsigned but well-worn spur trail quickly leads to this pretty descent.

OHANAPECOSH FALLS (U) ★★★★

MAGNITUDE: 56   ELEVATION: 2400 feet
WATERSHED: med (g)   USGS MAP: Chinook Pass (1987 nl)

This tiered punchbowl waterfall drops 50 to 75 feet along the grayish waters of the Ohanapecosh River. The color of the water is due to ground-up rock called glacial flour being carried by this glacier-fed stream. Continue south past Stafford Falls (described earlier) for 1.6 miles to the point where the East Side Trail crosses the Ohanapecosh River, a total of 3.5 miles from

S.R. 123, or 2.5 miles north of Olallie Creek Falls (described in the previous section). The best view is just south of the footbridge, a few feet off the trail.

Others: Nearby, a cross-canyon roadside vantage can be gained of the 100- to 130-foot double drop of *Upper Chinook Creek Falls* (u) ★ USGS Chinook Pass (1987 ns). Park at an unsigned turnout on the opposite side of a highway tunnel, located 2.3 miles north of Owyhee Lakes trailhead (described earlier). For safety's sake, drivers should continue farther until a clear U-turn can be made to backtrack to the turnout, which is located on the valley side of S.R. 123. Southbounders have it easier; simply drive 2.6 miles beyond Cayuse Pass and park just before the tunnel. The low rating is due to the distant view.

Ohanapecosh Falls

10 CAYUSE PASS

PASS FALLS (U) ★★

MAGNITUDE: 25

WATERSHED: vsm

ELEVATION: 4460 feet

USGS MAP: White River Park (1971 ns)

This is one of the best of the multitude of seasonal roadside waterfalls in the national park. Drive 1 mile north of Cayuse Pass and park along an unsigned turnout on the west side of the road. This triple-tiered drop totaling 30 to 50 feet is easy to miss for southbounders; it's safest to simply continue to Cayuse and backtrack.

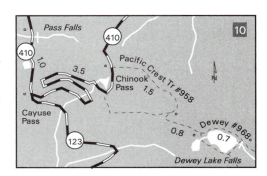

Others: Unless you happen to be hiking or just "have to" see every waterfall, you'll probably want to skip *Dewey Lake Falls* (u) ★ USGS Cougar Lake (1988 ns). The outlet from Dewey Lake is nothing more than a trickle down a 25- to 35-foot escarpment. From Chinook Pass, follow Pacific Crest Trail #958 eastward 2.3 miles to Dewey Lake Trail #968 and turn left. Hike past the north end of the lake to the falls in 0.7 mile. It is located within William O. Douglas Wilderness, administered by Wenatchee National Forest.

11 CAMP SHEPPARD

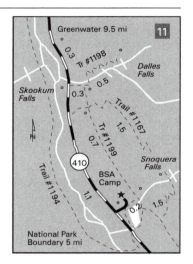

Camp Sheppard is a Boy Scouts of America site, but visitors are welcome to use the trail system. In fact, the Boy Scouts blazed the pathways for that purpose. The entrance to the camp is along S.R. 410, about 11 miles south of Greenwater and 5 miles north of Mount Rainier National Park.

SKOOKUM FALLS ★★

MAGNITUDE: 32 (l)
ELEVATION: 2920 feet
WATERSHED: vsm
USGS MAP: Sun Top (1986 nl)

Skookum Creek can be seen from a moderate distance as silvery threads descending 150 to 200 feet in two primary tiers. This falls is located within White River Ranger District of Mount Baker–Snoqualmie National Forest. Before entering Camp Sheppard, drive 1.4 miles north of the Boy Scout camp along S.R. 410 to an unsigned turnout. A cross-valley view of the cataract can be gained from this point.

An additional pair of cataracts occurs nearby. The impressiveness of the thin 200- to 300-foot *Snoquera Falls* ★ USGS Sun Top (1986 nl) decreases from spring to autumn. From the parking area of Camp Sheppard, follow Moss Lake Nature Trail to the east side of a small lake. Take the designated Snoquera Falls Loop Trail #1167 to the falls in 1.5 miles. Alternatively, hike from the north end of Trail #1167 via White River Trail #1199.

Also reduced to a trickle during the low-water periods of late summer is *Dalles Falls* (u) ★ USGS Sun Top (1986 ns). Each portion of this double waterfall can be viewed separately. Continue hiking past Snoquera Falls along Snoquera Falls Trail #1167 to its north end, where Dalles Creek Trail #1198 is met. This trail ascends steeply but safely through switchbacks to the top of The Dalles Gorge. In 0.3 mile, a short spur trail leads to the lower falls. In 0.2 mile more, the upper falls can be seen from the main trail. The return hike along White River Trail #1199 is 1.5 miles to the parking area, or 3.2 miles via the Snoquera Falls route.

12 RAINIER VALLEY

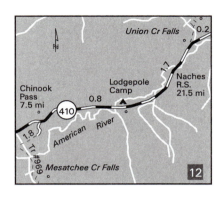

For an excellent example of a glacial trough shaped by the enormous erosive powers of an alpine glacier, look down from Chinook Pass and admire the characteristic steep-sided, U-shaped form of Rainier Valley. The glacier has long since disappeared, and the Rainier Fork American River flows along the valley floor. The pass was also formed by glacial activity and is what is known geomorphically as a "col," a notch eroded in a ridge by glaciers flowing from either side.

MESATCHEE CREEK FALLS ★★★

MAGNITUDE: 72   ELEVATION: 3840 feet
WATERSHED: sm   USGS MAP: Norse Peak (1988 nl)

Water shimmers 100 feet along Mesatchee Creek, which is located within William O. Douglas Wilderness, administered by Wenatchee National Forest. Drive 7.5 miles east from Chinook Pass on S.R. 410 and turn south at Wenatchee National Forest Road #1710. Drive 0.3 mile to the end of this gravel route to the trailhead for Mesatchee Creek Trail #969. After crossing Morse Creek and the American River, the trail steepens considerably and reaches an open vista of the descent after 1.5 miles.

UNION CREEK FALLS ★★★

MAGNITUDE: 64   ELEVATION: 3520 feet
WATERSHED: med   USGS MAP: Goose Prairie (1988)

This picturesque 40- to 60-foot drop along Union Creek is located within Norse Peak Wilderness, administered by Wenatchee National Forest. Turn into the parking and picnic area at Union Creek Trail #956, located 10 miles east of Chinook Pass. Follow the trail about 0.2 mile to a well-traveled but unmarked spur that quickly leads to the cataract.

13 NACHES

The following three waterfalls are situated within the rain shadow of the Cascades in ponderosa pine and Douglas-fir forests administered by Naches Ranger District, Wenatchee National Forest, and thus are best visited during a wet spell. The point of departure for all three is the junction of S.R. 410 and Little Naches Road #19, located 23.5 miles east of Chinook Pass and 38 miles northwest of Yakima.

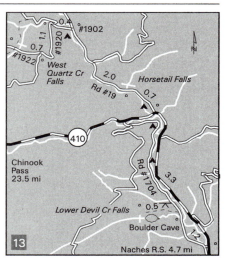

WEST QUARTZ CREEK FALLS ★★

MAGNITUDE: 35 (l)   ELEVATION: 3160 feet
WATERSHED: vsm   USGS MAP: Mount Clifty (1987 ns)

Low-volume West Quartz Creek plummets 150 to 175 feet into a canyon. Drive about 2.7 miles north along Little Naches Road #19 and turn left onto Road #1902, proceeding 0.4 mile to gravel Road #1920. Turn left again and drive 1.1 miles, then bear right onto Road #1922 and go 0.7 mile to the creek crossing. Walk down the trail 0.1 mile to trailside views back into the falls. Be careful at the unfenced canyon rim, which drops a sheer 200 feet.

Observant drivers will notice *Horsetail Falls* ★ USGS Cliffdell (1987) along Little Naches Road #19. Water from an unnamed tributary descends 40 to 50 feet from cliffs toward the Little Naches River. This is a pretty falls during wet periods from late autumn to early spring, but it is otherwise only a trickle. A short turnout to the falls is located 0.7 mile north of S.R. 410 along Little Naches Road #19.

LOWER DEVIL CREEK FALLS (U) ★★

MAGNITUDE: 16 (l)   ELEVATION: 2720 feet
WATERSHED: med   USGS MAP: Cliffdell (1987 nl)

By itself, this 20- to 30-foot falls would deserve a lower rating, but the unique geology of this area is not to be missed. The cataract is viewed from within a recess shaped like an amphitheater. Immediately downstream is Boulder Cave, which was formed when a landslide blocked the course of Devil Creek and the stream eventually eroded a tunnel through the debris. A flashlight is required to explore the cavern.

Drive south on S.R. 410 for 3.3 miles beyond the junction with Little Naches Road #19. Depart the main road here, turning right to cross the bridge over the Naches River, then turn right again, heading north on Naches River Road #1704. Park in 1.2 miles at Boulder Cave Picnic Area. Hike an easy 0.5 mile along the canyon rim, then drop down to the base of the descent.

14 RIMROCK LAKE

The Rimrock Lake area is administered by Tieton Ranger District, Wenatchee National Forest. Tieton Ranger Station, the primary reference point for the following falls, is located 34 miles west of Yakima or 17 miles east of White Pass on U.S. 12.

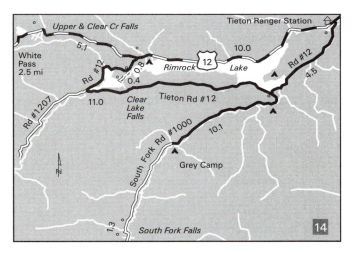

CLEAR LAKE FALLS ★★

MAGNITUDE: 33   ELEVATION: 2960 feet
WATERSHED: 1g   USGS MAP: Spiral Butte (1988 ns)

Water tumbles 40 to 60 feet at the outlet from Clear Lake and flows toward Rimrock Lake. Ten miles west of the ranger station turn south off U.S. 12 onto Tieton Road #12. Drive 0.8 mile to Clear Lake Road #740 and turn left. The pair of cascades is 0.4 mile away and is divided by a bridge spanning the drainage.

SOUTH FORK FALLS ★★★

MAGNITUDE: 66   ELEVATION: 3840 feet
WATERSHED: lg   USGS MAP: Pinegrass Ridge (1988 nl)

A misty vista makes this modest 30- to 40-foot curtain along the South Fork
Tieton River an unforgettable experience. Drive 0.5 mile west of the ranger
station, then turn south on Tieton Road #12. After 4.5 miles, turn left (south)
on South Fork Road #1000. Continue for 11.4 miles (1.3 miles past the bridge
over Bear Creek) to an unsigned turnout and a moderately steep trail that
leads to the river in 0.2 mile.

UPPER CLEAR CREEK FALLS (U) ★★★★

MAGNITUDE: 74   ELEVATION: 4000 feet
WATERSHED: med   USGS MAP: Spiral Butte (1988 nl)

Upper Clear Creek Falls

Every waterfall collector should see
this unusual configuration. One side
of the 60- to 80-foot falls horsetails,
while the other side veils downward
into a pool adjacent to the main portion of the creek. Drive 2.5 miles east
of White Pass along U.S. 12 to the
signed Clear Creek Falls parking
area. Take the short trail to the right
(west) a few yards past the parking
area to the fenced vista high above
the falls.

CLEAR CREEK FALLS ★★★★★

MAGNITUDE: 99
ELEVATION: 3800 feet
WATERSHED: med
USGS MAP: Spiral Butte (1988)

Enjoy a grand canyon-rim view of this
spectacular 300-foot plunge along
Clear Creek. From the Clear Creek
Falls parking area take the short trail
to the left to the fenced viewpoint.

Clear Creek Falls

15 LOWER OHANAPECOSH

Vacationers tend to zip past the northeast portion of Packwood Ranger District, Gifford Pinchot National Forest, on their way to Mount Rainier during the summer and to White Pass during the winter. Slow down. Better yet, stop and explore. The fine scenery includes, of course, waterfalls.

LAVA CREEK FALLS ★★★

MAGNITUDE: 86   ELEVATION: 2600 feet
WATERSHED: med   USGS MAP: Ohanapecosh Hot Springs
                                          (1989 nl)

These braids of water rushing 200 to 250 feet down the facing canyon wall
are hard to see on a sunny midday. Drive along U.S. 12 to an obscurely marked
turnout 7.6 miles west of White Pass or 4.8 miles east of the junction with
S.R. 123. A viewpoint overlooks the Clear Fork Cowlitz River canyon.

There is also easy access to *Grant Purcell Falls* ★ USGS Ohanapecosh Hot
Springs (1989). Purcell Creek slides 75 to 100 feet across sloping bedrock.
Enter La Wis Wis Campground, on the west side of U.S. 12, 0.5 mile south
of its junction with S.R. 123. Park at the C-Loop Tent Site Area. A sign directs you to the trail, which leads shortly to the stream and its waterfall.

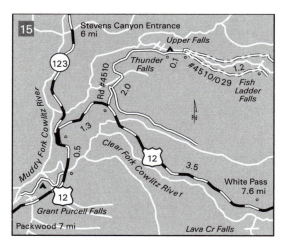

UPPER FALLS (U) ★★

MAGNITUDE: 35   ELEVATION: 2180 feet
WATERSHED: med   USGS MAP: Ohanapecosh Hot Springs
                                          (1989 ns)

Rushing water skips 25 to 35 feet across slabs of bedrock on Summit Creek.
From U.S. 12, 1.3 miles east of the junction with S.R. 123, turn north on Summit Creek Road #4510. Drive 2 miles farther and park at the unmarked turnout on the north side of the road. Follow the well-worn trail about 40 yards
to these cascades.

THUNDER FALLS ★★★

MAGNITUDE: 72   ELEVATION: 2120 feet
WATERSHED: med   USGS MAP: Ohanapecosh Hot Springs
                                 (1989 ns)

Close-up views of this 80-foot cataract spreading outward along Summit Creek are possible. From Upper Falls (described earlier) continue along the path in the downstream direction. The way becomes steep toward the end, so it is recommended only for nimble hikers.

FISH LADDER FALLS ★★★

MAGNITUDE: 48   ELEVATION: 2760 feet
WATERSHED: med   USGS MAP: Ohanapecosh Hot Springs (1989)

Peer from a canyon-rim vantage to enjoy this pristine 60-foot drop roaring along Summit Creek. Drive 0.1 mile past the trailhead for Thunder Falls (described earlier) and bear right on dirt Road #4510/029. When last traveled, most of the 1.2-mile route was overgrown with shrubs. Park at a dry ravine near the end of the road. Walk up the route a short distance and bear right at the junction, which continues 0.1 mile to the top of a small knoll at a fire pit. Bushwhack another 0.1 mile through a clear-cut to an open vista hundreds of feet above the falls at an unguarded cliff. You may need to walk along the wooded canyon rim in one direction or the other to find the unmarked viewpoint.

16 JOHNSON CREEK

RAINBOW FALLS ★★

MAGNITUDE: 21 (t)
ELEVATION: 2900 feet
WATERSHED: vsm
USGS MAP: Wahpenayo Peak (1989 nl)

This 100-foot drop from an unnamed tributary of Johnson Creek is reduced to a trickle in late summer. It is located in Packwood Ranger District, Gifford Pinchot National

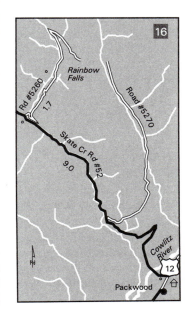

completion of Cowlitz Falls Dam, they have been drowned by the creation of Lake Scanewa reservoir.

2 NORTH ST. HELENS

The following cataracts are all in close proximity to the volcano. All but Iron Creek Falls are situated in the blast zone of the 1980 eruption.

HARMONY FALLS ★★

MAGNITUDE: 15 (l)   ELEVATION: 3480 feet
WATERSHED: vsm   USGS MAP: Spirit Lake East (1984)

This waterfall, which formerly fell 50 feet into Spirit Lake, was significantly altered in appearance by the catastrophic eruption of Mount St. Helens in 1980. The appearance of the falls will continue to change as its watershed matures along with successional changes in the accompanying vegetative cover.

Turn south off U.S. 12 about 1.3 miles west of the Randle Ranger Station onto Randle–Lewis River Road #25. Follow Road #25 for 20 miles until you reach Spirit Lake–Iron Creek Road #99, then turn right (west). In just under 5 miles enter the National Volcanic Monument and continue on Road #99 to Harmony Viewpoint, 4.2 miles south of the route's junction with Road #26. The current 40- to 60-foot cataract is located at the end of Harmony Falls Trail, a moderately steep hike of 1 strenuous mile.

Elsewhere in the vicinity is *Last Hope Falls* ★ USGS Spirit Lake East (1984 ns). Only a distant cross-valley view is available of an unnamed tributary steeply cascading 70 feet toward the headwaters of the Green River. It is located outside the National Volcanic Monument, but within another part of Randle Ranger District devastated by the eruption of Mount St. Helens. From the Cispus River on Road #25, turn right onto Road #26. Proceed 12.3 miles, then turn right onto Road #2612. Vantages of the falls are at the 2.5-mile end of the gravel road. Polar Star Mine is nearby, on your side of the valley. Look, but don't enter!

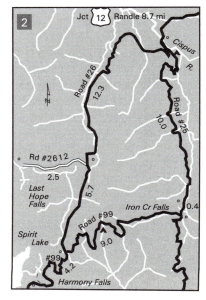

Iron Creek Falls ★★★

MAGNITUDE: 48
WATERSHED: med

ELEVATION: 2740 feet
USGS MAP: French Butte (1965 ns)

Iron Creek hurtles 25 to 35 feet into a small pool. Formerly accessible only to bushwhackers, this entry is now reachable by a short path constructed by the Randle Ranger District. Look for a signed turnout along the east side of Randle–Lewis River Road #25 (described earlier), located 0.4 mile past the junction with Big Creek Road #2517 and 0.4 mile before Spirit Lake–Iron Creek Road #99.

3 KALAMA RIVER ROAD

Marietta Falls ★★

MAGNITUDE: 30 (l)
WATERSHED: sm

ELEVATION: 60 feet
USGS MAP: Kalama (1990)

Marietta Creek tumbles 75 to 100 feet into the Kalama River. Depart I-5 onto Kalama River Road, located 0.5 mile north of the town of Kalama. Drive 4 miles east to a vantage point across the river from the falls. Unfortunately, the only safe roadside view is from the car window, as there are no parking turnouts. For better views, bring an inner tube or canoe and float down the main river. Launch your craft from access points 0.4 mile upstream from the falls.

For those who enjoy watching fish jump, continue on to *Lower Kalama River Falls* ★ USGS Woolford Creek (1993), a modest 15- to 25-foot cascade. Drive 4.4 miles eastward beyond Marietta Falls to the marked turnoff for Kalama Falls Salmon Hatchery. The view is from the top of the falls at the end of the side road.

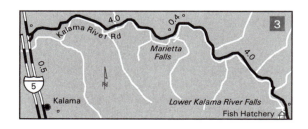

4 LAKE MERWIN

Lake Merwin is the first of three reservoirs along the Lewis River. The other two are Yale Lake and Swift Reservoir. The valley sides are steep, with three waterfalls accessible in the area. All are outside the national forest. Turn off I-5 at Woodland and drive east on S.R. 503.

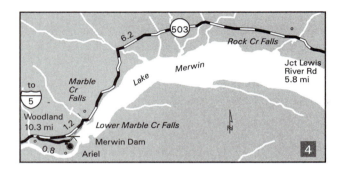

MARBLE CREEK FALLS (U) ★★

MAGNITUDE: 37   ELEVATION: 540 feet
WATERSHED: sm   USGS MAP: Ariel (1994 nl)

Marble Creek descends 40 to 60 feet in an undeveloped area. Take S.R. 503 east 11.5 miles past Woodland, 1.2 miles beyond the junction signed for Merwin Dam, to Marble Creek. Park at the turnout on the east side of the culvert. Walk upstream through the lush meadow, then along a short footpath through a wooded tract.

LOWER MARBLE CREEK FALLS (U) ★★

MAGNITUDE: 44   ELEVATION: 270 feet
WATERSHED: sm   USGS MAP: Ariel (1994 nl)

Marble Creek pours 25 to 35 feet into Lake Merwin. A wooden deck offers a moderately distant view that is partly obscured when the surrounding vegetation is in leaf. Boaters have a clearer vantage.

From the turnout for Marble Creek Falls (described earlier), backtrack westward 1.2 miles along S.R. 503 to Merwin Village Road, signed for Merwin Dam. Drive 0.8 mile to the picnic area at the end of the road, park, and head uplake until you reach the signed Marble Creek Trailhead. Maintained by Pacific Power and Light, the 0.4-mile route ends near the cataract.

ROCK CREEK FALLS ★★

MAGNITUDE: 72 (h)   ELEVATION: 480 feet
WATERSHED: med   USGS MAP: Amboy (1993 nl)

Peer down into a rugged gorge to see this 75- to 100-foot cataract as well as the creek making a 180-degree bend around a rock outcrop near the falls. Drive S.R. 503 east 17.7 miles past Woodland (6.2 miles past Marble Creek Falls, described earlier) and park at the large unsigned turnout on the west side of the new Rock Creek bridge. Look across the gorge from the fenced vista framed by trees for a moderately distant yet nice view of the waterfall.

5 KALAMA FALLS

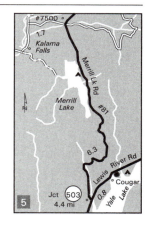

KALAMA FALLS ★★

MAGNITUDE: 57
ELEVATION: 1300 feet
WATERSHED: lg
USGS MAP: Cougar (1983)

The falls and the trail to it are owned by Weyer-haeuser Company, which invites visitation by the public. At the northeastern extreme of S.R. 503, turn east on Lewis River Road #90 and go 4.4 miles to Merrill Lake Road #81. Drive north 6.3 miles, then turn left (west) on Kalama River Road #7500. Continue 1.7 miles farther and park at any available turnout. A short trail leads down to the Kalama River, then upstream to the base of the falls.

6 SOUTH ST. HELENS

Understandably, most accounts have focused upon the destructive consequences of the 1980 eruption of Mount St. Helens. It is not so well known that the volcano also contributed to creating some new geographic features. Lava Canyon and its series of waterfalls, for instance, were unveiled when glacial meltwaters and mudflows sent forth by the eruption scoured away sediments that had long ago covered over prior lava flows. All of the following entries are within Mount St. Helens National Volcanic Monument, administered by Gifford Pinchot National Forest.

June Lake Falls (u) ★★★

MAGNITUDE: 61   ELEVATION: 3200
WATERSHED: vsm   USGS MAP: Mount St Helens (1983 ns)

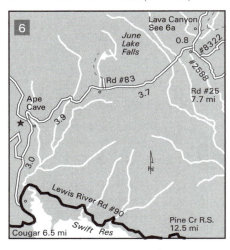

After several failed attempts to find the trail to June Lake, success was easily achieved in 2003, as the trail is now signed. Drive 6.5 miles eastward past the community of Cougar along Lewis River Road #90 (described earlier). Turn left (north) on Forest Road #83 and continue 6.9 miles to the turnoff marked for June Lake. Proceed 0.1 mile to the parking area. Hike 1.3 miles to see an unnamed stream pouring 60 to 80 feet into a tiny idyllic lake. Close-up views can be gained with an inflatable raft or other such portable watercraft.

Upper Lava Canyon Falls (u) ★★

MAGNITUDE: 50 (h)   ELEVATION: 2450 feet
WATERSHED: med (g)   USGS MAP: Smith Creek Butte (1983 nl)

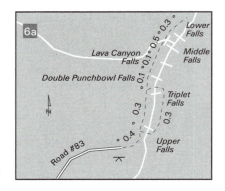

While June Lake Falls (described earlier) is an appropriate place for quiet reflection, the journey into Lava Canyon will get your heart pounding as the Muddy River roars through the gorge. Drive 4.5 miles eastward past the junction for June Lake along Forest Road #83 to the parking and interpretive area.

Six major waterfalls occur within Lava Canyon. Access to the first two is appropriate for children, but the hiking conditions for the latter four are too precarious even for skittish adults. The trail begins on paved and wooden surfaces, providing a pleasant 0.4-mile walk to this particular entry, which was named Lava Canyon Falls in the last edition of this guidebook. Protected viewpoints are provided for this 60- to 80-foot plummet.

Triplet Falls (u) ★★★

MAGNITUDE: 47 (h) ELEVATION: 2380 feet
WATERSHED: med (g) USGS MAP: Smith Creek Butte (1983 ns)

The Muddy River tumbles 50 to 70 feet over three steps of resistant rhyolite. From the Upper Falls (described earlier), the trail roughens but is still moderately easy to hike. Proceed down either side of the canyon 0.3 mile farther for full views from the excitement of a swinging footbridge.

Double Punchbowl Falls (u) ★★

MAGNITUDE: 40 (h) ELEVATION: 2280 feet
WATERSHED: med (g) USGS MAP: Smith Creek Butte (1983 ns)

Continuing downstream from the footbridge (described above), the path steepens and becomes much narrower. Don't go farther if you are wary of heights or have someone immature with you. Within 0.1 mile, a good trailside view is offered of Muddy River dropping a total of 25 to 35 feet.

Lava Canyon Falls (u) ★★★★

MAGNITUDE: 81 (h) ELEVATION: 2120 feet
WATERSHED: med (g) USGS MAP: Smith Creek Butte (1983 ns)

When hiking, sometimes it's good to have some fear. It makes one more cautious. And caution cannot be overstated when visiting this entry. The trail is very narrow, moderately steep, very crumbly, and situated along the side of a cliff. Continue past Double Punchbowl Falls (described earlier) for another 0.1 mile to an exhilarating trailside vantage of Muddy River plunging 110 to 135 feet downward in a double-drop.

Middle Lava Canyon Falls (u) ★★★

MAGNITUDE: 66 (h) ELEVATION: 2080 feet
WATERSHED: med (g) USGS MAP: Smith Creek Butte (1983 ns)

Muddy River plunges and cascades a total of 70 to 100 feet. Continue carefully beyond Lava Canyon Falls (described earlier) another 0.5 mile. The best views are from a small promontory adjacent to the trail.

LOWER LAVA CANYON FALLS (U) ★★

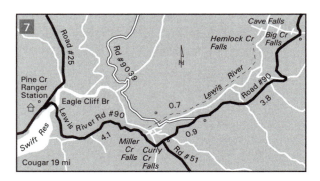

MAGNITUDE: 70 (h)   ELEVATION: 2050 feet
WATERSHED: med (g)   USGS MAP: Smith Creek Butte (1983 ns)

This waterfall deserves a higher rating, except views of it descending a total of 120 to 145 feet are obstructed. Proceed carefully beyond Middle Lava Canyon Falls (described above) for 0.3 mile. The best vantage will be after crossing a side creek and descending a steel ladder. A 20- to 25-foot-high chunk of volcanic rock will be next to you; perhaps someday a ladder will be attached to it, enabling a clear view of this tiered entry. From here, the small side creek can also be seen pouring 80 to 100 feet into the gorge.

From this location, it is 1.7 miles back to the trailhead, although some adventurers may wish to first go 0.2 mile farther and climb very steeply up a sentinel called "The Ship," a 100-foot-high volcanic erosional remnant.

---

7 EAGLE CLIFF

Located in close proximity to Mount St. Helens National Volcanic Monument, three of the following quartet of waterfalls are described in National Forest literature as points of interest. All of them are situated within a portion of Gifford Pinchot National Forest administered by the National Monument office.

CURLY CREEK FALLS ★★★★

MAGNITUDE: 66 (h)   ELEVATION: 1120 feet
WATERSHED: med   USGS MAP: Burnt Peak (1965 ns)

Despite its modest size, the natural arch that has been formed between the tiers of its 50- to 75-foot drop puts Curly Creek Falls on everyone's must-see list. Look closely; stream erosion is in the process of constructing a second arch from the bedrock. At the northeastern extreme of S.R. 503, turn east on Lewis River Road #90. Follow Lewis River Road #90 for 5 miles past the Eagle Cliff Bridge (19 miles east of Cougar). Turn left (west) on Road #9039 and drive about 0.7 mile to a parking area on the near side of the Lewis River. Walk across the bridge and follow the trail downstream for 0.3 mile to a view of the falls from across the river.

MILLER CREEK FALLS ★★

MAGNITUDE: 52   ELEVATION: 1120 feet
WATERSHED: sm   USGS MAP: Burnt Peak (1965 ns)

Miller Creek pours 40 to 60 feet into the Lewis River. Continue 0.1 mile beyond Curly Creek Falls (described earlier). Find the cataract on the opposite side of the river from the trail.

BIG CREEK FALLS ★★★★

MAGNITUDE: 76 (h)   ELEVATION: 1600 feet
WATERSHED: med   USGS MAP: Burnt Peak (1965 ns)

The view from the rim of this natural gorge is breathtaking as Big Creek plummets 125 feet into an obscured pool. Drive 3.8 miles beyond Road #9039 (described earlier) along Lewis River Road #90, a total of 8.8 miles east from Eagle Cliff Bridge. From the signed parking area, walk 0.1 mile down the trail to a vista from a wooden observation deck.

HEMLOCK CREEK FALLS ★★

MAGNITUDE: 32 (l)
ELEVATION: 1700 feet
WATERSHED: vsm
USGS MAP: Burnt Peak (1965 ns)

Here is a moderately distant, cross-canyon view of water plummeting 90

Big Creek Falls

to 120 feet down the side of Lewis River Canyon. This falls deserves a lesser rating during the very low flow of summer. Hike past Big Creek Falls (described earlier) for 0.5 mile to a fenced vantage along the gorge of Big Creek, where unfortunately only a dismal view is available of *Cave Falls* ★ USGS Burnt Peak (1965 ns) sliding down 80 to 100 feet. From here it is 0.2 mile farther to the end of the trail at an overlook of the canyon and the descent of Hemlock Creek.

Others: Documented in earlier editions as one tough bushwhack, *Rush Creek Falls* ★★★★ USGS Burnt Peak (1965 ns) is virtually inaccessible because of road closures. Hopefully someday the Forest Service, perhaps with the aid of a hiking club, will blaze a trail from Lewis River Road #90. That would most likely result in an awesome hike and make this waterfall one of the best in the region.

8 LEWIS RIVER

The scenic quality of the following falls within Mount Adams Ranger District tends to decrease as one progresses upstream. Therefore, the following entries are listed in reverse order of driving into the area. Drive all the way up along the Lewis River Road eastward, then visit the falls as you retrace the route.

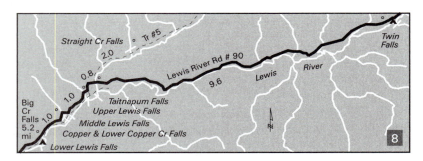

TWIN FALLS ★★

MAGNITUDE: 64 ELEVATION: 2660 feet
WATERSHED: sm USGS MAP: Steamboat Mtn (1970)

Twin Falls Creek is named for the successive 15- to 20-foot punchbowls that occur above its confluence with the Lewis River. Drive along Lewis River Road #90 for 17.6 miles past Big Creek Falls (described earlier), a total of 26.4 miles northeast of Eagle Cliff Bridge. Proceed down the access road to Twin Falls Camp and drive 0.3 mile to its end. The view of the falls is from across the Lewis River.

STRAIGHT CREEK FALLS ★★

MAGNITUDE: 33 (h)   ELEVATION: 1980 feet
WATERSHED: med   USGS MAP: Quartz Creek Butte (1965 ns)

This pleasant series of cascades along Straight Creek totals 30 to 60 feet. The highlight when the author surveyed this entry was the appearance of several elk along the trail. Drive along Lewis River Road to the parking area for Quartz Creek Trailhead #6, located 16.8 miles northeast of Eagle Cliff Bridge and 9.6 miles southwest of the access road to Twin Falls Camp (described earlier). Hike 2 miles, passing a logged area in 1.7 miles. Walk across the log bridge over Straight Creek, then pick up your own path upstream to a viewpoint.

TAITNAPUM FALLS ★★★

MAGNITUDE: 63   ELEVATION: 1720 feet
WATERSHED: lg   USGS MAP: Quartz Creek Butte (1965 ns)

The least well known waterfall on the Lewis River not only has the best name but also rivals the others in beauty. Find the spur path for Lewis River Trail #5, located across the road from the trailhead for Quartz Creek (described above). Walk down to the river, then proceed downstream for a total of 0.3 mile to a signed airy vista above and looking into this 80- to 100-foot-wide display dropping 20 to 25 feet.

UPPER LEWIS FALLS ★★★

MAGNITUDE: 65   ELEVATION: 1620 feet
WATERSHED: lg   USGS MAP: Quartz Creek Butte (1965)

Lewis River thunders 35 feet over a massive slab of bedrock. This waterfall and those described in the next four entries are all interconnected by the recently expanded Lewis River Trail system. For access, find Upper Falls Trail next to Lewis River Road as indicated by a sign 0.8 mile southwest of Quartz Creek Trail #5 (described earlier). The path is moderately steep but only 0.3 mile long. At its end are the falls and the junction with Lewis River Trail.

COPPER CREEK FALLS ★★

MAGNITUDE: 44   ELEVATION: 1680 feet
WATERSHED: vsm   USGS MAP: Quartz Creek Butte (1965 ns)

This sharp 40- to 60-foot drop along Copper Creek can be viewed by descending beneath a footbridge. Drive 1 mile southwest of Upper Falls Trail (described earlier) along Lewis River Road to the parking area for an unnamed trail that leads down to the Lewis River. After walking along the path for several hundred yards, look back toward the footbridge framing the cataract.

MIDDLE LEWIS FALLS ★★

MAGNITUDE: 56   ELEVATION: 1560 feet
WATERSHED: lg   USGS MAP: Quartz Creek Butte (1965)

This 30-foot descent along the Lewis River is the least inspiring of the three Lewis Falls. Take the trail to Copper Creek Falls (described earlier). Continue another 0.5 mile to Lewis River Trail and views of this cataract.

LOWER COPPER CREEK FALLS (u) ★★

MAGNITUDE: 29   ELEVATION: 1600 feet
WATERSHED: vsm   USGS MAP: Quartz Creek Butte (1965 ns)

Copper Creek slides steeply into the Lewis River. A footbridge along Lewis River Trail passes over this 20- to 30-foot drop. Walk a short distance downstream from Middle Lewis Falls (described earlier) to this entry.

LOWER LEWIS FALLS ★★★★

MAGNITUDE: 67   ELEVATION: 1480 feet
WATERSHED: lg   USGS MAP: Spencer Butte (1965)

Water crashes 35 feet over a broad expanse of the Lewis River in an especially scenic block form. Drive along Lewis River Road to Lewis River

Lower Lewis Falls

Campground, located 1 mile south of Copper Creek (14 miles northwest of Eagle Cliff Bridge) and 5.2 miles north of Big Creek Falls. Park in the southeast part of the campground. A short trail leads to good vistas overlooking the falls.

9 CHELATCHIE

All of the following waterfalls occur along Siouxon Creek and its tributaries, a drainage basin not explored previously by the author. Take an entire day hiking to eight delightful cataracts, all located on national forest land. Depart S.R. 503 at the hamlet of Chelatchie, turning east onto Northeast Healy Road. Drive 9.2 miles, passing the nearly perfectly symmetrical cinder cone of Tum Tum Mountain, then paralleling the gorge of Canyon Creek. Turn left onto Forest Road #57, motoring 1.2 miles up the ridge. Take another left onto Forest Road #5701, which descends down the other side, then along Siouxon Creek to the parking area near road's end 3.8 miles farther.

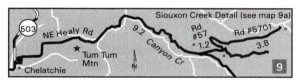

HORSESHOE CREEK FALLS ★★

MAGNITUDE: 46   ELEVATION: 1350 feet
WATERSHED: sm   USGS MAP: Siouxon Peak (1993 ns)

The first cataract encountered along Siouxon Trail #130 is this nice double horsetail totaling 35 to 50 feet. Follow the trail for 1.2 miles, crossing a footbridge over the falls. Continue another 0.1 mile to a signed spur, which leads to a good vantage in another 0.1 mile.

SIOUXON FALLS ★★

MAGNITUDE: 23 (h)   ELEVATION: 1250 feet
WATERSHED: lg   USGS MAP: Siouxon Peak (1993 ns)

A trailside bench enables hikers to rest their feet while admiring this classic 20- to 30-foot punchbowl falls. Continue past the spur junction for Horseshoe Creek Falls (described earlier) for 0.3 mile to this entry. Incidentally, numerous unmapped cascades and small falls occur along Siouxon Creek. Only the larger, accessible ones are listed here.

MIDDLE SIOUXON FALLS (U) ★★

MAGNITUDE: 26 (h)   ELEVATION: 1280 feet
WATERSHED: lg   USGS MAP: Siouxon Peak (1993 ns)

According to the topographic map, Trail #130 leaves the creek at Siouxon Falls (described earlier), passing over a small saddle. Apparently the path has been altered, because only 0.2 mile away the trail meets up with this 10- to 15-foot drop.

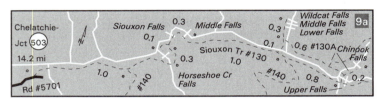

UPPER SIOUXON FALLS (U) ★★

MAGNITUDE: 37   ELEVATION: 1460 feet
WATERSHED: med   USGS MAP: Bare Mtn (1993 ns)

This is the last of the waterfalls along Siouxon Creek; taller ones can be seen along a pair of tributaries. Continue past Middle Siouxon Falls (described earlier) for 1.8 miles where a footbridge crosses the stream. Look upstream to see the 15- to 20-foot drop over rock slabs. Closer views are available farther up Trail #130.

CHINOOK FALLS ★★★

MAGNITUDE: 59   ELEVATION: 1560 feet
WATERSHED: med   USGS MAP: Bare Mtn (1993 nl)

Chinook Creek veils 50 feet down a rock wall into a pool below. Proceed across the footbridge (described earlier) up Chinook Trail #130A for 0.2 mile to the base of the falls.

WILDCAT FALLS ★★★★

MAGNITUDE: 66   ELEVATION: 1750 feet
WATERSHED: sm   USGS MAP: Siouxon Peak (1993 nl)

It's always nice to have the last waterfall on a hike be the best. Such is the case with this 100- to 120-foot beauty set in a serene setting. However, lack of signage makes it a bit of a challenge to find. Ford Chinook Creek (described earlier) immediately below the 2-foot block-shaped falls that just precedes Chinook Creek Falls. Pick up the trail here. After 0.1 mile is a junction; continue straight on the unnamed path instead of switchbacking up Chinook Trail #130A. Proceed an easy 0.6 mile and ford Wildcat Creek. Rejoin the path, which very quickly ends at unsigned Wildcat Trail. The route climbs steeply; partial views can be gained of *Lower Wildcat Falls* (u) ★ and *Middle Wildcat Falls* (u) ★, both USGS Siouxon Peak (1993 ns), along the way. Reach a superb vista 0.3 mile up this trail.

From here, it is 4.7 miles back to the parking area. However, 1.6 miles can be saved by taking a shortcut although it requires a ford of Siouxon Creek. Follow Wildcat Trail all the way down to Siouxon Creek and cross the creek to reach Siouxon Trail #130. Incidentally, the trail shown on the topographic map is not Wildcat Trail, which most closely parallels Wildcat Creek.

10 EAST FORK LEWIS RIVER

Four small waterfalls tumble along the East Fork Lewis River, with a more impressive specimen along one of its tributaries. Follow the marked route 3 miles from the town of Battle Ground to Battle Ground Lake State Park. Continue 2.8 miles northbound from the state park, passing the hamlet of Heisson, to Lucia Falls Road.

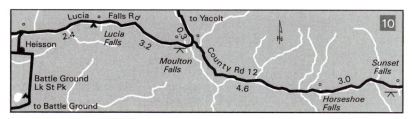

LUCIA FALLS ★★

MAGNITUDE: 44 (h)   ELEVATION: 400 feet
WATERSHED: lg   USGS MAP: Yacolt (1990)

The park surrounding this 15- to 25-foot waterfall is privately developed and has periodically been closed to the public. When last visited, there was an admittance fee. Drive 2.4 miles east along Lucia Falls Road and turn into Lucia Falls Park and Cafe.

Day-trippers can also visit a couple of smaller falls in the vicinity. *Moulton Falls* ★ USGS Yacolt (1990) occurs where East Fork Lewis River slides 15 to 25 feet. Continue eastward 3.2 miles past Lucia Falls along Lucia Falls Road to a public park to the descent. Turn southward onto County Road #12 and continue 4.6 miles farther to *Horseshoe Falls* ★ USGS Dole (1994). This appropriately named 15- to 20-foot, crescent-shaped waterfall deserves a higher rating if closer views were possible. Unfortunately, it is located on private property posted "No Trespassing" when last visited.

SUNSET FALLS ★★

MAGNITUDE: 60 (h) ELEVATION: 980 feet
WATERSHED: lg USGS MAP: Gumboot Mtn (1986 nl)

East Fork Lewis River splashes 20 feet within Wind River Ranger District. From Lucia Falls, follow Lucia Falls Road east for 3.5 miles to its end and turn right (southeast) onto County Road #12, which rises 100 to 200 feet above the East Fork. Drive 7.6 miles farther to the Sunset Picnic Area. Walk a short distance upstream to the descent.

BIG TREE CREEK FALLS (U)
★★★

MAGNITUDE: 56
ELEVATION: 980 feet
WATERSHED: med
USGS MAP: Dole (1986 nl)

This is a unique waterfall. The horsetail half so forcefully strikes part of the escarpment that it causes the water to plunge the rest of the way down. From the hamlet of Yacolt, specifically at the intersection of Railroad Road and Yacolt Road, proceed eastward on the latter road for 0.6 mile, where it becomes Falls Road. Here it makes a sweeping bend to the right. Continue an additional 1.6 miles and park at an unsigned turnout, but don't block the gate.

Walk down the gravel road for a flat 0.1 mile to an unmarked path to the right, just before the bridge cross-

Big Tree Creek Falls

ing over the falls. Go down the path a short distance to a nice unguarded vista above and views into the cataract, which is located on property owned by Weyerhaeuser.

11 WIND RIVER ROAD

Three of the most impressive waterfalls of the region are located within Wind River Ranger District and drainage basin.

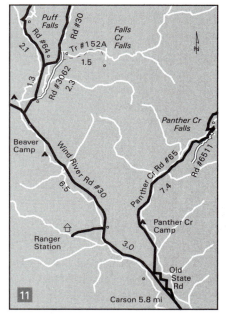

PANTHER CREEK FALLS
★★★★

MAGNITUDE: 74
ELEVATION: 1790 feet
WATERSHED: med
USGS MAP: Big Huckleberry Mtn (1983 ns)

This 50- to 75-foot waterfall is unique because it is actually two waterfalls dropping side by side from Panther Creek and Big Creek. From S.R. 14 turn north onto Wind River Road #30. Pass Carson in 1 mile and after another 5.8 miles turn right (east) on Old State Road. Almost immediately, take a left (north) onto Panther Creek Road #65. Drive 7.4 miles up this road and find a safe place to park near its junction with Road #6511. Walk about 100 yards up Panther Creek Road #65 to a faint unsigned path that drops sharply down (the most difficult part), then quickly leads to an unfenced vista overlooking the falls.

FALLS CREEK FALLS ★★★★★

MAGNITUDE: 99 (h)   ELEVATION: 2200 feet
WATERSHED: lg   USGS MAP: Termination Point (1983)

This fantastic triple-tiered waterfall totals 250 feet and is so outstanding one must wonder how it was given such a generic name. Several vantages are afforded toward the end of the trail, although the shape of the cataract is such that all three tiers cannot be viewed together.

Drive north on Wind River Road #30 and continue 9.5 miles past Panther Creek Road #65 (described earlier) to Road #3062–057. Turn right and

proceed 2.3 miles to Lower Falls Creek Trail #152A. The trail crosses Falls Creek in 0.8 mile. Half a mile beyond is a steeply sloping cascade, which can be forded easily during high-water periods, after which, the upper and middle portions of the falls soon come into view. The trail ends in front of the middle and lower falls 0.2 mile farther.

PUFF FALLS ★★★

MAGNITUDE: 65
ELEVATION: 1560 feet
WATERSHED: med
USGS MAP: Termination Point (1983 ns)

Dry Creek leaps 120 feet into a pool, which makes a good secluded swimming hole if you can bear the chilly water. Proceed 1.3 miles past Road #3062–057 (described earlier) along Wind River Road #30 to Dry Creek Road #64. Turn left onto #64 and proceed 2.1 miles to the point where the road crosses the creek. Proceeding upstream to the falls, also known as Dry Creek Falls, is not overly difficult, but the 0.8-mile route is slow going and requires perseverance. Hopefully, trail access will be improved in the future.

Falls Creek Falls

12 TROUT LAKE

The point of departure for these attractive waterfalls, all located within Gifford Pinchot National Forest, is Mount Adams District Ranger Station, located 0.5 mile west of Trout Lake on S.R. 141.

LITTLE GOOSE CREEK FALLS ★★★

MAGNITUDE: 80   ELEVATION: 3000 feet
WATERSHED: med   USGS MAP: Sleeping Beauty (1970 ns)

Opposite: Panther Creek Falls

Peer into a canyon, looking down on this 75- to 100-foot triplet descending from Little Goose Creek. Be careful at the rim; there is no fence and the sheer cliffs are dangerously abrupt! Drive about 1 mile west of the ranger station, then turn right (north) on Trout Lake Creek Road #88. After 8.3 more miles, park on the far (northwest) side of the gorge where the paved road leaves the creek. Although there is no trail, viewpoints at the canyon rim are easily and quickly reached.

Langfield Falls ★★★★

MAGNITUDE: 86   ELEVATION: 3400 feet
WATERSHED: med   USGS MAP: Sleeping Beauty (1970)

Mosquito Creek veils 110 feet, deep within the forest. The waterfall is named after a retired ranger who is credited with its discovery. Drive along Trout Lake Creek Road #88 for 4.4 miles past Little Goose Creek Falls (described earlier) to a marked turnout for Langfield Falls. A short trail leads to a viewpoint in front of the descent.

13 Mount Adams

These high-country waterfalls are all accessible from the Yakama Indian Reservation, adjacent to Mount Adams Wilderness. The best visiting period is from late summer to early autumn. The roads are rough and slow but usually navigable by passenger vehicles. Proceed north from Trout Lake along Road #23 for 1.3 miles, then bear right onto Road #80. Bear right again after 0.6 mile, this time onto Road #82. Stay on this route for 8.5 miles, then turn left (north) on Mount Adams Road #8290.

Bird Creek Falls ★★

MAGNITUDE: 16 (h)   ELEVATION: 4800 feet
WATERSHED: sm (g)   USGS MAP: King Mtn (1971 ns)

Spy a series of 5- to 10-foot cascades and punchbowls adjacent to both sides of the road on the way to Mount Adams. From the junction of Forest Roads #82 and #8290, proceed 2.7 miles north along #8290 to an unmarked turnout at the creek.

CROOKED CREEK FALLS ★★★

MAGNITUDE: 50
ELEVATION: 6100 feet
WATERSHED: sm (g)
USGS MAP: Mount Adams East
(1970)

Water pours 35 to 50 feet from a small cliff, then steeply cascades along the stream course. Lots of flowering plants and miniature waterfalls make the 1-mile hike absolutely charming. Proceed northward past Bird Creek Falls (described earlier) along Road #8290 for 1.9 miles. Turn left at Mirror Lake and drive 1 mile to Bird Lake and the trailhead at the end of this access road.

HELLROARING FALLS ★★

MAGNITUDE: 68
ELEVATION: 6800 feet
WATERSHED: sm (g)
USGS MAP: Mount Adams East
(1970 nl)

Distant views of several 100- to 150-foot cataracts, unofficially named Hellroaring Basin Falls in the previous edition of this book, are dwarfed by the specter of Mount Adams in the background. A roadside vista is afforded from Hellroaring Falls overlook, which is located 2 miles beyond Mirror Lake. A better, yet still-distant vantage is available from Hellroaring Viewpoint, a moderately strenuous 1-mile hike. The shortest trail to the viewpoint starts at Bird Creek Picnic Area. Reach the picnic site by backtracking 0.9 mile from the overlook along Road #8290.

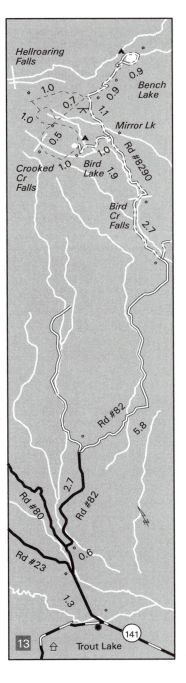

14 GLENWOOD

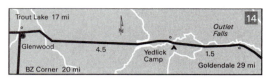

OUTLET FALLS ★★★★★

MAGNITUDE: 74   ELEVATION: 1600 feet
WATERSHED: med   USGS MAP: Outlet Falls (1970)

Outlet Creek roars toward Klickitat Canyon in an exciting 120- to 150-foot plummet. The gorge-rim vista into the cataract and its large natural amphitheater is unguarded, making it very dangerous. From BZ Corner, which is north of White Salmon on S.R. 141, drive northeast for 20 miles on BZ Corner–Glenwood Road to the town of Glenwood (alternatively drive 17 miles east of Trout Lake on Trout Lake–Glenwood Road). From the corner of Ash and Main, proceed eastward for 5.7 miles (updated from the 6-mile total shown on the map) to a small, unsigned turnout to the left. For further reference, the turnout is located 0.2 mile after you pass a gated road on the right, signed "Hancock Forest Management." The viewpoint is only a few steps away.

Outlet Falls

THE INLAND EMPIRE, WASHINGTON

The eastern half of the state of Washington is known locally as the Inland Empire. The name was popularized in the late 1800s, when the region ceased to be part of the frontier. Since then it has grown into a substantial producer of agricultural products, timber, minerals, and hydroelectric power. Railroads played a vital role in developing the Inland Empire and establishing Spokane as its center of commerce. The region's rail passenger service is still known as "The Empire Builder."

There are fifty-three falls recognized within this region; thirty of them are described on the following pages. Waterfalls are distributed throughout the Inland Empire, being found in the Selkirk Mountains, Okanogan Highlands, and the Channeled Scablands.

The Selkirks are composed of old sedimentary rocks that range from 80 million to 500 million years old. Recent folding and faulting, 1 million to 3 million years ago, was followed by glaciation, giving the range its present appearance.

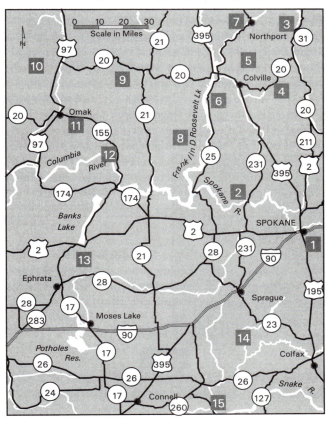

Boardman Road, located about 0.7 mile past the bridge over the Spokane River. Turn left and follow the dusty road 1.3 miles, then bear right (north) on Road #13. Proceed another 0.7 mile and turn right on a dirt road. Watch for an old sign tacked to a tree at a turnoff 0.3 mile farther. Park at this junction and walk toward the creek. Hike 0.5 mile down to the end of this road and find a small picnic area with the cataract a short distance upstream.

Little Falls ★★★

MAGNITUDE: 51 (h)   ELEVATION: 1400 feet
WATERSHED: lg (d)   USGS MAP: Little Falls (1973 ns)

The Spokane River pours from the uniquely V-shaped Little Falls Dam, then cascades downward 20 to 30 feet over a jumble of boulders. From Reardon, travel northward for 11 miles, then turn left (west) onto the access road signed for Little Falls. Drive 2.4 miles to an unsigned turnout on the near (east) side of the river. There are good views adjacent to the bridge.

3 BOUNDARY DAM

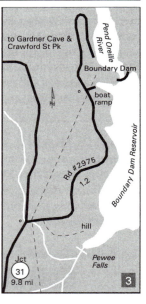

The following descent is one of the largest in eastern Washington, but unless visited by watercraft, it is accessible only to bushwhackers. Other visitors can still enjoy attractions such as Boundary Dam and Gardner Cave.

Pewee Falls ★★★★

MAGNITUDE: 78
ELEVATION: 2270 feet
WATERSHED: med
USGS MAP: Boundary Dam (1986)

Pewee Creek ribbons 150 to 200 feet down a vertical rock wall into Boundary Dam Reservoir. Talk about your misleading names! This starkly beautiful waterfall was actually originally called Periwee Falls in 1895 by a French-Canadian hunter and prospector, but the name was later shortened.

Turn northward off S.R. 31 onto Crawford Park Road #2975, which is located about 1 mile southwest of the town of Metaline Falls. Drive 11 miles to a boat launch site just below Boundary Dam. Boaters can follow the shoreline southward along the west shore of the lake approximately 1.5 miles to the falls.

Pewee Falls

Bushwhackers can gain a hilltop vista of the cataract as follows: Backtrack 1.2 miles by car from the boat ramp to an unsigned parking spot just west of the powerlines. Walk back up the road a short distance in order to avoid a marsh, then turn left, following the powerlines into the woods. After a few hundred yards, bear left (east) and progress 0.3 mile toward the top of a small knob. *Warning:* Do not attempt to get close to the waterfall, its stream, or the lake. Slopes in this area are dangerously unstable and cannot be walked upon.

4 PARK RAPIDS

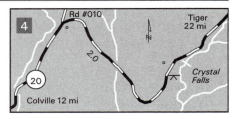

Formerly located on private land, the following waterfall is now a part of day-use Crystal Falls State Park.

CRYSTAL FALLS ★★★

MAGNITUDE: 75 (h)   ELEVATION: 2780 feet
WATERSHED: lg   USGS MAP: Park Rapids (1986)

The Little Pend Oreille River shoots 60 to 80 feet in tiered fashion. Look for a marked turnout along S.R. 20 approximately 14 miles east of Colville and 22 miles southwest of the ghost town of Tiger.

5 COLVILLE

The small city of Colville developed from old Fort Colville, a U.S. Army outpost from 1859 to 1882. The following falls are nearby.

MARBLE CREEK FALLS (U) ★★

MAGNITUDE: 41
ELEVATION: 3120 feet
WATERSHED: sm
USGS MAP: Gillette Mountain (1986 nl)

Marble Creek descends 25 to 35 feet and is located within Colville National Forest. Drive 1.2 miles east of Colville along S.R. 20 and turn left (north) on signed County Road 700. After 2 miles, bear right onto Alladin Road and proceed 11 miles. Look for obscurely marked Forest Road #200 to the left (west). Park along this primitive route, which quickly deteriorates into a well-worn path that leads in a short distance to the falls.

DOUGLAS FALLS ★★★

MAGNITUDE: 71   ELEVATION: 1800 feet
WATERSHED: lg   USGS MAP: Colville (1986)

Mill Creek veils downward 60 feet within historic Douglas Falls Grange Park (Washington State Department of Natural Resources). In 1855, R. H. Douglas harnessed the cataract for a grist mill, which he later converted into a sawmill. Failing to negotiate a lumber contract with Fort Colville, Douglas abandoned the project, but not his entrepreneurship. He turned his talents to the production of distilled spirits!

From the junction of County Road 700 and Alladin Road (described earlier), bear left onto Douglas Falls Road. It is 3 additional miles to the entrance of the park. The falls can be seen from an enclosed viewpoint adjacent to the picnic and playground areas.

Waterfall enthusiasts can also seek out *Mill Creek Falls* (u) ★ USGS Park Rapids (1986 nl), where water tumbles 30 to 50 feet along a wide breadth of South Fork Mill Creek. From the junction of County Road 700 and Alladin Road, drive 5.5 miles and turn right onto a gravel road. After 2 more miles park at an unsigned turnout near the bridge crossing South Fork Mill Creek. Make your way downstream through the woods to a view of the rapids.

---

6 KETTLE FALLS

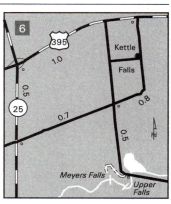

Kettle Falls is now only the name of a town. A cascade used to tumble nearby along the Columbia River, but the river's once mighty waters have been pacified by Grand Coulee Dam, which created Franklin D. Roosevelt Lake. However, two other waterfalls still exist in the vicinity.

MEYERS FALLS ★★★

MAGNITUDE: 60   ELEVATION: 1510 feet
WATERSHED: lg (d)   USGS MAP: Kettle Falls (1969)

Colville River crashes down 60 to 100 feet although some of the water is diverted to run a small Washington Water Power facility beneath the falls. The cataract is named for Louther Walden Meyers, a pioneer who lived here in the 1860s.

Turn off U.S. 395 and drive south through Kettle Falls. After 0.8 mile, turn left (south) on a paved road, then right on a dirt road 0.5 mile farther. Park at the unsigned parking area and walk down the road a short distance to good vantages. Please respect the landowner's privacy by not driving down the access road and by making your midday visit brief. Along the way, you will also see *Upper Falls* (u) ★ USGS Kettle Falls (1969 ns), where the Colville River drops 15 to 20 feet into a small rock basin.

7 NORTHPORT

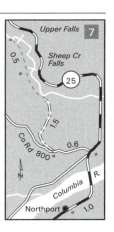

Correspondence has been received reporting difficulties finding the following pair of waterfalls. The author has not had the opportunity to revisit this part of the state, and thus far no one in the area has responded to his queries. Surf to *The Computer Companion*, described in the Introduction, for the latest information.

SHEEP CREEK FALLS ★★★★

MAGNITUDE: 63 (h)   ELEVATION: 1600 feet
WATERSHED: lg   USGS MAP: Northport
                    (1982)

Sheep Creek Falls

Sheep Creek explodes 125 to 150 feet over a sharp escarpment. Drive north along S.R. 25 to the village of Northport. Cross the Columbia River and turn left (west) on County Road 800. Continue approximately 0.6 mile to the first dirt road to the right (north). Park here and hike along this route about 1 mile to the canyon rim. An old railroad grade picks up from here and passes above and adjacent to the falls in another 0.5 mile.

UPPER FALLS ★★

MAGNITUDE: 59 (h)
ELEVATION: 1800 feet
WATERSHED: lg
USGS MAP: Northport (1982)

Sheep Creek roars 40 to 60 feet downward below a collapsed railroad trestle. Continue 0.5 mile on the railroad grade along the canyon rim beyond Sheep Creek Falls (described earlier) to the Upper Falls near the end of the route, 2 miles from the county road.

8 FRANKLIN D. ROOSEVELT LAKE

Both of the following waterfalls can be accessed by boat, and one can be easily reached by land. Given the great length of the reservoir, nautical maps should be taken along to aid in lake orientation. They can be obtained at the marinas in Kettle Falls or Seven Bays, where boat rentals are also available.

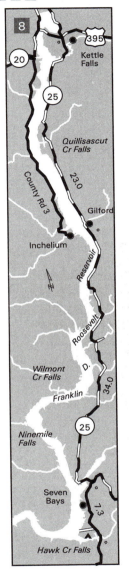

HAWK CREEK FALLS ★★

MAGNITUDE: 46
ELEVATION: 1320 feet
WATERSHED: lg
USGS MAP: Olsen Canyon (1985 nl)

This nice 35- to 50-foot drop next to Hawk Creek Campground is sheltered in a narrow crevice. Depart S.R. 25 at the sign for Seven Bays. Proceed 7.3 miles to an access road for the lake and turn right, reaching the camp and falls in 0.7 mile. Boaters may also gain a view by proceeding to the head of the embayment of Hawk Creek.

Also situated adjacent to FDR Lake is *Quillisascut Creek Falls* (u) ★ USGS Rice (1985 nl). Low streamflow limits the impressiveness of this 20- to 30-foot cataract. Try visiting right after wet weather. From the boat ramp and picnic area immediately north of Barnaby Island, head almost due east to a cove along the eastern shore of the lake. After dropping anchor, follow a jeep trail 0.3 mile to a very short path leading to the base of the falls.

9 SHERMAN CREEK

Both of the following entries are located within Colville National Forest.

UPPER SHERMAN CREEK FALLS ★★

MAGNITUDE: 26   ELEVATION: 3800 feet
WATERSHED: med   USGS MAP: Sherman Peak (1985 nl)

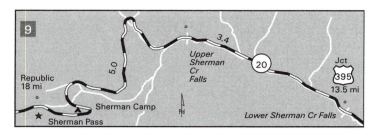

Sherman Creek drops 15 to 25 feet next to the highway. Take S.R. 20 eastward for 5 miles beyond Sherman Pass to an unsigned turnout preceding the falls. Walk along the highway for a short distance to a vantage of the cataract.

LOWER SHERMAN CREEK FALLS ★★

MAGNITUDE: 42 ELEVATION: 3090 feet
WATERSHED: lg USGS MAP: So Huckleberry Mountain
(1985 nl)

Water drops 35 to 50 feet along Sherman Creek; this entry requires a short, steep bushwhack for the best views. Continue eastward past the Upper Falls (described earlier) for 3.4 miles to another unsigned turnout. A moderately distant vista is available from the road. Close-up vantages require a scramble down the slope to the creek.

10 CONCONULLY

Conconully is a small resort town 22 miles northwest of Omak in north-central Washington. The following waterfall is located in the vicinity.

SALMON FALLS ★★

MAGNITUDE: 38 ELEVATION: 3130 feet
WATERSHED: lg USGS MAP: Conconully West (1989)

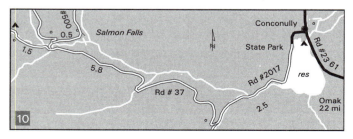

West Fork Salmon Creek drops 300 feet over a 0.2-mile length of the stream. This falls is located within Okanogan National Forest. Starting at the hamlet of Conconully, drive west on Road #2017, which becomes Forest Road #37 after 2.5 miles. Proceed another 5.8 miles, then bear right onto Road #500. Go another 0.5 mile to a jeep trail on the right. Park here. Walk down this dirt road for 0.3 mile to several paths leading to the various descents. Be careful! The ground tends to be somewhat steep and crumbly.

11 St. Mary's

Near the town of Omak, the past education of Native Americans intersects with the present. Drive 4 miles east of town, turning left (south) off of S.R. 155 at the sign for Omak Lake/St. Mary's Mission. Drive 1.1 miles and bear left, up the paved road signed for historic St. Mary's Mission. It was founded in 1886 by Jesuit Father Etienne de Rouge to minister to the bands of the Colville Federation. The present Catholic church was built in 1910 and remains active today. Next to it is the modern Pascal Sherman Indian School, the only boarding school for Native Americans in Washington. It is managed by the Colville Confederated Tribes.

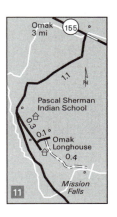

Mission Falls ★★

MAGNITUDE: 38   ELEVATION: 1500 feet
WATERSHED: lg   USGS MAP: Omak Lake (1980)

Omak Creek descends in a series within a small canyon. From the second sign for St. Mary's Mission, proceed 0.3 mile, passing by the church and school. Just beyond, turn left at the Omak Longhouse sign. Find the first dirt road to the right (south) in 0.1 mile and take it to its end in 0.4 mile. It's a moderately easy rock hop of a couple hundred feet to vantages of the drops totaling 20 to 30 feet within the gorge.

12 Nespelem

Over the years, the author has taken many waterfall expeditions. None of them happened to pass through this part of Colville Indian Reservation—until 2003. And the trio of waterfalls found along the Nespelem River was certainly worth the visit. Drive along S.R. 155 to the north end of Colville Indian Agency. Turn west onto an unmarked road, although a sign may be seen pointing in that direction advertising the Nespelem Junior Rodeo.

Spray Falls ★★

MAGNITUDE: 42   ELEVATION: 1600 feet
WATERSHED: lg   USGS MAP: Armstrong Creek (1989)

Nespelem River rushes 15 to 20 feet into a large plunge pool. From the junction with S.R. 155, drive down the road 1.4 miles and find a dirt road on the left. Turn here and park. From here, the way splits two ways. Walk up the route to the left for 0.1 mile where a beaten path leads to full side views of the descent.

Spray Falls

Nespelem Falls (u) ★★★

MAGNITUDE: 53   ELEVATION: 1540 feet
WATERSHED: lg   USGS MAP: Armstrong Creek (1989 nl)

It is ironic the most scenic falls along the Nespelem River is the one not officially named. From the dirt road (described earlier), walk down the route to the right. Follow it 0.5 mile to an overlook directly into water tumbling 50 to 70 feet. Rock outcrops mask parts of the cataract.

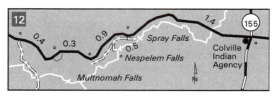

Multnomah Falls ★★

MAGNITUDE: 50   ELEVATION: 1140 feet
WATERSHED: lg   USGS MAP: Armstrong Creek (1989)

Who knew there was more than one Multnomah Falls? While many orders of magnitude smaller than its more famous namesake in Oregon, it nevertheless possesses scenic value. Continue along the paved road from the turnout (described earlier) for 0.9 mile to another unsigned turnout on the left. Park here and walk down the road an additional 0.3 mile to a moderately distant view of ribbons of water dropping 40 to 60 feet before cascading onward.

13 COULEE CITY

One of the engineering feats of the modern world was the construction of Grand Coulee Dam. One of the engineering feats of planet Earth is just to the south at Dry Falls.

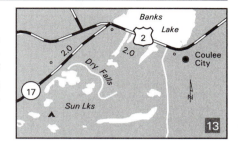

DRY FALLS ★★★★

MAGNITUDE: 174 (10,000 years ago: h, today: 0)

ELEVATION: 1510 feet

USGS MAP: Coulee City (1965)

At one time the largest waterfall ever known plunged 400 feet over cliffs in five sweeping horseshoes totaling 3.5 miles in width! The discharge was 40 times mightier than Niagara Falls. Follow U.S. 2 west from Coulee City and turn south on S.R. 17. Stop at the scenic turnout, viewpoint, and interpretive site 2 miles farther.

Dry Falls

Interpreters at the Visitor Center have reported that *Summer Falls* ★ USGS Coulee City (1965) is no longer accessible to the public. Water was formerly fed from Banks Lake through Trail Lake Coulee, resulting in a thundering 70- to 100-foot monster. It was even worthy of the establishment of a state park, which has since been retired because almost all of the water has been diverted elsewhere.

14 ROCK CREEK COULEE

ROCK CREEK FALLS ★★

MAGNITUDE: 50   ELEVATION: 1700 feet
WATERSHED: lg   USGS MAP: Texas Lake (1964)

This cooling 10- to 15-foot sheet of water in a sagebrush setting along Rock Creek is located on private property. Fortunately, as the posted signs indicate, permission to hike can be obtained from the adjacent landowner. From Ewan, drive west along S.R. 23 for about 1.3 miles. Find a dusty back road to the left (south). Walk along this route for 1.5 miles to the stream and the falls.

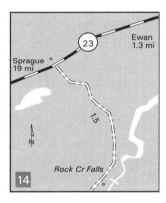

Rock Creek Falls

15 PALOUSE CANYON

The third, and largest, waterfall described below is part of a state park, but the other two are located on federal land leased for grazing.

PALOUSE FALLS ★★★★★

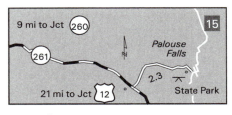

MAGNITUDE: 86   ELEVATION: 770 feet
WATERSHED: lg   USGS MAP: Palouse Falls (1981)

The Palouse River hurtles 185 feet into Lower Palouse Canyon in a thundering display. The Wilkes Expedition of 1841 called this descent Aputapat Falls. In 1875 W. P. Breeding erected a flour mill at the falls, envisioning a vibrant Palouse City at the site, but it never came to be.

From Washtucna follow S.R. 260 south to S.R. 261, turn left, and drive 9 miles southeast to the marked access road to Palouse Falls State Park. You can also reach the park entrance from the south by turning west onto S.R. 261 from U.S. 12 about 15 miles north of Dayton. The picnic area and falls are 2.3 miles from the entrance.

"No Trespassing" signs are now at both *Little Palouse Falls* ★★ USGS Palouse Falls (1981) and *Upper Palouse Falls* (u) ★ Palouse Falls (1981 nl), making them inaccessible to the public. This is a shame, since this is a geologically significant area where the Spokane Floods diverted the Palouse River into an extensive joint/fracture zone. Perhaps someday its federal owner, the Bureau of Land Management, will develop it as an interpretive site for public day-use.

Palouse Falls

THE COLUMBIA GORGE, WASHINGTON AND OREGON

The Columbia Gorge is a haven for waterfall lovers. Although it is the smallest of the fourteen regions in this book, it has the greatest density of waterfalls. There are 115 recognized falls in this area of 1700 square miles; descriptions of 72 are given in this chapter. The others cannot be viewed either because no trails lead to them or because they are in watersheds in which travel is restricted.

The majority of the falls along the Oregon side of the gorge were formed by the same geological events that shaped the region. Two major lava flows, which covered much of the Pacific Northwest, impacted this area, one over 30 million years ago and the other about 15 million years ago.

As the layers of lava cooled, they mainly formed a type of rock called basalt. The Cascade Range was formed when this bedrock material was uplifted by internal earth forces. Because basalt is relatively resistant to erosion by running water, the rise of the Cascades diverted the course of most rivers. But the Columbia River was powerful enough to erode through the rising bedrock to shape the Columbia Gorge. The small streams that flow into the Columbia from the adjacent upland cannot effectively erode the basalt, so their courses are interrupted by the sharp, vertical breaks of the gorge, resulting in spectacular waterfalls.

Because landslides have modified the steepness of relief on the Washington side these great waterfalls are limited to the south side of the gorge, with those on the Washington side being smaller and fewer in number than those in Oregon. Sections 1 through 12 below cover the Oregon side of the Gorge; sections 13 through 18 the Washington side.

A federal law that went into effect in 1986 designated most of this region, over 225,000 acres, as the Columbia River Gorge National Scenic Area. The first of its kind, the National Scenic Area legislation was the result of two primary concerns: first, to protect and provide for the enhancement of the scenic, cultural, recreational, and natural resources of

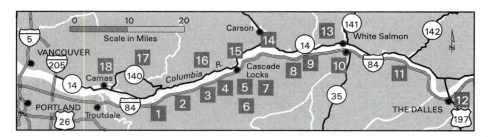

the area and, second, to protect and support the economy of the Gorge by encouraging growth to occur in existing urban areas, and by allowing future economic development outside these areas where it is compatible with Gorge resources.

1 BRIDAL VEIL

The Columbia Gorge Scenic Highway is accessible from I-84 (formerly I-80) for eastbounders at Troutdale (Exit 17), Lewis and Clark State Park (Exit 18), Corbett (Exit 22), or Bridal Veil (Exit 28). Westbounders can access the area at Dodson (Exit 35) or Warrendale (Exit 37).

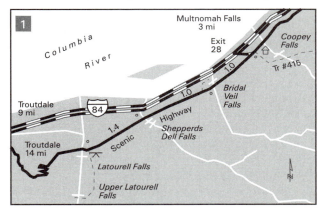

LATOURELL FALLS ★★★★★

MAGNITUDE: 83   ELEVATION: 400 feet
WATERSHED: sm   USGS MAP: Bridal Veil (1994)

This 249-foot waterfall along Latourell Creek is within Guy W. Talbot State Park, the land for which was donated to the state of Oregon in 1929 by Mr. and Mrs. Guy W. Talbot. The waterfall was named in August 1887, after Joseph Latourell, a prominent local settler. From Exit 28 on I-84 drive 3.4 miles west on the Scenic Highway to the day-use park. It is a very short walk from the picnic area to the viewpoint.

Latourell Falls

Upper Latourell Falls ★★★

MAGNITUDE: 65   ELEVATION: 680 feet
WATERSHED: sm   USGS MAP: Bridal Veil (1994)

It is possible to walk behind this 75- to 100-foot cataract on Latourell Creek. Continue along the upper trail past the top of Latourell Falls (described earlier) for 0.8 mile to the upper falls.

Shepperds Dell Falls (u) ★★

MAGNITUDE: 30 (l)   ELEVATION: 200 feet
WATERSHED: sm   USGS MAP: Bridal Veil (1994 nl)

A roadside view of a pair of falls is available by looking upstream from the bridge crossing at Shepperds Dell State Park. The lower tier is of the horsetail form and drops 40 to 60 feet. The 35- to 50-foot plunge of the upper portion is not as clearly visible. The day-use park is located 2 miles west of Exit 28 on the Columbia Gorge Scenic Highway.

Bridal Veil Falls ★★★

MAGNITUDE: 59   ELEVATION: 200 feet
WATERSHED: sm   USGS MAP: Bridal Veil (1994)

Bridal Veil Creek drops abruptly twice, the upper portion falling 60 to 100 feet and the lower portion 40 to 60 feet. Along the trail to the falls, you can look across the Columbia River to distant views of some seasonal cataracts descending from the Washington side of the gorge. Drive to a parking area located about 2.4 miles east of Latourell Falls (described earlier), or 1 mile west of Exit 28 on the Columbia Gorge Scenic Highway. A short trail winds down to the base of the cataract.

Coopey Falls ★★

MAGNITUDE: 59   ELEVATION: 360 feet
WATERSHED: sm   USGS MAP: Bridal Veil (1994)

This waterfall drops 150 to 175 feet along Coopey Creek, which is named for Charles Coopey, who once owned the adjacent land. It is located on the Columbia Gorge Scenic Highway just east of Exit 28.

A convent owned by the Franciscan Sisters of the Eucharist is located at the base of the falls. Meals are served to the public and guests are invited to stroll up to the falls. Partial views can also be gained above the descent by hiking 0.6 mile up nearby Angels Rest Trail #415.

2 MULTNOMAH FALLS

Multnomah Falls is the most famous waterfall in Oregon. In the same vicinity are several other falls that are worth a visit; all can be accessed from the Columbia Gorge Scenic Highway or from the rest area at Exit 31 on I-84.

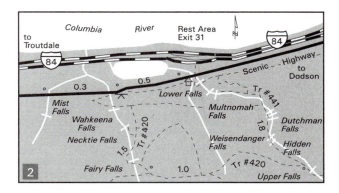

WAHKEENA FALLS ★★★★

MAGNITUDE: 59   ELEVATION: 560 feet
WATERSHED: sm   USGS MAP: Bridal Veil (1994)

Wahkeena Creek glistens 242 feet down the mountainside. It was once known as Gordan Falls and was renamed by the Mazamas outdoor recreation association in 1915. *Wahkeena* is a Yakama Indian word meaning "most beautiful." To view the falls, drive to the signed Wahkeena Picnic Area 0.5 mile west of Multnomah Falls Lodge on the Columbia Gorge Scenic Highway.

Only those travelers who know where to look are likely to see aptly named *Mist Falls* ★ USGS Bridal Veil (1994), as water spirals down hundreds of feet from tiny Mist Creek. Go 0.3 mile west of Wahkeena Falls and peer up the cliffs near mile marker 19.

NECKTIE FALLS ★★

MAGNITUDE: 49   ELEVATION: 800 feet
WATERSHED: sm   USGS MAP: Multnomah Falls (1986 ns)

This aptly named cataract veils 30 to 50 feet along Wahkeena Creek. Embark upon the moderately steep Wahkeena Trail #420 from Wahkeena Picnic Area (described earlier). After 0.8 mile, a spur trail quickly leads to the falls.

FAIRY FALLS ★★★

MAGNITUDE: 45   ELEVATION: 1000 feet
WATERSHED: sm   USGS MAP: Multnomah Falls (1986 ns)

Wahkeena Creek tumbles 20 to 30 feet in pleasant fashion. Continue 0.3 mile past the spur path for Necktie Falls (described earlier) to the point where Wahkeena Trail #420 crosses in front of the base of this cataract.

Fairy Falls

MULTNOMAH FALLS ★★★★★

MAGNITUDE: 93   ELEVATION: 620 feet
WATERSHED: med   USGS MAP: Multnomah Falls (1986 l)

Descending a total of 620 feet, Multnomah Falls is the tallest waterfall in the United States easily accessible year-round. The main portion plunges 542 feet off a sheer cliff, while below a stone masonry footbridge erected by Simon Benson in 1914 *Lower Multnomah Falls* drops 69 feet.

One of most popular tourist attractions in Oregon, the falls is accessible from both the historic Columbia Gorge Scenic Highway and I-84 via a rest area (Exit 31) built expressly for visiting here. The place can also be accessed via the Columbia Gorge Scenic Highway. Adjacent to the cataract is Multnomah Falls Lodge. Constructed in 1925, it now houses a visitor center, restaurant, and gift shop.

The falls occur due to Multnomah Creek flowing over the basalt cliffs of the Columbia Gorge, as the Columbia River managed to maintain its course during the rise of the Cascade Range millions of years ago. Nature alters the appearance of Multnomah Falls, sometimes slowly, sometimes abruptly. On September 4, 1995, a 400-ton slab of rock fell 225 feet into the upper pool. Twenty persons sustained minor injuries from flying, gravel-sized rock chips from a 100-foot-high splash that soaked the footbridge and beyond.

Native American folklore has a different account of the origin of Multnomah Falls; below is excerpted from a plaque at the waterfall:

"Many years ago, a terrible sickness came over the village of the Multnomah people and many died. An old medicine man of the tribe told the Chief that a pure and innocent maiden must go to a high cliff above the Big River and throw herself on the rocks below and the sickness would leave at once. The Chief did not want to ask any maiden to make the sacrifice. But when his daughter saw the sickness on the face of her lover, she went to the high cliff and threw herself on the rocks below. The sickness went away. As a token of the maiden's welcome, the Great Spirit took water, silvery white, and streamed it over the cliff, breaking it into a floating mist."

DUTCHMAN FALLS (U) ★★

MAGNITUDE: 37   ELEVATION: 840 feet
WATERSHED: sm   USGS MAP: Multnomah Falls (1986 ns)

In this series of three falls along Multnomah Creek, the lower and upper falls drop 10 to 15 feet while the middle section tumbles 15 to 20 feet. Embark upon Larch Mountain Trail #441, which begins to the left of Multnomah Falls Lodge (described earlier). The steep trail offers a variety of views of

DRY CREEK FALLS (U) ★★★

MAGNITUDE: 49   ELEVATION: 1400 feet
WATERSHED: sm   USGS MAP: Carson (1994 nl)

Dry Creek plunges 50 to 70 feet. The drainage is a part of the watershed for the city of Cascade Locks. Obey the signs posted near the falls. From Bridge of the Gods, hike 2 miles along Pacific Crest Trail #2000 to Dry Creek. For those departing from the Work Center or Herman Camp, take the appropriate spur trail to the Crest Trail and go 2.3 miles westward to Dry Creek. Once at the drainage, follow a dirt road 0.3 mile upstream to the base of the descent.

In the vicinity, one can also look a fair distance up an unnamed drainage for an obscured view of *Pacific Crest Falls* (u) ★ USGS Carson (1994 nl) dropping 25 to 40 feet. Hike 1.9 miles eastward past the Dry Creek drainage crossing of Pacific Crest Trail; or 0.4 mile west from its junction with Herman Bridge Trail #406-E. If it weren't for this nearby entry being mapped, it would probably be ignored.

CAMP CREEK FALLS (U) ★★★

MAGNITUDE:59   ELEVATION:900 feet
WATERSHED:vsm   USGS MAP:Carson (1994 ns)

An 80- to 100-foot ribbon of water splashes just a few feet from a trail. Easiest access to this specific entry is from Herman Creek Camp. Westbounders depart I-84 at Herman Creek (Exit 47). Eastbound traffic will need to use Wyeth (Exit 51) as a U-turn. Once off the interstate ramp, cross under the freeway and turn right (west) along the frontage road, named Forest Lane. Proceed 0.6 mile and turn left for Herman Camp (signs may also be seen for the Columbia Gorge Work Center). Go up the road, which quickly leads to the camp and trailhead on the west end. Park here.

Embark upon the route signed for both Herman Creek Trail #406 and Pacific Crest Trail #2000. After a fairly steep walk for 0.3 mile, crossing some powerlines along the way, a junction will be met. Turning right goes toward Pacific Crest Falls (described earlier), so bear left. The way is less steep for the next 0.2 mile, where a most confusing junction of multiple paths is encountered. The best way to describe it is to stay straight, bearing eastward, where the route steepens considerably as an old dirt road. A horse camp is 0.5 mile farther down the way, with another junction maze. Once again, proceed straight ahead although your bearing will now be toward the southeast. The directions are simple from here, as Herman Creek Trail parallels its namesake. During moist conditions, a trailside view of *Falls Creek Falls* (u) ★ USGS Carson (1994 nl) will be gained in 0.8 mile with Camp Creek and its cataract reached 0.5 mile farther. From the destination, it's 2.3 miles back to the trailhead.

8 WYETH

GORTON CREEK FALLS ★★★

MAGNITUDE: 70   ELEVATION: 500 feet
WATERSHED: sm   USGS MAP: Carson (1994 ns)

Gorton Creek pours 120 to 140 feet from cliffs of the Columbia Gorge. Some vantages reveal a 20- to 30-foot upper tier along the stream. Depart I-84 at Wyeth (Exit 51) and drive 0.4 mile through Wyeth Campground. Proceed to route's end at the parking area for Wyeth Trail #411 and begin walking; after a few hundred yards the way becomes a dirt road. Do not take either of the two signed trails; instead, continue along the dirt road. In 0.3 mile the road again becomes a path, crossing the creek once. After another 0.2 mile, you will need to negotiate a few large boulders before reaching the base of the cataract.

9 STARVATION CREEK STATE PARK

Turn off I-84 at the eastbound-only exit for day-use Starvation Creek State Park and rest area. West-bounders must make a U-turn at Wyeth (Exit 51) to enter, then make a similar turn at Viento Park (Exit 56) when leaving.

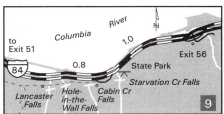

STARVATION CREEK FALLS ★★★★

MAGNITUDE: 62   ELEVATION: 280 feet
WATERSHED: sm   USGS MAP: Mount Defiance (1994 nl)

The name of this 186-foot waterfall and its stream came from an event in December 1884. Two trains were snowbound nearby on the recently completed railroad. The stranded passengers called the area "Starveout," although no one perished during the incident. Walk a very short distance from the southeast side of the picnic area to view the falls.

CABIN CREEK FALLS ★★

MAGNITUDE: 32 (l) ELEVATION: 300 feet
WATERSHED: vsm USGS MAP: Mount Defiance (1994 nl)

Water trickles 175 to 200 feet from Cabin Creek. Starting at the rest area, hike 0.3 mile west along Mount Defiance Trail #413 to a trailside view in front of the cataract.

HOLE-IN-THE-WALL FALLS ★★★

MAGNITUDE: 42 ELEVATION: 200 feet
WATERSHED: sm USGS MAP: Mount Defiance (1994 nl)

This 75- to 100-foot descent once sprayed onto the old highway, so the course of Warren Creek was diverted by blasting a tunnel through the adjacent basaltic cliff. The falls was originally named. Walk 0.3 mile past Cabin Creek Falls (described earlier) along Mount Defiance Trail #413.

LANCASTER FALLS ★★

MAGNITUDE: 29 (l) ELEVATION: 400 feet
WATERSHED: vsm USGS MAP: Mount Defiance (1994)

This 200- to 250-foot cataract descends seasonally from Wonder Creek. It was named in 1970 after Samuel C. Lancaster, who designed the beautiful Columbia River Scenic Highway prior to World War I. Continue 0.2 mile past Hole-in-the-Wall Falls (described earlier) for a total of 0.8 mile along Mount Defiance Trail #413.

---

10 HOOD RIVER VALLEY

The area around Hood River is known for sailboarding and fruit orchards. The town and its surrounding valley can be accessed from I-84 via Exits 62 and 64 or from Mount Hood via S.R. 35.

WAH GWIN GWIN FALLS ★★★

MAGNITUDE: 65 ELEVATION: 280 feet
WATERSHED: med USGS MAP: Hood River (1994)

This 207-foot plunge along Phelps Creek is located on the grounds of the luxuriant Columbia Gorge Hotel. *Wah Gwin Gwin* is a Native American phrase meaning "tumbling or rushing waters." Leave I-84 at West Hood River/Westcliff Drive (Exit 62), turning left (west) at Westcliff Drive and reaching the hotel and falls in 0.2 mile.

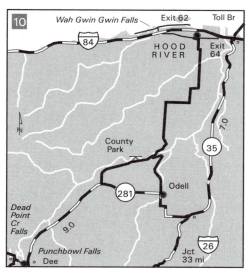

Punchbowl Falls ★★★

MAGNITUDE: 41 (h)   ELEVATION: 840 feet
WATERSHED: lg   USGS MAP: Dee (1994)

Hood River drops 10 to 15 feet into a large pool flanked by sheer cliffs of columnar basalt. Drive to the lumber processing facility at Dee, located on S.R. 281. Turn right on Punchbowl Road and continue 1.4 miles to an unsigned parking area on the near (east) side of the river. Take a short walk down the dirt road to pathways leading to unguarded vistas at the rim of the small canyon.

Dead Point Creek Falls (u) ★★

MAGNITUDE: 23 (l)   ELEVATION: 840 feet
WATERSHED: med   USGS MAP: Dee (1994 nl)

Look across the Hood River to view this 40- to 50-foot double falls. It is located immediately downstream from Punchbowl Falls (described earlier) and can be seen from the same viewpoints. The USGS topographic map erroneously labels this previously unnamed cataract as Punchbowl Falls.

11 MOSIER

MOSIER CREEK FALLS (U) ★★★

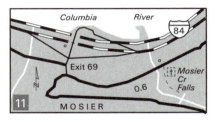

MAGNITUDE: 57
WATERSHED: lg

ELEVATION: 160 feet
USGS MAP: White Salmon (1978 nl)

Mosier Creek slides into a small gorge, falling a total of 125 to 150 feet. Turn off I-84 at Mosier (Exit 69) and drive 0.6 mile east, passing the town of Mosier. A short, easy path on the right (east) side of Mosier Creek bridge leads past a cemetary to an unguarded overlook.

Others: A brief glimpse of *Rowena Dell Falls* (u) ★ USGS Lyle (1994 nl) is possible while driving eastbound just prior to Rowena (Exit 76) along I-84. Go online to *The Computer Companion* (described in the Introduction) to see a map for this entry.

12 THE DALLES

Turn off I-84 at The Dalles East/U.S. 197 (Exit 87). Drive south 0.2 mile, then turn right (west) and go 0.2 mile to Southeast Frontage Road.

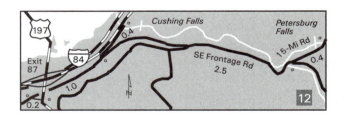

CUSHING FALLS ★★

MAGNITUDE: 13
WATERSHED: lg

ELEVATION: 140 feet
USGS MAP: Petersburg (1994)

This modest 10- to 15-foot drop along Fifteenmile Creek occurs in a setting that is markedly drier than those of its counterparts to the west. The eastern flank of the Columbia Gorge is characterized by a climatological phenomenon called the "rain-shadow effect." The rain shadow results from the fact that most of the region's precipitation falls on the western, windward side of the Cascade Mountains. Drive 1 mile along Southeast Frontage Road, then turn left and continue for 0.4 mile. Cross the bridge and turn right on an unimproved road. The descent is a very short, easy walk heading upstream.

Petersburg Falls (u) ★ USGS Petersburg (1994 nl) can be visited by proceeding 2.5 miles past the junction for Cushing Falls, staying on Southeast Frontage Road. Turn left and drive 0.4 mile along Fifteenmile Road. Park just before the bridge and walk a short distance to the creek and its 5- to 10-foot rapids. It was named by the author after a nearby unincorporated hamlet.

13 WHITE SALMON

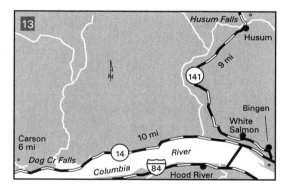

HUSUM FALLS ★★

MAGNITUDE: 41 (h)   ELEVATION: 400 feet
WATERSHED: lg   USGS MAP: Husum (1994 nl)

White Salmon River rushes 5 to 10 feet right in downtown Husum. The community is located 9 miles north of Bingen along S.R. 141. The falls can be seen from the bridge; park at the turnout on the north side where there is an interpretive sign about rafting on the White Salmon National Scenic River.

DOG CREEK FALLS (U) ★★

MAGNITUDE: 32 (h)   ELEVATION: 120 feet
WATERSHED: sm   USGS MAP: Mount Defiance (1994 nl)

Dog Creek sprays 15 to 20 feet downward in a narrow fan shape. Stop at the unsigned parking area just west of mile marker 56, located 6 miles east of Carson and 10 miles west of Bingen. Walk a short distance upstream to a view.

14 CARSON

The Carson area is best known for St. Martin Hot Springs, but the owners of the springs have periodically closed the waters to the public. The lesser known Shipherd Falls was, however, open to visitation at the time of the author's last visit.

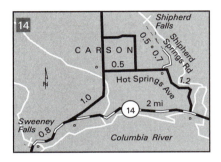

SHIPHERD FALLS ★★

MAGNITUDE: 55	ELEVATION: 160 feet
WATERSHED: lg	USGS MAP: Carson (1994)

This 40- to 60-foot series of cascades along the Wind River is next to a fishway, gauging station, and (locked) footbridge. Follow Hot Springs Avenue 0.5 mile east from Carson or 1.2 miles north from S.R. 14 to Shipherd Springs Road and turn north, following the graveled route 0.7 mile farther. A trail at the road end leads to a pair of views in 0.3 mile and 0.5 mile.

SWEENEY FALLS ★★

MAGNITUDE: 45	ELEVATION: 300 feet
WATERSHED: sm	USGS MAP: Carson (1994 ns)

Motorists zipping along S.R. 14 will certainly miss this 45- to 60-foot cataract, since it is camouflaged from the highway by vegetation and there are no signs. Drive to a turnout on the cliff side of the road, located at mile 46.6 based on mile markers 46 and 47. Find the path next to the turnout. A steep slope must first be negotiated—the most difficult part of the journey. When last visited, there was a rope to make the descent easier. From there, it's an easy 0.1 mile along the path that ends at the base of the falls along Smith Creek.

15 ROCK CREEK

ROCK CREEK FALLS (U) ★★★

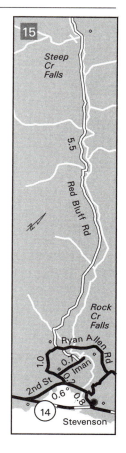

MAGNITUDE: 39 (l)
ELEVATION: 240 feet
WATERSHED: lg
USGS MAP: Bonneville Dam (1994 nl)

A short, well-worn path leads to side views of Rock Creek, shimmering as it drops 35 to 50 feet over a wide ledge. Turn off S.R. 14 onto Second Street either in Stevenson or 1 mile west of town. Turn west off Second Street onto Ryan Allen Road. In 0.2 mile, turn right on Iman Cemetery Road. Continue on this road to its end in 0.7 mile. Look for a path leading down to the stream.

STEEP CREEK FALLS (U) ★★

MAGNITUDE: 48   ELEVATION: 1160 feet
WATERSHED: sm   USGS MAP: Bonneville
                                          Dam (1994 nl)

Gain a roadside view of Steep Creek tumbling 30 to 40 feet into Rock Creek. Follow the directions to Rock Creek Falls (described earlier) but instead of turning on Iman Cemetery Road, continue along Ryan Allen Road for 1 more mile. Turn left on Red Bluff Road and drive 5.5 miles to the point where the gravel road crosses Rock Creek next to the cataract.

16 BEACON ROCK

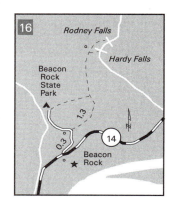

The 600-foot projection of Beacon Rock is one of the major landmarks of the Columbia River Gorge. Beacon Rock State Park is located next to S.R. 14 about 18 miles east of Washougal and 4 miles west of North Bonneville.

RODNEY FALLS ★★

MAGNITUDE: 51   ELEVATION: 1000 feet
WATERSHED: sm   USGS MAP: Beacon Rock (1994)

Hardy Creek plunges and cascades a total of 100 to 150 feet in two major sections. Drive 0.3 mile from the highway to the picnic area of Beacon Rock State Park. Begin hiking along Hamilton Mountain Trail. After a moderate climb of nearly 1.25 miles, you will encounter two short spur paths. The lower spur provides a view of the lower tier of the falls. Proceed on the main trail to a footbridge crossing and another short spur to the upper portion.

HARDY FALLS ★★★

MAGNITUDE: 63   ELEVATION: 800 feet
WATERSHED: sm   USGS MAP: Beacon Rock (1994)

The more scenic of two descents along Hardy Creek, this one pours 80 to 120 feet downward. Instead of taking the lower spur to Rodney Falls (described earlier), choose the upper way to the far right. This spur leads quickly to a viewpoint for this entry.

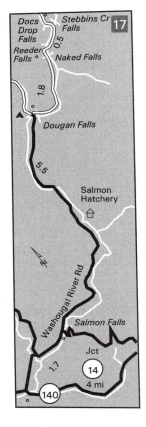

17 WASHOUGAL RIVER

Remember how hot it was in the Northwest during the summer of 2003? When the author visited the region that June, bathers were *en masse* along the Washougal River, cooling off in its refreshing waters. To his delight, all but the first of the following quintet of modest waterfalls are next to swimming holes.

SALMON FALLS ★★

MAGNITUDE: 29
ELEVATION: 380 feet
WATERSHED: lg
USGS MAP: Bridal Veil (1994 ns)

Obtain a bridge-side view of Washougal River pouring 10 to 15 feet into a pool below. A cement structure on the left side of the falls detracts from the scenery. Turn north off S.R. 14 onto S.R. 140, 10 miles east of Washougal or 12 miles west of North Bonneville. Drive up the hill and after 4 miles, turn right (north) onto Washougal River Road. Proceed 1.7 miles and turn right onto Salmon Falls Road. Cross the bridge and park at the unmarked turnout. This entry is probably located on private property.

DOUGAN FALLS ★★

MAGNITUDE: 32   ELEVATION: 640 feet
WATERSHED: lg   USGS MAP: Bobs Mtn (1994)

This stairstep series of block-type falls totals 30 to 60 feet along the Washougal River. Water also slides 20 to 30 feet into the river from nearby Dougan Creek. Located on public land maintained by the state of Washington, the waterfall is located 5.5 miles upstream from Salmon Falls (described earlier), where the Washougal River Road crosses the river for a second time.

NAKED FALLS ★★

MAGNITUDE: 43   ELEVATION: 730 feet
WATERSHED: lg   USGS MAP: Bobs Mtn (1994 ns)

This is a series of small falls and cascades as the Washougal River tumbles a total of 15 to 25 feet. Turn right at the road junction immediately past the

Naked Falls

bridge at Dougan Falls (described earlier). Proceed 1.8 miles and park along a wide spot in the road. You have gone a few hundred yards too far if you meet another bridge, which incidentally provides a view upstream of *Reeder Falls* ★ USGS Bobs Mtn (1994 ns). Looking downstream from the bridge, the top of Naked Falls can be seen. Meanwhile back along the road, look for a path that initially requires a brief descent with "root-holds" (the hardest part), then leads quickly 0.1 mile to rock slabs above and adjacent to the main display. Reportedly its name is based on the bare rock rather than some cultural phenomenon.

STEBBINS CREEK FALLS (U) ★★

MAGNITUDE: 25   ELEVATION: 820 feet
WATERSHED: med   USGS MAP: Beacon Rock (1994 ns)

Also unofficially known as Mad Dog Falls, this 15- to 20-foot display pours directly into the Washougal River. Continue 0.5 mile past Naked Falls (described earlier) to turnouts next to a bridge crossing over this entry.

DOCS DROP FALLS (U) ★★

MAGNITUDE: 27   ELEVATION: 780 feet
WATERSHED: lg   USGS MAP: Beacon Rock (1994 ns)

Drive or walk 0.1 mile beyond Stebbins Creek Falls (described earlier) to rivulets of water descending 15 to 25 feet along the Washougal River.

18 CAMAS

Lacamas Park, located within the lumber town of Camas, harbors three modest falls. From downtown, drive 1.4 miles north on S.R. 500 from its junction with Business S.R. 14. Turn left into the parking area.

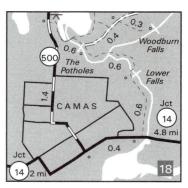

THE POTHOLES ★★

MAGNITUDE: 30   ELEVATION: 240 feet
WATERSHED: lg (d)   USGS MAP: Camas (1993 ns)

Rivulets of Lacamas Creek pour 15 to 20 feet along a wide expanse of bedrock. Views are obscured when the foliage is in leaf. Walk past the park's small playground and turn right, taking a path following tiny Round Lake. Cross a footbridge over a generator, then in 0.3 mile walk over the concrete dam. Parallel the lake for another 0.2 mile, then select the middle trail at a three-pronged fork. Proceed 0.1 mile to a grassy area above the cataract.

Woodburn Falls ★ USGS Camas (1993 ns) occurs where water trickles 35 to 45 feet along an unnamed intermittent creek. At The Potholes, find the service road and hike up it for 0.3 mile, passing a trail sign and a path to the left that goes back to Round Lake. Do not turn here; instead, continue another 0.1 mile to an unsigned path to the right. Take this path for 0.3 mile until it ends directly in front of the small cataract.

LOWER FALLS ★★

MAGNITUDE: 29   ELEVATION: 120 feet
WATERSHED: lg (d)   USGS MAP: Camas (1993 nl)

Lacamas Creek slides 25 to 35 feet over an escarpment in two segments. Continue past The Potholes (described earlier), following Lacamas Creek downstream. In 0.6 mile reach a footbridge over the top of the falls. Better views require a bit of a bushwhack. Backtrack from the bridge, looking for a faint path where the trail begins to leave the creek. Follow it down to open views below the base of the falls.

NORTHERN COAST RANGE, OREGON

The Coast Range extends from the northwestern lobe of Oregon southward to California. For convenience, the region has been divided into two chapters, entitled "Northern Coast Range" and "Southern Coast Range." This chapter describes waterfalls found in association with the moist, montane environment stretching from the Columbia River, between Portland and Astoria, to an arbitrarily chosen southern limit along U.S. 20, which connects Newport and Corvallis.

During the author's travels along the coast, evidence was found suggesting that the Pacific Northwest has an enormous number of unmapped waterfalls. The density of mapped falls in the Northern Coast Range is comparable to the other regions of the Northwest (USGS topographic maps show sixty-four, of which nineteen are described in the following pages). How-

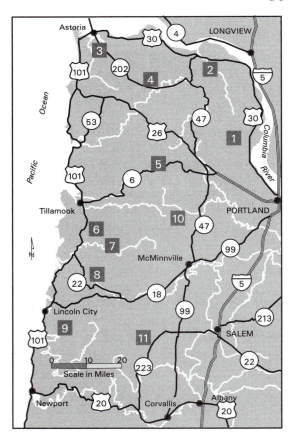

ever, it appears likely that many more falls occur in the area. Cal Baker, an employee of Siuslaw National Forest, has surveyed and recorded ninety-nine drops exceeding 5 feet just in the Hebo Ranger District alone. Much of Idaho, Oregon, and Washington is more rugged and wild than the Coast Range, so if a similar proportion of cataracts are unlisted in those areas, the entire Northwest probably has over 10,000 falls versus the 1411 falls I have personally mapped. It would require an encyclopedia-sized document to describe every waterfall!

SCAPPOOSE

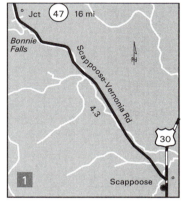

BONNIE FALLS ★★

MAGNITUDE: 44
ELEVATION: 330 feet
WATERSHED: lg
USGS MAP: Chapman (1990)

North Scappoose Creek tumbles 15 to 25 feet over a basalt escarpment. Turn off U.S. 30 at the north end of Scappoose and drive 4.3 miles northwest along Scappoose–Vernonia Road. A small parking turnout immediately precedes the falls. A fish ladder has been built next to them.

Bonnie Falls

2 BEAVER CREEK

Motorists driving along old U.S. 30 pass by two waterfalls between Rainier and Clatskanie. The route has changed, so few travelers see them unless they turn off the main highway. Drive 6.2 miles west from Rainier on U.S. 30 to the marked Delena turnoff, located 1.2 miles west of the turnoff to Vernonia.

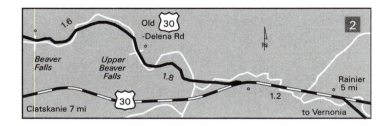

BEAVER FALLS ★★★

MAGNITUDE: 64   ELEVATION: 230 feet
WATERSHED: lg   USGS MAP: Delena (1985)

Water pours 60 to 80 feet from Beaver Creek. Be careful. There are no guardrails at the viewpoint from the top of the waterfall. Turn westward off U.S. 30 onto Old Highway 30/Delena Road. After 1.8 miles, a roadside view will be reached of the 10- to 15-foot drop comprising *Upper Beaver Falls* (u) ★ USGS Delena (1985 ns). Continue 1.6 additional miles to an unsigned parking area to the left (south). Walk down the short dirt road to a path leading shortly to side views above the descent.

3 OLNEY

YOUNGS RIVER FALLS ★★★

MAGNITUDE: 54
ELEVATION: 90 feet
WATERSHED: lg
USGS MAP: Olney (1973)

Youngs River curtains 30 to 50 feet into the Klaskanine Valley. The author remembers seeing a commercial showing Clydesdales

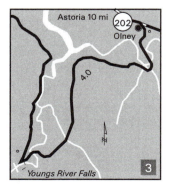

high-stepping near the base of the falls. Drive 10 miles southeast from Astoria on S.R. 202, or 20 miles northwest from Jewell. At Olney junction drive 3.8 miles down the road marked for the falls. Turn left upon the old roadgrade to its end in 0.1 mile. A roadside vista has recently been built or you can walk 0.1 mile down to the base of the cataract.

4 JEWELL

FISHHAWK FALLS ★★

MAGNITUDE: 33   ELEVATION: 770 feet
WATERSHED: med   USGS MAP: Vinemaple (1984)

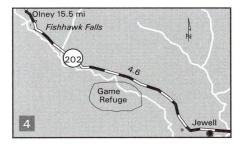

Fishhawk Creek ripples 40 to 60 feet downward within Lee Wooden County Park. Located between Jewell and Fishhawk Falls is Jewell Meadows Wildlife Area. Elk and deer are often seen browsing in this state game refuge. There are marked viewpoints next to the highway.

Drive 4.4 miles northwest from Jewell along S.R. 202 to the park. Trails lead upstream to the base of the falls in 0.2 mile. You can also drive 0.2 mile farther to an unsigned viewpoint above the descent.

5 WILSON RIVER

S.R. 6 is *the* highway for travelers accessing the coast from Portland. And traffic tends to speed, so be careful when turning on and off for the following trio of pleasant waterfalls.

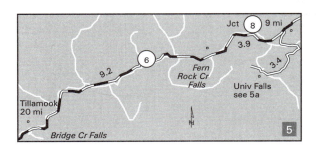

University Falls ★★★

MAGNITUDE: 59   ELEVATION: 1640 feet
WATERSHED: sm   USGS MAP: Woods Point (1979)

Water curtains 40 to 50 feet within Tillamook State Forest. Be cognizant of the signs for the falls as you drive, as there are a lot of road junctions along the way. Take S.R. 6 for 9 miles west of its junction with S.R. 8. Just past mile marker 33, turn onto Rogers Camp Road, also marked for University Falls. Go 0.1 mile, turn right, and proceed 3.3 miles to the trailhead sign for the falls. Find a wide spot to park. Hike for 0.5 mile, avoiding the dirt road junctions that are used by ATVs. The footpath ends at the base of this delightful display along Elliot Creek.

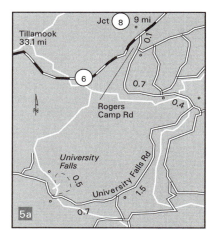

University Falls

FERN ROCK CREEK FALLS ★★

MAGNITUDE: 35   ELEVATION: 1100 feet
WATERSHED: vsm   USGS MAP: Woods Point (1979 ns)

A small stream veils 15 to 25 feet adjacent to the highway. Drive 3.9 miles southwest of the junction for University Falls (described earlier) along S.R. 6. Look
for the large turnout on the south side of the road with the generic sign sheep-
ishly signed as "falls." It is situated 0.2 mile east of mile marker 29.

BRIDGE CREEK FALLS (U) ★★

MAGNITUDE: 25   ELEVATION: 480 feet
WATERSHED: vsm   USGS MAP: Jordan Creek (1984 ns)

Bridge Creek tumbles a total of 40 to 60 feet over three ledges of rock. Take
S.R. 6 for 9.2 miles southwest of Fern Rock Creek Falls (described earlier),
20 miles northeast of Tillamook, to a large turnout on the south side of the
highway just west of mile marker 20. A nice trail with a series of concrete
and wooden steps quickly leads to the base of the cataract. Such features make
one wonder why the place is not signed.

   Others: The following pair of small cascades can be seen along the Nehalem
River. *Little Falls* ★ USGS Elsie (1984) occurs where water rushes 5 to 10 feet
over the 75- to 100-foot breadth of the river. Depart U.S. 26 near Elsie at the
southbound turn marked Spruce Run County Park. Drive 5.2 miles to the park,
then 1 mile farther to a sharp right (west) turn in both the road and the river.
Park where the road widens and follow the fishermen's paths quickly leading
to the descent. *Nehalem Falls* ★ USGS Foley Peak (1985) slides 5 to 10 feet within
Nehalem Falls Park. Turn northeast off U.S. 101 onto S.R. 53 near Wheeler.
In 1.3 miles turn right (southeast) on Nehalem River Road and drive 7 miles to
the entrance to the park. Stop along the road about 100 yards inside the entrance adjacent to the falls. Go online to *The Computer Companion* (described
in the Introduction) to see a map for these entries.

---

6 TILLAMOOK

Compared to the relatively
modest falls of this region,
the following entry will
surely impress. Buy some
crackers and the famous
Tillamook cheese and take in
the highest waterfall of the entire Coast Range.

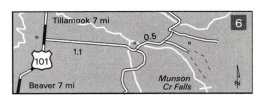

MUNSON CREEK FALLS ★★★★

MAGNITUDE: 75   ELEVATION: 760 feet
WATERSHED: sm   USGS MAP: Beaver (1985)

This fine-lined cataract drops 266 feet as a triple horsetail. The descent and its stream are named after Goran Munson, a native of Michigan who settled

Munson Creek Falls

nearby in 1889. Turn off U.S. 101 about halfway between Tillamook and Beaver at the sign for Munson Creek Falls County Park. Follow the signs 1.6 miles to the parking area and trailhead. The easily hiked Lower Trail traverses through a lush forest to the base of the falls. For full views, follow the Upper Trail for 0.5 mile to an excellent gorge vista. (Reportedly, this way has not been maintained and is overgrown with vegetation.) The steep trails were built as part of youth programs in 1960–62 and 1978–79.

7 BLAINE

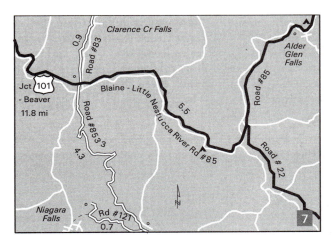

CLARENCE CREEK FALLS (U) ★★

MAGNITUDE: 27   ELEVATION: 560 feet
WATERSHED: med   USGS MAP: Blaine (1984 nl)

Clarence Creek slides 46 feet next to the road. Turn left (north) off U.S. 101 at Beaver onto the Blaine–Little Nestucca River Road #85. Drive for 11.8 miles, then turn left (north) on Clarence Creek Road #83. The gravel route ascends steeply before leveling off to a gentle slope in 0.9 mile at the falls.

Waterfall seekers can also easily access *Alder Glen Falls* (u) ★ USGS Dovre Peak (1984 ns), where an unnamed creek tumbles 15 to 25 feet into the Nestucca River. This falls is located within Nestucca Recreation Area. Drive 5.5 miles east of Road #8533 (described earlier) along Blaine–Little Nestucca River Road #85 to Alder Glen Camp. The cataract is situated across the river from the north end of this Bureau of Land Management campground.

take the latter highway eastward for 4.5 miles. Turn right onto Bear Creek Road and follow it for 3.5 miles, then stay straight where the way is renamed Forest Road #17. The signed parking area and trailhead is 7 miles farther.

It's a 1.5-mile hike from here along Drift Creek Falls Trail #1378. A salute goes out to the trailblazers who constructed an extremely consistent grade over the entire route. Eventually arrive at a footbridge, which affords views to the right looking down into the cataract and the gorge bottom 100 feet below.

Here we have a very unconventional geographic naming of the creeks. Usually when a smaller stream meets a larger one, the name of the larger one is kept. In this case, despite Drift Creek plunging over the side of the gorge, its name is surprisingly retained farther downstream.

---

10 CHERRY GROVE

Cherry Grove is a small community nestled in the eastern foothills of the Coast Range. Two small waterfalls descend nearby along the refreshing waters of the Tualatin River.

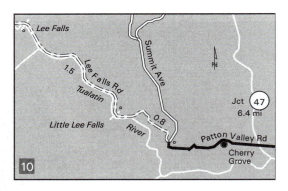

LEE FALLS ★★

MAGNITUDE: 37   ELEVATION: 390 feet
WATERSHED: lg   USGS MAP: Turner Creek (1979)

The Tualatin River pours 10 to 20 feet from a rocky escarpment adjacent to the gravel road. Turn west off S.R. 47 at Patton Valley Road 6 miles south of Forest Grove and 11 miles north of Yamhill. Drive 6 miles to Cherry Grove, staying on the main road through the village. At a sweeping curve to the right, the route becomes Summit Avenue. Continue to the end of the paved surface and turn left (west) on a dirt road, located 0.4 mile west of town. A gate prevents further driving, so start walking.

Little Lee Falls ★ USGS Turner Creek (1979) occurs where the Tualatin

River splits into three parts before cascading 6 to 10 feet into a large pool. It will be encountered in 0.8 mile. Continue another 1.5 miles to a roadside view of Lee Falls.

---

11 FALLS CITY

FALLS CITY FALLS (u) ★★

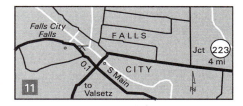

MAGNITUDE: 57   ELEVATION: 380 feet
WATERSHED: lg   USGS MAP: Falls City (1974 nl)

The Little Luckiamute River sharply drops 25 to 35 feet into a tight gorge. This falls is located within Michael Harding Park, where only partially obscured side views are possible. Turn off S.R. 223 onto a road signed for Falls City, 6 miles south of Dallas and 20 miles north of U.S. 20. Drive 4 miles to town. After crossing a bridge over the river, turn right at the South Main Street sign and drive 0.1 mile to the park.

Falls City Falls

SOUTHERN COAST RANGE, OREGON

The southern portion of Oregon's Coast Range extends from the north along S.R. 34, which connects Waldport and Corvallis, south to the California border, where the range transitions into the Klamath Mountains. There are ninety-five waterfalls mapped in this region; thirty-five of them are included here.

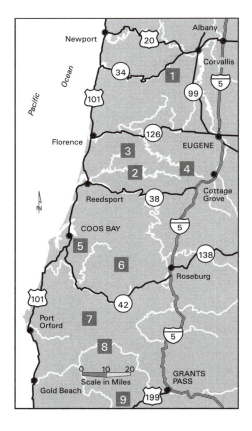

The landscape of the Southern Coast Range is geomorphically youthful. Its geology includes each of the three major classes of rocks. Igneous rocks, such as basalt, are common, as are sedimentary layers of sandstone and siltstone. Heat and pressure have transformed some of these rocks into the third category, metamorphic rocks, of which gneiss and quartzite are examples. Each type of rock has a varying degree of resistance to the erosive effects of running water.

This region was once characterized by low relief, but between 1 million and 3 million years ago internal earth forces uplifted and deformed the flat, coastal plains. The courses of most of the rivers flowing to the Pacific Ocean from the western flank of the Cascade Range were altered by this evolution of the Coast Range. Only two waterways, the Rogue River and the Umpqua River, were powerful enough to maintain their passages to the sea. On these two rivers falls were shaped where rising bedrock with a slow rate of erosion met the less resistant streambeds.

Additional descents formed where tributary creeks connected with larger rivers. As uplifting progressed, smaller streams generally eroded the rock beneath them less effectively than did the main channels. Therefore, a vertical drop is often seen near a tributary's confluence with the larger waterway. *Elk Creek Falls* is an example.

1 ALSEA

Alsea is located near three waterfalls along the eastern flank of the Coast Range. The town is 25 miles southwest of Corvallis and 40 miles east of Tidewater on S.R. 34.

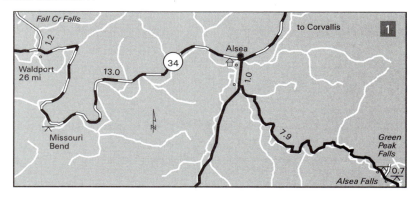

FALL CREEK FALLS ★★

MAGNITUDE: 14   ELEVATION: 160 feet
WATERSHED: lg   USGS MAP: Grass Mtn (1984 nl)

Although Fall Creek drops only 5 to 10 feet, a fish ladder has been constructed to bypass it. Follow S.R. 34 west of Alsea for 13 miles and turn right (north) on Fall Creek Road. Look for the cataract to the left in 1.2 miles.

ALSEA FALLS ★★

MAGNITUDE: 30   ELEVATION: 780 feet
WATERSHED: med   USGS MAP: Glenbrook (1984)

South Fork Alsea Creek cascades 30 to 50 feet downward. This entry is located within Alsea Falls Picnic Area. A short trail leads to the river at the base of the descent. Turn off S.R. 34 at Alsea and drive south for 1 mile. Then turn left (east) onto South Fork Road and continue 8.6 miles to the picnic area. The route is marked all the way from town.

GREEN PEAK FALLS ★★

MAGNITUDE: 55   ELEVATION: 740 feet
WATERSHED: med   USGS MAP: Glenbrook (1984)

Water veils 30 to 40 feet downward along the South Fork Alsea River. When the author last visited it, he had to bushwhack to get to this entry. The official website for Alsea Falls Picnic Area now indicates trail access, which has been field-truthed by waterfall-seeker Greg Lief. Drive 0.7 mile beyond the entrance to the picnic area (described earlier) and turn into Herbert K. McBee Memorial Park. The trailhead is at the far end of the parking area. Walk 0.8 mile down its length to the small plunge pool at the base of the falls. It is also reported a loop trail links up with Alsea Falls (described earlier).

2 SMITH RIVER

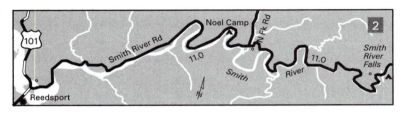

SMITH RIVER FALLS ★★

MAGNITUDE: 54   ELEVATION: 70 feet
WATERSHED: lg   USGS MAP: Smith River Falls (1984)

This 5- to 10-foot drop along the otherwise placid Smith River is located on publicly accessible Federal Bureau of Land Management property. The features are named for Jedediah Strong Smith, an early nineteenth-century fur trader and explorer.

North of Reedsport turn east off U.S. 101 onto Smith River Road. Continue east for 22 miles, passing the junction with North Fork Road #48 (do not turn at the junction) at 11 miles. The waterfall, which is less impressive in summer, is located just before Smith River Falls Campground.

3 MAPLETON RANGER DISTRICT

Five scenic waterfalls are nestled deep within Mapleton Ranger District, Siuslaw National Forest. All of them were inaccessible when earlier editions of this guidebook were prepared.

SWEET CREEK FALLS ★★

MAGNITUDE: 40   ELEVATION: 440 feet
WATERSHED: lg   USGS MAP: Goodwin Peak (1984)

Depart S.R. 126 in the town of Mapleton, next to the
Siuslaw Bridge, southward onto Sweet Creek Road. Follow it 11 miles to the Homestead/Sweet Creek trailhead.
Drive another 0.6 mile and park in the area signed for the
Sweet Creek Falls Trailhead. A short spur trail leads
quickly down to Sweet Creek Trail #1319. Turn left at the
junction and head 0.3 mile upstream to the lower 25- to
35-foot segment of the cataract spilling over igneous rock.
The way continues up another 0.1 mile to a fenced vista of
the 50- to 60-foot upper portion, but the narrow gorge prevents a full view.

A Forest Service flyer mentions that nine additional
waterfalls can be seen along the trail. According to other
sources, they drop from slabs of sandstone over a 1-mile
stretch downstream from the main falls.

BEAVER CREEK FALLS ★★★

MAGNITUDE: 44   ELEVATION: 630 feet
WATERSHED: med   USGS MAP: Goodwin Peak (1984)

Beaver Creek and Sweet Creek combine to create this interestingly shaped
25- to 35-foot waterfall. (It's probably named after the first stream because
the other joins it halfway down the descent.) Drive southward beyond the
trailhead for Sweet Creek Falls (described earlier) for 0.9 mile. Turn left
(east) onto the spur road signed for Beaver Creek trailhead. Park near road's
end in 0.5 mile. Embark upon the path where there is a close-up vantage in
0.1 mile.

Beaver Creek Falls

UPPER KENTUCKY FALLS ★★★

MAGNITUDE: 66   ELEVATION: 1400 feet
WATERSHED: sm   USGS MAP: Baldy Mtn (1984 ns)

This is the first of three waterfalls to be found along Kentucky Falls Trail #1376. This route is not recommended for young children, as part of the way is unprotected on the side of cliffs. From the junction of the Beaver Creek Falls access road (described earlier), drive approximately 8 miles southward on Sweet Creek Road and North Fork Road #48 to Forest Road #23. For those coming from the south, follow Smith River Road (described in the previous subsection) east from U.S. 101 for 11 miles to North Fork Road #48; turn north and continue 7.6 miles to Forest Road #23.

Turn east on Road #23. After an additional 10.5 miles, turn left (northwest) on Forest Road #919 and proceed 2.8 miles to the trailhead.

The first 0.7 mile of the hike is fairly easy, then it begins to follow down along the small gorge of Kentucky Creek. Here you will gain a trailside view of the 80- to 100-foot upper descent of the stream.

LOWER KENTUCKY FALLS ★★★★

MAGNITUDE: 48   ELEVATION: 920 feet
WATERSHED: sm   USGS MAP: Baldy Mtn (1984 ns)

Kentucky Creek plunges 50 to 60 feet before diverging into a pair of 15- to 20-foot horsetails. A viewing platform has been built near the base of the falls. Kentucky Creek Trail (described earlier) steepens considerably in the portion from the upper falls to its end 1.3 miles farther, 2 miles from the trailhead.

NORTH FORK FALLS ★★★

MAGNITUDE: 26 (l)   ELEVATION: 820 feet
WATERSHED: med   USGS MAP: Baldy Mtn (1984)

The North Fork Smith River curtains 60 to 80 feet over a large escarpment. During periods of low discharge, these falls appear in a segmented form. This entry is also visible from the end of Kentucky Creek Trail (described earlier). The cataract can be seen in tandem with Lower Kentucky Falls from selected vantages.

Others: *The Horn* ★ USGS Mapleton (1984 nl) is only a 3- to 5-foot drop along a 20- to 30-foot breadth of Lake Creek among a long series of rapids. Travel 1 mile northeast of the hamlet of Swisshome along S.R. 36 to an unsigned wide turnout on the river side of the highway. Walk a short distance along the road in the downstream direction for a partially obscured vantage. This entry is listed as a "falls" in the USGS's Geographic Names Information System. Go online to *The Computer Companion* (described in the Introduction) to access a map.

4 LORANE

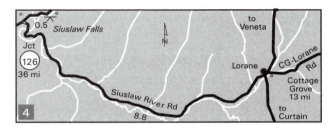

SIUSLAW FALLS ★★

MAGNITUDE: 22   ELEVATION: 570 feet
WATERSHED: lg   USGS MAP: Letz Creek (1984)

Water stairsteps 5 to 10 feet over a 70-foot-wide expanse of the Siuslaw River. From Cottage Grove drive 13 miles northwest on the Cottage Grove–Lorane

Siuslaw Falls

Road to the hamlet of Lorane. Continue west on Siuslaw River Road for 8.8 miles to an unnamed county park. Stop after 0.5 mile along the park access road. The falls is a short walk away. Look for a fish ladder along the south side of the falls.

---

5 MILLICOMA RIVER

Waterfalls are abundant on the various tributaries of the Millicoma River. Unfortunately, most of them are inaccessible. But all is not lost. The most impressive falls of the area and indeed of the region are the star attractions at Golden and Silver Falls State Park. Turn left off U.S. 101 south of downtown Coos Bay on a road signed for Eastside and the state park. Drive through Eastside and continue on to the logging community of Allegany in 14 miles. The day-use state park is at the road's end 10 miles farther.

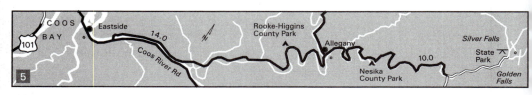

SILVER FALLS ★★

MAGNITUDE: 21 (t)   ELEVATION: 520 feet
WATERSHED: sm   USGS MAP: Golden Falls (1990)

Silver Creek trickles 80 to 120 feet over an unusual dome-shaped projection of weathered bedrock. Follow the marked trail from the picnic area for a gently sloped 0.3 mile to the falls.

GOLDEN FALLS ★★★

MAGNITUDE: 34   ELEVATION: 480 feet
WATERSHED: med   USGS MAP: Golden Falls (1990)

Glenn Creek plummets 126 to 160 feet over a rock wall. It is named after Dr. C. B. Golden, First Grand Chancellor of the Knights of Pythias of Oregon. Take the second marked trail from the end of the park road, an easy 0.3 mile to the base of the falls.

Others: Ranking as one of the smallest officially named falls of stature in the Northwest, *Laverne Falls* ★ USGS Daniels Creek (1971) consists of

Opposite: Golden Falls

a modest series of miniature falls ranging from 3 to 6 feet high along the North Fork Coquille River. These child-sized falls are located within Laverne County Park. Leave S.R. 42 at Coquille and drive 9 miles northeast to Fairview. Continue north 5.6 miles past the community to the county park. Look for the rapids near the camping area, located downstream from the park entrance. Go online to *The Computer Companion* (described in the Introduction) to access a map of this entry.

6 EAST FORK COQUILLE RIVER

There are many small waterfalls along the scenic East Fork Coquille River, and the historic Coos Bay Wagon Road follows beside it. Be careful when driving this narrow route: Logging trucks have replaced horse-drawn buggies! Be sure to find a safe place to park off the road when you locate each descent. The Wagon Road can be accessed from the west at Fairview and from the east at Tenmile.

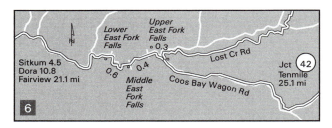

LOWER EAST FORK FALLS (U) ★★

MAGNITUDE: 19   ELEVATION: 880 feet
WATERSHED: lg   USGS MAP: Sitkum (1990 nl)

East Fork Coquille River tumbles 15 to 20 feet along a bend in the stream. The farthest downstream of a trio of descents, this waterfall is located 4.5 miles east of Sitkum, 10.8 miles east of Dora, and 26.4 miles west of Tenmile.

MIDDLE EAST FORK FALLS (U) ★★

MAGNITUDE: 36   ELEVATION: 920 feet
WATERSHED: lg   USGS MAP: Sitkum (1990 nl)

Water pours 15 to 20 feet over a small rock escarpment. Drive 0.6 mile upstream from the lower falls (described earlier). Continuing 0.4 mile onward, one will encounter *Upper East Fork Falls* (u) ★ USGS Sitkum (1990 nl). This low-lying 5- to 10-foot descent occurs where the East Fork Coquille River spreads downward next to a small, primitive campsite off the main road.

7 POWERS

Siskiyou National Forest is a largely primitive portion of southwest Oregon's Coast Range. Many waterfalls here are currently inaccessible and unmapped. Also, seasonal descents are often seen along canyon roads during moist periods. Three of the most easily accessible cataracts located in the Powers Ranger District area are listed here.

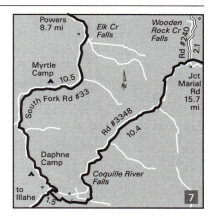

ELK CREEK FALLS ★★★

MAGNITUDE: 32 (l)   ELEVATION: 480 feet
WATERSHED: sm   USGS MAP: China Flat (1986)

Elk Creek drops 80 to 120 feet over a bluff, next to which is a picnic table. This entry is not as impressive during dry spells. Turn south off S.R. 42 onto South Fork Coquille River Road #33, 3 miles southeast of Myrtle Point. Drive 19 miles to the ranger station at Powers, then continue 8.7 miles south to the parking area for Elk Creek Falls Trail #1150. Follow the path to the left, toward the stream. It is a short stroll to the falls.

COQUILLE RIVER FALLS ★★★

MAGNITUDE: 46   ELEVATION: 1280 feet
WATERSHED: lg   USGS MAP: Illahe (1989)

This waterfall is superb year-round, as water crashes 40 to 60 feet along the Coquille River. At trail's end, miniature falls can also be seen sliding into the river from Drowned Out Creek. Drive 10.5 miles past Elk Creek Falls (described earlier) and turn left (east) on Forest Road #3348 soon after crossing the river. Continue for 1.5 miles to the trailhead. Coquille River Trail #1257 steadily switchbacks down the steep valley side for 0.5 mile to a streamside vantage below the falls.

WOODEN ROCK CREEK FALLS (U) ★★

MAGNITUDE: 45   ELEVATION: 2480 feet
WATERSHED: med   USGS MAP: Eden Valley (1990 nl)

Wooden Rock Creek Falls

A curtain of water slides 40 to 60 feet over bulging bedrock. Continue eastward 10.4 miles past Coquille River Falls Trailhead (described earlier) along Forest Road #3348. Turn left (north) onto Forest Road #240. Proceed 2.1 miles to an unsigned turnout just before the bridge crossing Wooden Rock Creek. Peer over the rim of the small gorge for partial views.

8 THE WILD ROGUE

The lower Rogue River cuts through the Klamath Mountains portion of the Coast Range, creating a 2000-foot-deep canyon. A 35-mile stretch of it is designated a National Wild and Scenic River, a federal classification intended to provide river recreation in a primitive setting and to preserve the natural, untamed integrity of the river and its surrounding environment. The following waterfalls can all be visited within a half-day's hike.

Access the area by departing from I-5 at Merlin (Exit 61). Drive westward along Merlin–Galice Road, where the small hamlet of Galice is met

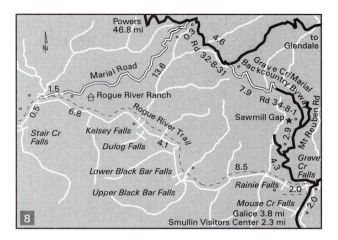

after 16.5 miles. The road has now turned north; continue 1.5 miles to the Smullin Visitors Center at Rand.

Mouse Creek Falls (u) ★★

MAGNITUDE: 19 (l)   ELEVATION: 900 feet
WATERSHED: vsm   USGS MAP: Galice (1989 nl)

The most easily accessible waterfall in the area is ironically the most obscure. Some of the locals aren't even aware of its 35- to 45-foot descent over a wall of bedrock. Drive 2.3 miles north of Smullin Visitors Center (described earlier) to an unsigned turnout at Mouse Creek. If you look closely, the cataract can be seen from the road. For better views, it's only a 50-yard bushwhack in. Best seen during wet periods, it deserves a lower rating in summer.

Rainie Falls ★★

MAGNITUDE: 32 (h)   ELEVATION: 580 feet
WATERSHED: lg   USGS MAP: Mount Reuben (1989)

Five falls occur along the Rogue River within this canyon. All but this one are more like rapids than waterfalls. Drive 2 miles beyond Mouse Creek Falls (described earlier) and park along the turnout just before the bridge crossing the Rogue. Rainie Falls Trail begins toward the left. After walking an easy 0.3 mile, a 2- to 5-foot interruption known as *Grave Creek Falls* ★ USGS Mount Reuben (1989) will be visible. After an additional 1.7 miles of moderate hiking, this 10- to 15-foot drop extending 120- to 150-feet wide will be seen near trail's end.

STAIR CREEK FALLS ★★★

MAGNITUDE: 65   ELEVATION: 340 feet
WATERSHED: lg   USGS MAP: Marial (1989)

Stair Creek Falls

It is a rugged drive before hiking to this entry, but it's a good adventure. Have a full tank before leaving, because there are no gas stations anywhere in this wildernesslike area. From the bridge crossing (described earlier), proceed over the Rogue, then turn left onto the Grave Creek/Marial Backcountry Byway (BLM Road 34-8-1). Proceed 4.3 miles to Mount Reuben Road and bear right. After another 2.9 miles, turn left toward Sawmill Gap (BLM Road 34-8-1). This road ends 7.9 miles farther; turn left (west) onto Road #32-8-31. Drive 4.6 miles and turn left for the access road to the back-country outpost of Marial. Take another left in 0.3 mile. Travel is quite slow from this point onward, but usually passable for passenger vehicles. Pass Rogue River Ranch in 13.6 miles. The route turns to dirt the final 1.5 miles beyond Mule Creek Bridge to road's end at a parking area for hiking on the Rogue River Trail.

Embark upon the trail, where it soon parallels the river in a narrow gorge. Watch rafters and kayakers chute the many rapids in this picturesque reach. After 0.5 mile, Stair Creek enters in from across the gorge as a double punchbowl totaling 40 to 60 feet. Here the trail is cut into the gorge, so those fearful of heights need to be wary. Those not afraid of heights—don't stray from the trail!

9 ILLINOIS RIVER

Though it doesn't carry the notoriety of the Rogue, the Illinois River also carries the status of National Wild and Scenic River. Two modest drops occur along its reaches.

ILLINOIS RIVER FALLS ★★

MAGNITUDE: 40   ELEVATION: 1000 feet
WATERSHED: lg   USGS MAP: Pearsoll Peak (1989)

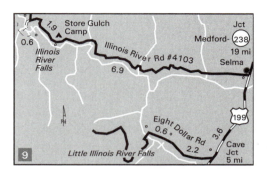

A 15- to 20-foot drop occurs where the river negotiates an extensive jumble of igneous rock. Drive to the crossroads named Selma, located along U.S. 199 approximately 19 miles south of S.R. 238 in Grants Pass, or 8.6 miles north of Cave Junction. At the crossroads, turn west onto Illinois River Road #4103, following it 8.8 miles (1.9 miles past Store Gulch Camp) to an unsigned dirt road on the left. Passenger cars can carefully drive down it for 0.3 mile to the parking area and trailhead.

The walk begins across an attractive wooden suspension footbridge. Notice the scars on the landscape on the other side of the canyon; fires in 1992 and 2002 have ravished many tracts of Siskiyou National Forest. After crossing, turn left, following Fall Creek Trail #1221 upstream. Don't go down the path immediately to the left, as that only goes to the riverbank. Walk just a bit farther before turning. From here it is 0.3 mile to a variety of rockside vantages of the cascades.

Several miles downstream, *Little Illinois River Falls* ★ USGS Cave Junction (1989) drops 10 to 15 feet over more igneous obstructions. From the junction of Illinois River Road (described earlier), drive 3.6 miles south along U.S. 199 to Eight Dollar Road #4701. Turn right onto this route and proceed 2.2 miles to an unsigned turnout. A clear, but somewhat distant, view of the descent is available here.

Others: *Cave Creek Falls* (u) ★ USGS Oregon Caves (1996 ns) was unexpectedly encountered on a trip to Oregon Caves National Monument. From Cave Junction, drive 20 miles along S.R. 46 to road's end at the parking lot. Walk 0.1 mile up toward the visitors center. To the right is a magnificent wooden building called "The Chateau." On the opposite side of it you will find springs issuing out of the mountainside, descending into a double tier totaling 15 to 20 feet.

THE MIDDLE CASCADES, OREGON

This chapter describes waterfalls located in an area that ranges from Mount Hood, located a few miles south of the Columbia Gorge, through the Cascades to Mount Washington, 75 miles to the south. There are 147 cataracts known to occur throughout the region, with 49 of them mentioned here.

The major peaks of the Cascades are actually volcanoes. The appearance of each snow-topped mountain shows the relative time since it last experienced volcanic activity. The smooth slopes of Mount Hood (11,236 feet) indicate its youth, while Mount Jefferson (10,496 feet) is slightly older and hence more rugged. Three Fingered Jack (7841 feet) and Mount Washington (7802 feet) have very jagged features, suggesting that their volcanic activity ceased even longer ago, allowing glacial erosion to greatly modify their once-smooth form.

Glaciation created most of the waterfalls associated with the volcanic mountains of the high Cascades. The alpine glaciers that top these peaks today once extended to lower elevations. Today, streams descend from adjacent rock walls into these glacially carved valleys. *Switchback Falls* is an

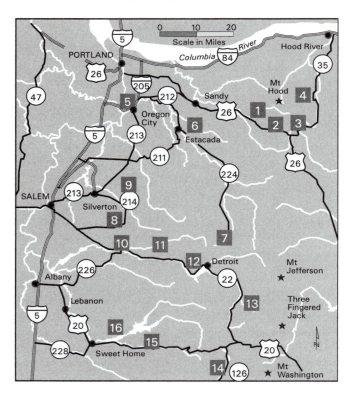

example. Some cataracts are found on valley floors where glaciers eroded unevenly, as at *Gooch Falls,* or where the present stream cuts over a highly resistant rock escarpment, as at *Downing Creek Falls*.

The many falls along the western flank of the Cascades reflect the circumstances of the development of the entire range. About 20 million to 30 million years ago, lava flows and accumulations of ashfalls alternately covered the region. The lava hardened to become basaltic bedrock, while the volcanic ash mixed with dust to create rock layers called tuffaceous sandstone. Twelve million years ago the area was uplifted and folded, forming the Cascade Range. As streams carved courses from the high Cascades westward, their flowing waters eroded the softer sandstone much more rapidly than the resistant basalt. Good examples of this process are the descents at Silver Falls State Park and along the McKenzie River, which plunge over ledges of basalt. Recesses beneath the falls are open amphitheaters where sandstone layers have been eroded away by the running water.

1 MOUNT HOOD WILDERNESS

One of twelve wilderness areas in Oregon, Mount Hood Wilderness, preserving over 35 square miles of pristine sanctuary, is just a few miles from metropolitan Portland.

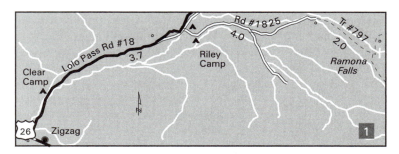

RAMONA FALLS ★★★

MAGNITUDE: 54   ELEVATION: 3520 feet
WATERSHED: sm (g)   USGS MAP: Bull Run Lake (1980)

The Sandy River veils 60 to 80 feet downward and is located within Mount Hood Wilderness in the Zigzag Ranger District, Mount Hood National Forest. Turn north off U.S. 26 at Zigzag onto Lolo Pass Road #18. In 3.7 miles bear right on Muddy Fork Road #1825, driving to its end in 2 miles (formerly 3 miles). Sandy River Trail #797 begins at the road's end. Hike 3 miles (formerly 2 miles) to the falls.

2 ZIGZAG RIVER

All of the following cataracts are in the southwest sector of Mount Hood Wilderness in the Zigzag Ranger District of Mount Hood National Forest.

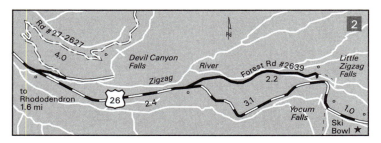

DEVIL CANYON FALLS (U) ★★

MAGNITUDE: 54   ELEVATION: 2840 feet
WATERSHED: sm   USGS MAP: Government Camp (1980 nl)

An unnamed stream plunges 60 to 76 feet within Devil Canyon. Only a distant view is possible. Drive 1.6 miles east of Rhododendron along U.S. 26 to Zigzag Mountain Road #27-2627 and turn north. The road soon deteriorates into a dirt surface, but is usually navigable by automobiles during the summertime. Drive 4 miles to an overlook of the Zigzag River Valley and the falls, 0.6 mile up the canyon.

YOCUM FALLS ★★

MAGNITUDE: 48   ELEVATION: 3360 feet
WATERSHED: sm   USGS MAP: Government Camp (1980)

Camp Creek slides over 100 feet down into the valley. The waterfall is named after Oliver C. Yocum, who in 1900 opened a hotel and resort in nearby Government Camp. Drive along U.S. 26 to a Sno-Park wayside about 7 miles east of Rhododendron and 1 mile west of the entrance to SkiBowl Resort. The cataract is immediately downstream from Mirror Lake Trailhead. The only view is from the parking area, where you can look down upon the upper portion of the falls.

LITTLE ZIGZAG FALLS ★★★

MAGNITUDE: 45   ELEVATION: 3200 feet
WATERSHED: sm (g)   USGS MAP: Government Camp (1980 ns)

The Little Zigzag River tumbles 35 to 45 feet downward. Turn off U.S. 26 onto signed Forest Road #2639, located 2.4 miles east of the turn for Devil Canyon and 3.1 miles west of Yocum Falls (described earlier). Drive 2.2 miles to the road's end at Little Zigzag Falls Trail #795C. Hike 0.3 mile to a vista immediately in front of the cataract.

---

3 BENNETT PASS

Since the first printing of this edition, highway reconfiguration has modified access to the following waterfalls within Mount Hood National Forest. Go online to *www.mymaps.com/nwfalls/mc/mc3.htm* for updated directions and map.

SAHALIE FALLS ★★★

MAGNITUDE: 67   ELEVATION: 4590 feet
WATERSHED: sm (g)   USGS MAP: Mt. Hood South (1980)

Bright water tumbles 60 to 100 feet along the East Fork Hood River within Hood River Ranger District. The cataract was named many decades ago by George Holman as part of a competition sponsored by the Portland Telegram. *Sahalie* is a Chinook word meaning "high." From S.R. 35 turn north at the entrance to Mount Hood Meadows Ski Area. An old road that leads 0.6 mile to the descent is now only open to hikers. See the online map for an alternate vehicular route.

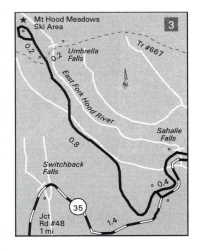

Back on S.R. 35, *Switchback Falls* ★ USGS Mt. Hood South (1980) occurs where North Fork Iron Creek cascades steeply 100 to 200 feet. The descent is aptly named for a winding turn in the highway within Zigzag Ranger District. Drive to the unsigned turnout along S.R. 35, 1 mile past Road #48 and now 1.0 mile from the entrance to Mount Hood Meadows Ski Area. Look for the falls immediately above the road. It can be easily missed due to the heavy foliage.

UMBRELLA FALLS ★★

MAGNITUDE: 51   ELEVATION: 5250 feet
WATERSHED: sm (g)   USGS MAP: Mt. Hood South (1980)

8 SILVER FALLS STATE PARK

This is a paradise for waterfall seekers. Silver Creek Canyon is a waterfall haven, all of them within moderate walking distances of the main highway via the "Trail of Ten Falls." S.R. 214 goes through the park 14 miles southeast of Silverton and 25 miles east of Salem.

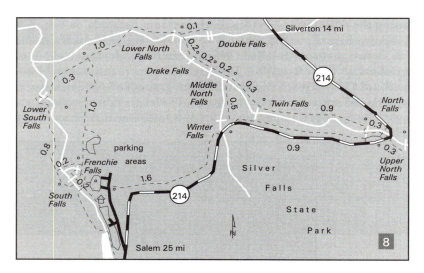

UPPER NORTH FALLS ★★★

MAGNITUDE: 68   ELEVATION: 1520 feet
WATERSHED: lg   USGS MAP: Elk Prairie (1985)

North Silver Creek drops 65 feet in the first of a series of nice falls that get better as you progress through the park. Find the trail at the south side of the parking lot at the east end of the park. Cross under the highway and walk east 0.3 mile to path's end at the falls.

NORTH FALLS ★★★★

MAGNITUDE: 76   ELEVATION: 1400 feet
WATERSHED: lg   USGS MAP: Elk Prairie (1985)

There are exciting views both beside and behind this impressive 136-foot waterfall, located along North Silver Creek. Take the trail mentioned in the previous entry 0.3 mile westward to trailside vantages.

Twin Falls ★★

MAGNITUDE: 45   ELEVATION: 1230 feet
WATERSHED: lg   USGS MAP: Drake Crossing (1985)

North Silver Creek diverges in two parts as it tumbles 31 feet over weathered bedrock. Follow the trail 0.9 mile downstream from North Falls (described earlier), a total of 1.2 miles from the trailhead.

Middle North Falls ★★★

MAGNITUDE: 42   ELEVATION: 1120 feet
WATERSHED: lg   USGS MAP: Drake Crossing (1985)

This unique waterfall hurtles through the air for two-thirds of its 106-foot drop, then veils over bedrock along the final portion. A side trail goes behind and around this descent from North Silver Creek. Walk 0.5 mile downstream from Twin Falls (described earlier), a total of 1.7 miles from the trailhead, or 0.7 mile past Winter Falls (described later) to view this entry.

Drake Falls ★★

![icons]

MAGNITUDE: 35   ELEVATION: 1060 feet
WATERSHED: lg   USGS MAP: Drake Crossing (1985)

North Silver Creek drops 27 feet in a curtain of water. Gain trailside views by hiking 0.2 mile downstream from Middle North Falls (described earlier) to this entry.

Double Falls ★★★

![icons]

MAGNITUDE: 37 (l)   ELEVATION: 1220 feet
WATERSHED: sm   USGS MAP: Drake Crossing (1985)

Water drops a total of 178 feet in tiered fashion. The lower portion descends four times as far along Hullt Creek as the upper part. Walk 0.3 mile past Drake Falls (described earlier) to the signed spur trail. Walk up the side path a short distance for views.

LOWER NORTH FALLS ★★

MAGNITUDE: 63   ELEVATION: 1030 feet
WATERSHED: lg   USGS MAP: Drake Crossing (1985)

This is the last major falls, descending 30 feet, along North Silver Creek. Walk a few yards downstream from the spur path for Double Falls (described earlier) along the main trail. It is 1 mile back to Winter Falls Trailhead, or 2 miles to the trailhead near North Falls.

WINTER FALLS ★★

MAGNITUDE: 33 (l)   ELEVATION: 1360 feet
WATERSHED: vsm   USGS MAP: Drake Crossing (1985)

Winter Creek falls 134 feet in two forms. Initially it plunges down, then it becomes a horsetail. Walk a short distance north from the signed turnout 0.9 mile west of the trailhead for North Falls (described earlier).

SOUTH FALLS ★★★★

MAGNITUDE: 82   ELEVATION: 1200 feet
WATERSHED: med   USGS MAP: Drake Crossing (1985)

This is the highlight of the park. South Silver Creek drops 177 feet over a ledge of basalt. Several vistas, including a trailside view behind the cataract, reveal the many faces of this entry. Walk about 0.4 mile west from the parking areas in the western portion of the park.

About one-half way along this trail, a sign now directs hikers to a short spur to tiny *Frenchie Falls* ★ USGS Drake Crossing (1985 ns). Since Frenchie Falls is seldom more than a trickle over an unnamed drainage, perhaps Oregon State Parks should consider recycling a sufficient volume of water to make its 48-foot drop worth visiting. Until then, it's just as well it is not indicated on any of the park's maps or brochures.

LOWER SOUTH FALLS ★★★

MAGNITUDE: 75   ELEVATION: 980 feet
WATERSHED: med   USGS MAP: Drake Crossing (1985)

The trail passes behind this 93-foot plummet along South Silver Creek. Continue 0.8 mile downstream from South Falls (described earlier), a total of 1.2 miles from the trailhead.

9 SCOTTS MILLS

McKay Falls (u) ★★

MAGNITUDE: 38	ELEVATION: 420 feet
WATERSHED: lg	USGS MAP: Scotts Mills (1985 ns)

Within a town park, water pours 10 to 15 feet over a 35- to 50-foot breadth of Butte Creek. Drive to Scotts Mills via S.R. 213 and Scotts Mills Road. Turn right on Third Street, then proceed a couple blocks and turn left into Scotts Mills Park. Views are a very short distance away. This waterfall was unofficially named by Bryan Swan after Thomas McKay, who long ago built a mill (now gone) for which the town is named.

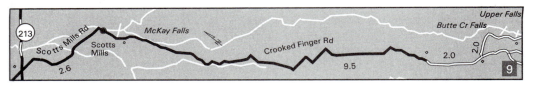

UPPER BUTTE CREEK FALLS ★★★

MAGNITUDE: 49	ELEVATION: 1760 feet
WATERSHED: med	USGS MAP: Elk Prairie (1985 ns)

Within Santiam State Forest, Butte Creek plunges 15 to 25 feet into a pool. From Third Street in Scotts Mills (described earlier), the street turns into

Upper Butte Creek Falls

Butte Creek Falls

Crooked Finger Road upon leaving town. Continue 9.5 miles southeastward to the end of the pavement, then 2 miles farther on gravel. Turn left onto another gravel road (not signed). Travel 2 miles down this route to a turnout to the left. A sign now exists at the trailhead. After a short distance, take the right fork at a junction. The path descends 0.2 mile down to an excellent vista. Behind the falls is a grotto, or cavernlike recess, that can be explored. The author erroneously identified this as Butte Creek Falls (described later) in earlier editions.

BUTTE CREEK FALLS ★★★★

MAGNITUDE: 56   ELEVATION: 1720 feet
WATERSHED: med   USGS MAP: Elk Prairie (1985)

Water plummets 60 to 80 feet in a lush setting of Santiam State Forest. From the Upper Falls (described earlier), hike another 0.2 mile down the trail. The viewpoints are beautiful, as they are from the top of unguarded rock outcrops. Be careful.

10 MEHAMA

Vehicular accessibility has recently changed for the following trio of waterfalls within Santiam State Forest. You can avoid walking an additional 2.8 miles by following the updated directions and map online at *www.mymaps.com/nwfalls/mc/mc10.htm.*

LOWER SHELLBURG FALLS ★★

OR

MAGNITUDE: 46   ELEVATION: 1250 feet
WATERSHED: sm   USGS MAP: Lyons (1985)

Shellburg Creek tumbles 20 to 40 feet. At Mehama turn north off S.R. 22 onto Fenn Ridge Road. Drive uphill 1.2 miles, then take a sharp right (east) turn into a small unsigned parking area. Embark along the gated gravel road, walking 1.4 miles to the top of the cataract.

Continuing along the road, waterfall collectors can catch a glimpse of *Stasel Falls* ★ USGS Lyons (1985). This 100- to 125-foot descent along Stout Creek would deserve a higher

rating, but the side view is partly obstructed by the gorge. Drive 0.2 mile farther and park next to a dirt road junction. Follow this unimproved route about 100 yards to paths leading to the top of abrupt and unprotected cliffs with a partial view upstream to the falls.

SHELLBURG FALLS ★★★★

MAGNITUDE: 61   ELEVATION: 1340 feet
WATERSHED: sm   USGS MAP: Lyons (1985)

This 80- to 100-foot plume along Shellburg Creek descends over bulging basalt so you can walk behind the waterfall. From Lower Shellburg Falls

Shellburg Falls

(described earlier), find the unmarked trail on the north side of the road. The gentle trail reaches this upper counterpart in 0.2 mile.

11 NORTH FORK RIVER

Access to the pleasant Elkhorn Valley and the waterfalls upstream is easiest via North Fork Road #2209, which joins S.R. 22, 1 mile east of Mehama. Alternatively, adventurous drivers with reliable brakes may wish to tackle (in low gear) Gates Hill Road. Beginning in the town of Gates, this gravel route proceeds up, up, up, then down, down, down on its route to the Elkhorn Valley.

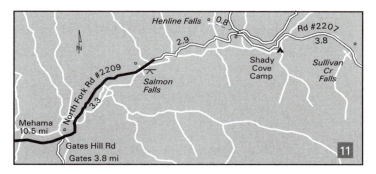

SALMON FALLS ★★★

MAGNITUDE: 56 (h)   ELEVATION: 1120 feet
WATERSHED: lg   USGS MAP: Elkhorn (1985)

Located within Salmon Falls County Park, this high-volume 25- to 35-foot waterfall drops down along the Little North Santiam River. A fish ladder bypasses the cataract. Drive 3.3 miles up the valley (east) from the junction of Gates Hill Road and North Fork Road #2209. Turn at the sign for the county park.

If the clear-cut has healed around *Sullivan Creek Falls* (u) ★ USGS Elkhorn (1985 ns), perhaps this steep 40- to 60-foot cascade is deserving of a higher rating. Continue 2.9 miles past Salmon Falls along Road #2209, making a right turn onto Road #2207. Proceed along this gravel road for 3.8 miles to a roadside view of the cataract directly above a bridge over Sullivan Creek. This falls is located on a square-mile section of private land surrounded by Willamette National Forest.

HENLINE FALLS ★★★★

MAGNITUDE: 74   ELEVATION: 1880 feet
WATERSHED: sm   USGS MAP: Elkhorn (1985)

Henline Creek shimmers 75 to 100 feet over the mountainside. The falls is located within the Detroit Ranger District of Willamette National Forest. The entrance to the old Silver King Mine is near the base of the falls. Look, but do not enter! A listing for Silver King Falls USGS Elkhorn (1985 ns) can be found in the federal government's Geographic Names Information System. But because it shows the same geographic coordinate, this is almost surely a second official name for Henline, which is a rarity.

Continue past Salmon Falls (described earlier) for 2.9 miles, then bear left, staying on Road #2209 and go 0.1 mile. Park and walk up the tributary road to the left. After about 0.5 mile, turn left onto a dirt road, which quickly becomes a well-worn trail. Reach the falls in 0.3 mile.

Waterfall enthusiast Tom Kloster uncovered an obscure series of eight waterfalls in a hidden gorge above Henline Falls. Collectively known as "Family Falls," they were described in the book *Treasures of the Oregon Country,* by Maynard Drawson. Go online to *The Computer Companion* (described in the Introduction) for more information about their unofficial names and the strenuous bushwhack required to find them.

---

12 NIAGARA PARK

Niagara Park was the site of a small town from 1890 to 1934. A rubble masonry dam was built in the late 1890s to provide power for a paper mill, but difficulties in constructing the dam caused the mill project to be abandoned and the village faded. Historic remnants of the town can be seen at a marked turnout along S.R. 22, 4.2 miles east of Gates and 13 miles west of Detroit.

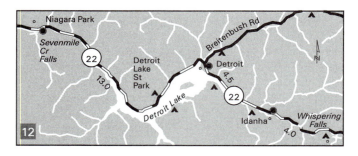

SEVENMILE CREEK FALLS (U) ★★

MAGNITUDE: 29   ELEVATION: 1050 feet
WATERSHED: sm   USGS MAP: Elkhorn (1985 ns)

Look across the North Santiam River where Sevenmile Creek slides into the main river. Walk down a short pathway from Niagara Park to the river. Scramble on interesting rock formations to get a vantage of the falls.

Farther along the highway, *Whispering Falls* ★ USGS Idanha (1985 ns) can be viewed where Misery Creek tumbles 40 to 60 feet into the North Santiam River. An across-the-river vista is gained at Whispering Falls Campground, located 4 miles east of Idanha on S.R. 22 in Detroit Ranger District, Willamette National Forest.

13 MARION FORKS

As you head farther up the drainage basin of Marion Forks, located within the Detroit Ranger District of Willamette National Forest, the waterfalls become increasingly scenic.

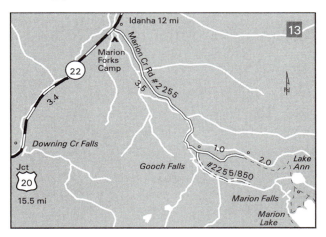

GOOCH FALLS ★★★★

MAGNITUDE: 85   ELEVATION: 2810 feet
WATERSHED: lg   USGS MAP: Marion Forks (1988)

An absolutely beautiful 75- to 100-foot display drops from Marion Creek. The federal government's Geographic Names Information System lists *Gatch Falls* USGS Marion Lake (1993 ns) at a location different from that of this entry, but "Gatch Falls" has also been documented elsewhere as an alternative name for this feature. So are they the same or different?

Turn southeast off S.R. 22 at Marion Forks Camp onto Marion Creek Road #2255. Follow the gravel road for 3.5 miles, then turn right on Road #2255/850. Park where the dirt road widens in less than 0.2 mile. Walk carefully toward the creek for a natural, unfenced view above and into the falls.

Meanwhile, along the main highway *Downing Creek Falls* (u) ★ USGS Marion Forks (1988 nl) can be found flowing 20 to 30 feet down a chute. Drive 3.4 miles south from Marion Forks Camp on S.R. 22 to an unsigned turnout and camping site on the left (east) side of the highway. Bushwhack upstream until the falls come into view.

MARION FALLS ★★★

MAGNITUDE: 81 (h)   ELEVATION: 3980 feet
WATERSHED: med   USGS MAP: Marion Lake (1993)

The outlet of Marion Lake plunges 120 to 160 feet in the form of two power-ful descents along Marion Creek. Located within Mount Jefferson Wilder-ness in the Detroit Ranger District, this cascade is recommended for adults only. Drive 1 mile past the turnoff for Gooch Falls (described earlier) to the end of Marion Creek Road #2255. Hike 1.5 miles along Marion Trail #3493 to Lake Ann. Continue 0.3 mile farther to a trail junction; bear right on Marion Outlet Trail #3495. Proceed about 0.1 mile to an unsigned path to the right. If you encounter a rocky slope along Trail #3495, you have passed the junction by 100 to 200 yards and will need to backtrack. Follow the path 0.1 mile to its end at an unguarded cliff at the top of the falls. Best views are from a faint path along the east side of the canyon.

Marion Falls

14 McKenzie River

The waterfalls along the McKenzie River descend with fury, except for Tamolitch Falls, which has been artificially turned off. They all occur within the McKenzie Ranger District, Willamette National Forest.

Sahalie Falls ★★★★

MAGNITUDE: 99 (h)
ELEVATION: 2800 feet
WATERSHED: lg (d)
USGS MAP: Clear Lake (1988)

This roaring 140-foot torrent can be seen from several developed viewpoints. The smaller of the two segments disappears

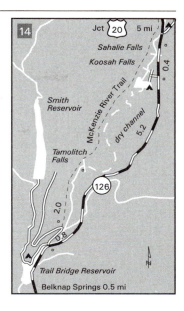

Sahalie Falls

during periods of lower discharge. *Sahalie* is a Chinook word meaning "high." Depart S.R. 126 at the point-of-interest sign located 5 miles south of U.S. 20 and 6.1 miles north of Belknap Springs.

KOOSAH FALLS ★★★★

MAGNITUDE: 95 (h)   ELEVATION: 2680 feet
WATERSHED: lg (d)   USGS MAP: Clear Lake (1988)

The McKenzie River thunders 80 to 120 feet over a sharp escarpment. The cataract usually appears in a segmented form during late summer. Drive 0.4 mile south of Sahalie Falls (described earlier) along S.R. 126 to the entrance marked Ice Cap Campground. Turn here and proceed to the parking area and developed viewpoints in 0.3 mile.

Koosah Falls

Tamolitch Falls ★★

MAGNITUDE: 0   ELEVATION: 2380 feet
WATERSHED: none   USGS MAP: Tamolitch Falls (1989)

A 60-foot dry rock wall is the only thing left where water once poured from the McKenzie River. But by all means, visit this location! This circular basin inspired the name *Tamolitch,* which is Chinook for "tub" or "bucket." At this site, you will see a rare phenomenon: a full-sized river beginning at a single point. Springs feed the plunge pool at the base of the dry cataract. What happened to the falls? The river's water has been diverted 3 miles upstream at Carmen Reservoir, where a tunnel directs the water to Smith Reservoir and the power-generating facilities in the adjacent drainage.

Turn off S.R. 126 at the north end of Trail Bridge Reservoir, 0.5 mile north of Belknap Springs or 5.2 miles south of Koosah Falls (described earlier). Drive about 0.8 mile to the McKenzie River Trailhead. Hike up the trail along the river for 2 miles to a crystal-clear, cyan-colored pool with the dry falls at its head (and a dry channel above it).

Others: *House Rock Falls* (u) ★ USGS Harter Mtn (1984 nl) is unusual in that its 20- to 30-foot drop along the South Santiam River is nearly covered by several large boulders that have fallen into the stream from the north slope of the gorge. In this case being unusual does not correspond with being scenic. Drive to House Rock Campground, located 2 miles east of Upper Soda along U.S. 20. Proceed 0.4 mile into the camp and park just before a creek crossing at House Rock Loop Trail #3406. It is a 0.3-mile walk to the site along a nice trail situated within Sweet Home Ranger District, Willamette National Forest. Go online to *The Computer Companion* (described in the Introduction) to see a map for this entry.

---

15 Cascadia

Lower Soda Falls ★★★

MAGNITUDE: 25 (l)   ELEVATION: 1270 feet
WATERSHED: sm   USGS MAP: Cascadia (1985)

Soda Creek tumbles 150 to 180 feet in three tiers among moss-covered rocks. The falls is located within Cascadia State Park. Start at the state park, located 13 miles east of Sweet Home along U.S. 20. Find the unmarked trail at the far north end of the campsite area and hike a moderately steep 0.5 mile to the descent.

An obscure entry, *High Deck Falls* (u) ★ USGS Cascadia (1985 ns) is located in the vicinity, probably on private property. It is unofficially named after a nearby mountain where water cascades steeply for more than 100 feet along an unnamed creek. Continue east along U.S. 20 for 1.7 miles past Swamp Mountain Road (described later) to Moose Creek Road #2027. Follow the turns as shown on the accompanying map to Road #505 and the cataract in 1.3 miles.

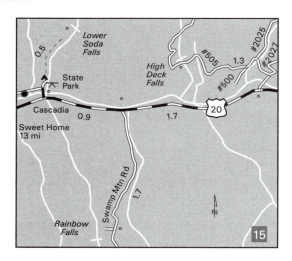

RAINBOW FALLS ★★

MAGNITUDE: 40   ELEVATION: 1460 feet
WATERSHED: sm   USGS MAP: Cascadia (1985)

Dobbin Creek pours 20 to 30 feet into a pool. The waterfall lies outside national forest land, most likely on private property. Drive 0.9 mile east of the community of Cascadia, then turn right (south) off U.S. 20 onto Swamp Mountain Road. Follow this gravel route for 1.7 miles, parking at an unsigned, old dirt road to the right. Follow the dirt road for about 100 feet, then descend along the top of a small ridge to an open view of the falls.

16 MCDOWELL CREEK FALLS COUNTY PARK

Four of the five waterfalls described in this section are within McDowell Creek Falls County Park, a pleasant and thoughtfully planned day-use recreation area. Turn off U.S. 20 at Fairview Road. Proceed east for 1 mile, then turn left onto McDowell Creek Road. The county park and first parking turnout are 6.5 miles farther east.

LOWER FALLS ★★

MAGNITUDE: 45   ELEVATION: 800 feet
WATERSHED: med   USGS MAP: Sweet Home (1984 nl)

This minor pair of descents drops 5 to 10 feet along McDowell Creek. Park at the southern access point of the park's trail system. This entry is located a very short walk away, immediately downstream from the first footbridge.

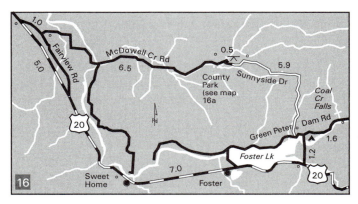

ROYAL TERRACE FALLS ★★★

MAGNITUDE: 39 (l)   ELEVATION: 1000 feet
WATERSHED: vsm   USGS MAP: Sweet Home (1984 ns)

Fall Creek sprays 119 feet down in a fountainlike tiered display. A marked spur path ascends to a viewpoint above the top of the cataract. Walk an easy 0.3 mile upstream from Lower Falls (described earlier) to this waterfall.

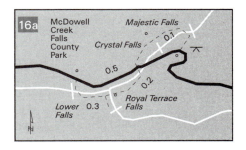

MAJESTIC FALLS ★★★

MAGNITUDE: 58   ELEVATION: 980 feet
WATERSHED: med   USGS MAP: Sweet Home (1984 nl)

A porchlike overlook allows a close-up view of this 30- to 40-foot drop tumbling from McDowell Creek. Drive to the north end of the park. A stairway leads a short distance to the vista. Hikers can also reach it by continuing northward along the main trail from Royal Terrace Falls (described earlier). Hikers on this route will also encounter a vista for modest *Crystal Falls* ★ USGS Sweet Home (1984 nl), about 0.1 mile past Majestic Falls.

COAL CREEK FALLS (U) ★★

MAGNITUDE: 32 (l)   ELEVATION: 920 feet
WATERSHED: sm   USGS MAP: Green Peter (1984 nl)

Coal Creek drops 40 to 60 feet in a waterfall located outside McDowell Creek Falls County Park. It is most likely situated on private property. Depart U.S. 20 at the east end of Foster Lake and drive north on Sunnyside Drive to Green Peter Dam Road. You can also reach this road by following Sunnyside Drive for 6 miles southeast of McDowell Creek Falls County Park. Once you reach the Middle Santiam River, drive east 1.6 miles and park at the dirt road to the left (north). Walk to the end of the road, then scramble up the crumbly slope to a faint path. A short distance farther will be a fairly distant view of this entry.

THE SOUTH CASCADES, OREGON

South-central Oregon presents a collage of scenic outdoor settings typical of the Cascade Range. The area's major peaks include Three Sisters, Bachelor Butte, Diamond Peak, and Mount McLoughlin—all of them volcanic in origin. The region also boasts five national forests, four wilderness areas, an abundance of mountain lakes, and Crater Lake National Park. Waterfalls are well distributed throughout the South Cascades. Most of the 123 recognized falls in the region are relatively accessible; 79 of them are listed in this book.

Many of this region's waterfalls are among the most majestic of the Pacific Northwest. They often occur streaming down the walls of canyons carved by alpine glaciers. During the last major Ice Age, 10,000 to 14,000 years ago, these glaciers extended their range to areas below 2500 feet in elevation in the South Cascades. Large, U-shaped glacial troughs

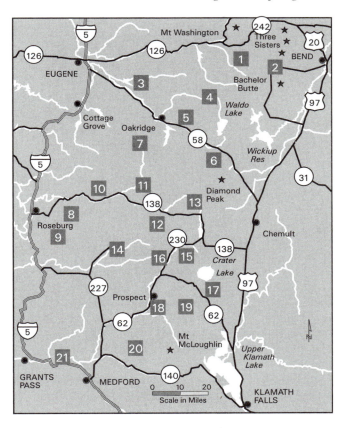

remain as evidence of the intense erosive powers of these glaciers. To-day, rivers follow the valleys abandoned by the retreating glaciers. As tributary streams flow into the troughs, they often drop sharply as waterfalls. Rainbow Falls, Proxy Falls, and Vidae Falls are examples. Many physical geographers and geologists refer to this type of descent as a ribbon falls.

The western portion of the South Cascades formed in the same manner as the central portion described in the preceding chapter. Where layers of resistant basalt and weak sandstone meet along a stream's course, the sandstone erodes faster than the basalt. The graceful *Toketee Falls* and idyllic *Grotto Falls* are good examples of cataracts shaped in this way.

1 MCKENZIE HIGHWAY

The peaks of North Sister (10,085 feet), Middle Sister (10,047 feet), and South Sister (10,358 feet) dominate the Cascade scenery along S.R. 242. The following waterfalls are just inside Three Sisters Wilderness, which is located within the McKenzie Ranger District of Willamette National Forest, and are readily accessible.

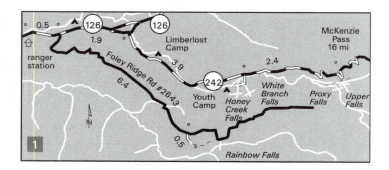

RAINBOW FALLS ★★★

MAGNITUDE: 85 (h) ELEVATION: 2960 feet
WATERSHED: med USGS MAP: Linton Lake (1988)

The peaks of the Three Sisters provide a background to a cross-valley view of Rainbow Creek distantly descending 150 to 200 feet. About 0.5 mile east of McKenzie Bridge Ranger Station turn south off S.R. 126 onto Foley Ridge Road #2643. Follow Road #2643 for 6.4 miles, then turn right on the marked dirt road and proceed 0.5 mile to the start of Rainbow Falls Trail #3543. The moderately gentle trail ends in 0.8 mile at an unfenced, distant view of the cataract.

White Branch Falls ★★

MAGNITUDE: 21 (l)   ELEVATION: 2560 feet
WATERSHED: vsm (?)   USGS MAP: Linton Lake (1988 nl)

It's okay to visit this moss-framed 35-
to 50-foot veil located on private
property as long as you check in first.
Depart S.R. 126 onto S.R. 242 and
drive 3.9 miles to White Branch
Youth Camp. Turn right and proceed 0.3 mile to an unsigned turnout
and trailhead. Walk up to the camp
buildings and ask permission to hike.

Follow the spur trail 0.2 mile
down to its end. If desired, take the
right fork, signed for the 15- to 25-foot
ribbon of *Honey Creek Falls* ★ USGS
Linton Lake (1988 ns). It's another 0.2
mile, with an upper loop trail to the
main falls. Taking the left fork, it's 0.2
mile to the display along an unnamed
tributary of White Branch.

White Branch Falls

Upper Falls ★★

MAGNITUDE: 28 (l)   ELEVATION: 3000 feet
WATERSHED: vsm (?)   USGS MAP: Linton Lake (1988 ns)

Water cascades steeply 100 to 125 feet from springs issuing from a high canyon
wall. Continue 2.4 miles eastward past White Branch Youth Camp (described
earlier) along S.R. 242 to the signed parking area for Proxy Falls trailheads. The
trails have recently been reconfigured into an interpretive loop. In order to save
the best falls for last, start on the entrance to the left and hike clockwise. After
0.4 mile, a short spur will quickly lead you to the base of the Upper Falls.

Proxy Falls ★★★★

MAGNITUDE: 91   ELEVATION: 3000 feet
WATERSHED: med (?)   USGS MAP: Linton Lake (1988)

Proxy Falls

As trees surround you, gain a windowlike view of Proxy Creek pouring 200 feet in impressive fashion. These falls are also called Lower Falls. From the Upper Falls (described earlier), continue 0.2 mile to another spur to the left, ending 0.1 mile farther at the vista. From here, it is 0.8 mile to complete the trail loop at the west end of the parking area.

2 CASCADE LAKES HIGHWAY

Drive west from Bend for 28 miles on the Cascade Lakes Highway, also known as Century Drive and County Road #46. Turn at the signed access for Green Lakes Trail. There are two parking areas: the one to the right (east) accesses waterfalls along Soda Creek Trail; the other leads to Green Lakes Trail and its cataract. This area is a part of Bend Ranger District, Deschutes National Forest.

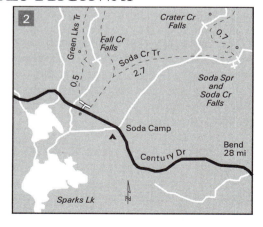

SODA CREEK FALLS (U) ★★

MAGNITUDE: 39   ELEVATION: 5900 feet
WATERSHED: sm   USGS MAP: Broken Top (1988 nl)

Soda Creek drops 5 to 10 feet in block form before fanning downward another 20 to 30 feet. The minor descent of *Soda Spring Falls* (u) ★ USGS Broken Top (1988 ns) will be encountered a few hundred yards before reaching this entry.

    Hike along Soda Creek Trail for 2.1 miles through a lava field, then a meadow. After the trail reaches a wooded area, it is 0.6 mile farther to both falls. The main display is situated just upstream from the point where the trail departs the stream and switchbacks uphill.

CRATER CREEK FALLS (U) ★★

MAGNITUDE: 41   ELEVATION: 6240 feet
WATERSHED: sm   USGS MAP: Broken Top (1988 nl)

Water sprays 40 to 50 feet downward along Crater Creek. This route is recommended for adults only. After passing Soda Creek Falls (described earlier), the trail steepens considerably. After 0.7 mile, Crater Creek will come into view. Leave the trail and proceed down the ridge top for about 100 yards. Stay off the steep slopes in the canyon!

FALL CREEK FALLS ★★★

MAGNITUDE: 61   ELEVATION: 5500 feet
WATERSHED: med   USGS MAP: Broken Top (1988 nl)

Fall Creek explodes 25 to 35 feet over a rock escarpment. Starting at Green Lakes Trail (described earlier), walk up the moderately steep path for 0.5 mile. The sound of the falls will be plainly heard. Find the short side trail, which leads above the cataract and to several paths that take you below to full views.

---

3 BIG FALL CREEK

CHICHESTER FALLS ★★★

MAGNITUDE: 34   ELEVATION: 1100 feet
WATERSHED: med   USGS MAP: Saddleblanket Mtn (1986)

5 SALMON CREEK

Reach the following trio of waterfalls by turning north off S.R. 58 at Fish Hatchery Road, which is located on the east side of Oakridge. Follow the route 1.4 miles to its end, then proceed right (east) on Salmon Creek Road #24. They are all located within Oakridge Ranger District, Willamette National Forest.

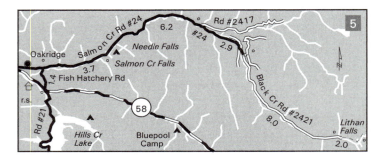

SALMON CREEK FALLS ★★

MAGNITUDE: 47 (h)   ELEVATION: 1440 feet
WATERSHED: lg   USGS MAP: Huckleberry Mtn (1986)

Water tumbles a total of 10 to 15 feet along a 60- to 80-foot breadth of Salmon Creek. Drive 3.7 miles east of Fish Hatchery Road (described earlier) along Salmon Creek Road #24 to Salmon Creek Falls Camp. Vantages are available from both the picnic area and the campground.

Found behind campsite #4 is a view of *Needle Falls* (u) ★ USGS Huckleberry Mtn (1986 nl), skirting in segmented fashion 35 to 50 feet along an unnamed stream into Salmon Creek. This entry deserves a higher rating during wet periods.

Needle Falls

LILLIAN FALLS ★★

MAGNITUDE: 25   ELEVATION: 3980 feet
WATERSHED: sm   USGS MAP: Waldo Lake (1997)

Nettie Creek steeply cascades 60 to 80 feet. Follow Salmon Creek Road #24 eastward past Salmon Creek Falls (described earlier). After 6.2 miles, the paved road crosses Salmon Creek and becomes a single lane. Continue 2.7 additional miles to a crossing at Black Creek. About 0.2 mile farther, bear right (south) on graveled Black Creek Road #2421. The road ends in 8 more miles at the start of Black Creek Trail #3551. Hike the moderately steep route to a trailside view of the falls in 2 miles. It was named after Lillian Ryker McGillvrey, who was a cook on the trail construction crew. Prior editions of this book list the entry as Lithan Falls, as that is how it is labeled on the 1986 USGS map (since updated). Apparently the name was transcribed incorrectly, with "lli" mistaken as "th."

6 SALT CREEK

A concentration of six impressive cataracts occurs within an area of only 2 square miles in the Oakridge Ranger District of Willamette National Forest. Drive 21 miles east from Oakridge or 6 miles west from Willamette Pass along S.R. 58. Park at the Salt Creek Falls turnout or in Salt Creek Falls Picnic Area.

SALT CREEK FALLS ★★★★★

MAGNITUDE: 98 (h)
ELEVATION: 4000 feet
WATERSHED: lg
USGS MAP: Diamond Peak (1986)

This cascade is the gem of the South Cascades, as Salt Creek plummets 286 feet into a gorge. Trails and a fenced vista provide a variety of views of the cataract, which was first seen by Anglos (Frank S. Warner and Charles Tufti) in March 1887. The falls is easily accessible from the turnout or the picnic area (described earlier).

Salt Creek Falls

LOWER DIAMOND CREEK FALLS ★★

MAGNITUDE: 82   ELEVATION: 4000 feet
WATERSHED: med   USGS MAP: Diamond Peak (1986 nl)

Although it is 200 to 250 feet high, this entry's scenic rating is diminished by obscured views. In past visits, a couple of trees prevented a clear vantage of the bottom portion of the falls. From Salt Creek Picnic Area (described earlier), follow Diamond Creek Falls Trail #3598 for a gentle 0.7 mile along the rim of Salt Creek Canyon to one of several viewpoints.

DIAMOND CREEK FALLS ★★★★

MAGNITUDE: 72   ELEVATION: 4240 feet
WATERSHED: med   USGS MAP: Diamond Peak (1986 nl)

This superb cataract occurs where Diamond Creek pours 70 to 90 feet downward. Follow Trail #3598 for 0.6 mile beyond Lower Diamond Creek Falls
(described earlier). A trail provides a good viewpoint above the descent, plus

Diamond Creek Falls

a short spur trail quickly leads to its base. A loop route can be taken back to Salt Creek Picnic Area by continuing a short distance, bearing left onto Vivian Lake Trail #3662, and walking 1 mile.

LOWER FALLS CREEK FALLS (U) ★★

MAGNITUDE: 45   ELEVATION: 4440 feet
WATERSHED: sm   USGS MAP: Diamond Peak (1986 ns)

This double waterfall along Falls Creek totals 30 to 50 feet. At the junction of Diamond Creek Falls Trail #3598 with Vivian Lake Trail #3662 (described earlier), turn right onto Trail #3662. Cross some railroad tracks and proceed 0.8 mile up the moderately steep path to views just off the trail.

FALLS CREEK FALLS ★★

MAGNITUDE: 54   ELEVATION: 4780 feet
WATERSHED: sm   USGS MAP: Diamond Peak (1986)

Falls Creek plunges 40 to 60 feet. Continue climbing steeply for 1 mile past Lower Falls Creek Falls (described earlier). A sign tacked to a tree points to a moderately distant view of this entry.

UPPER FALLS CREEK FALLS (U) ★★★

MAGNITUDE: 69   ELEVATION: 5000 feet
WATERSHED: sm   USGS MAP: Diamond Peak (1986 ns)

This is the best of the cataracts along Falls Creek, descending 50 to 80 feet. Hike 0.2 mile past Falls Creek Falls (described earlier) to a trailside vantage. From here, it is 3 miles back to Salt Creek Picnic Area.

---

7 ROW RIVER

The recreation staff at Umpqua National Forest is a waterfall-lover's best friend. They always seem to be blazing trails to more and more descents. They have even copublished a twenty-page color pamphlet entitled "Thundering Waters" with the Roseburg Bureau of Land Management District, guiding travelers to the area's falls. (This author was pleased to note this guidebook is cited in it.)

Several waterfalls are to be found within the Row River drainage basin of the Cottage Grove Ranger District of Umpqua National Forest. Access

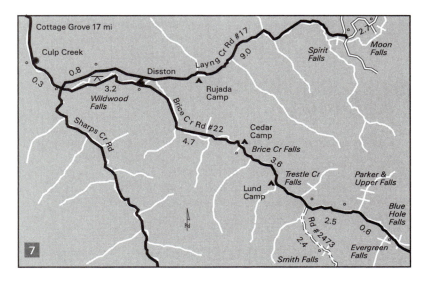

the area by departing I-5 at Cottage Grove (Exit 174) and driving east on Cottage Grove–Dorena Road for 17 miles to the community of Culp Creek. All but Wildwood Falls are situated within the national forest.

WILDWOOD FALLS ★★

MAGNITUDE: 34   ELEVATION: 1000 feet
WATERSHED: lg   USGS MAP: Culp Creek (1986)

The course of the Row River is interrupted by this 10- to 15-foot drop. Drive to the east side of Culp Creek townsite, then bear left in 0.3 mile onto an unsigned road, remaining on the north side of the Row River. Views of the descent are available at the Wildwood Falls Picnic Area in 0.8 mile, and at a developed roadside vista just before.

SPIRIT FALLS ★★★

MAGNITUDE: 34 (l)   ELEVATION: 1920 feet
WATERSHED: sm   USGS MAP: Rose Hill (1986)

This aptly named 60-foot veil, located where Alex Creek gouges into a bulging mass of moss-covered substrate, has a surrealistic feel. From Wildwood Falls (described earlier), drive 2.4 miles to the crossroads of Disston. Stay on the north side of the Row River; the route changes its name to Layng Creek Road #17. Proceed 9 miles to a signed trailhead and a path that leads moderately steeply 0.5 mile to a picnic table at the base of this entry.

MOON FALLS ★★

MAGNITUDE: 24 (t)   ELEVATION: 3000 feet
WATERSHED: vsm   USGS MAP: Holland Point (1986)

The upper reaches of Alex Creek drop 120 feet. The approach is an easy 0.5-mile walk, complete with a picnic table. Continue 0.2 mile past the trailhead for Spirit Falls (described earlier) to Road #1702. Turn left and drive 2.7 miles; then bear right on Road #1702–728. Drive along this unimproved surface for 0.3 mile before turning left on Road #1702–203; in another 0.1 mile the trailhead will be reached.

BRICE CREEK FALLS ★★

MAGNITUDE: 29   ELEVATION: 1510 feet
WATERSHED: lg   USGS MAP: Rose Hill (1986 ns)

A sequence of falls and cascades occurring along this particular reach of Brice Creek is highlighted by this 5- to 10-foot segmented punchbowl. At the junction of Layng Creek Road #17 and Brice Creek Road #22 (described earlier), continue along the latter route for 4.7 miles to Cedar Creek Camp. Park here and walk across the footbridge to Brice Creek Trail #1403. It's a 0.3-mile march to the right (upstream) for this particular entry.

TRESTLE CREEK FALLS ★★★

MAGNITUDE: 58   ELEVATION: 2240 feet
WATERSHED: sm   USGS MAP: Rose Hill (1986 ns)

Water sprays downward 60 feet in a moss-covered setting. Continue 3.6 miles past Cedar Creek Camp (described earlier) along Brice Creek Road #22. Park at the turnout near the bridge crossing. Walk across the bridge, meeting Brice Creek Trail #1403. Turn left (west) and hike 0.4 mile to Trestle Creek Falls Trail #1403C to the right. The hike steepens considerably the final 0.3 mile up Trestle Creek to viewpoints of the cataract.

SMITH FALLS ★★

MAGNITUDE: 42   ELEVATION: 2640 feet
WATERSHED: med   USGS MAP: Fairview Peak (1986)

Champion Creek tumbles 15 to 25 feet along a route dubbed the "Tour of the Golden Past," which was once a thoroughfare leading to the historic Bohemia Mining District, only remnants of which remain. A sign indicating the location of Jerome #9 Placer Claim is posted near the falls. Adjacent to the parking area for Trestle Creek Falls (described earlier) is Champion Creek Road #2473. Vehicles with decent clearance can usually drive up the road during summer, though the 2.4-mile journey will be slow.

PARKER FALLS ★★★

MAGNITUDE: 41   ELEVATION: 2620 feet
WATERSHED: sm   USGS MAP: Holland Point (1986 ns)

Parker Creek splits into two rivulets dropping 35 feet off a rock escarpment. From the parking area for Trestle Creek Falls (described earlier), continue along Brice Creek Road #22 for 2.5 miles and stop just before the next bridge crossing. Trek up Parker Falls Trail #1415 for 0.5 mile to this entry, also known as Lower Parker Falls.

UPPER PARKER FALLS ★★

MAGNITUDE: 22   ELEVATION: 2700 feet
WATERSHED: sm   USGS MAP: Holland Point (1986 ns)

Water slides 40 feet along Parker Trail. Proceed beyond Parker Falls (described earlier); the trail steepens for 0.3 mile to a viewpoint of this display.

EVERGREEN FALLS (U) ★★

MAGNITUDE: 35   ELEVATION: 2600 feet
WATERSHED: vsm   USGS MAP: Holland Point (1986 ns)

An unnamed creek skips a total of 30 to 40 feet among the mosses. This unofficial name was coined by Bryan Swan during one of his waterfall excursions. Drive 0.6 mile past the trailhead for Parker Falls (described earlier) along Brice Creek Road #22 to this roadside cataract.

BLUE HOLE FALLS (U) ★★★

MAGNITUDE: 39   ELEVATION: 2540 feet
WATERSHED: med   USGS MAP: Holland Point (1986 ns)

Blue Hole Falls

This is one of the prettiest punchbowls in the Northwest. From the turnout at Evergreen Falls (described earlier), walk a short distance up Brice Creek Road #22 to fisherman's paths that lead a short 0.1 mile to the river. A variety of natural vantages are available of this entry, with another nice descriptive name given by Bryan Swan.

8 LITTLE RIVER

As you progress up the Little River Valley you will pass one waterfall after another. Access the area by turning southeast off S.R. 138 at Glide onto Little River Road #27. All but the next descent are located within North Umpqua Ranger District, Umpqua National Forest.

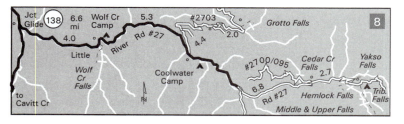

WOLF CREEK FALLS ★★★

MAGNITUDE: 26 (l)   ELEVATION: 1280 feet
WATERSHED: med   USGS MAP: Red Butte (1989)

Water slides down a mountainside in two parts. The upper portion drops 75 feet and the lower 50 feet. The trail to the falls is courtesy of the Bureau of Land Management. Drive southeast 10.6 miles from S.R. 138 along Little River Road #27 and stop at the signed parking area across the road from Wolf Creek Trailhead. It is a gently sloping 2-mile trip to the falls.

HEMLOCK FALLS ★★

MAGNITUDE: 63   ELEVATION: 2800 feet
WATERSHED: med   USGS MAP: Quartz Mtn (1989)

Water rushes 80 feet along the lower reaches of Hemlock Creek. Drive along Little River Road #27 for 14.8 miles past Wolf Creek Falls (described earlier). About 12.1 miles along the way, you should see a sign for *Cedar Creek Falls* ★ USGS Taft Mtn (1989 ns), a 40- to 60- foot cliff-side trickle 1 mile up Road #2700/095 where there is a sharp switchback in the road. Wet your head if you dare! For Hemlock Falls, continue 2.7 miles along Road #27, turning into Lake in the Woods Camp. Hemlock Falls Trail #1520 begins just before you reach the campsites. Follow a steep path for 0.5 mile down to this entry.

TRIBUTARY FALLS (U) ★★

MAGNITUDE: 40   ELEVATION: 3260 feet
WATERSHED: vsm   USGS MAP: Quartz Mtn (1989 ns)

Dropping 20 to 30 feet along an unnamed creek, this is the first of a trio of waterfalls visible along the recently reconstructed Hemlock Trail #1505. Drive 0.1 mile eastward past Lake in the Woods Camp (described earlier). Turn right (south) on a dirt road and proceed an additional 0.1 mile to the trailhead. Hike up the moderately steep route for 0.5 mile to a viewing platform.

MIDDLE HEMLOCK FALLS (U) ★★

MAGNITUDE: 41   ELEVATION: 3340 feet
WATERSHED: sm   USGS MAP: Quartz Mtn (1989 nl)

From the trail, only the upper portion of this descent can be seen tumbling 30 to 40 feet from Hemlock Creek. Hike the steep trail past Tributary Falls (described earlier) for 0.3 mile to trailside vantages.

UPPER HEMLOCK FALLS (U) ★★★

MAGNITUDE: 43   ELEVATION: 3580 feet
WATERSHED: sm   USGS MAP: Quartz Mtn (1989 nl)

This is the best of the cataracts along Trail #1505, as water hurtles 30 to 40 feet along Hemlock Creek. Follow the steep trail another 0.2 mile past Middle Hemlock Falls (described earlier) to a trailside view. It is 1 mile back down the mountain to the trailhead.

YAKSO FALLS ★★★

MAGNITUDE: 71   ELEVATION: 3100 feet
WATERSHED: sm   USGS MAP: Quartz Mtn (1989)

Yakso Falls

This is a classic example of a fan form, as the Little River takes a 70-foot drop. Yakso Falls Trail #1519 starts across the road from the entrance to Lake in the Woods Camp (described earlier). Proceed 0.7 mile down to the base of the falls.

GROTTO FALLS ★★★

MAGNITUDE: 37 (l)
ELEVATION: 3120 feet
WATERSHED: med
USGS MAP: Mace Mtn (1989)

The shimmering waters of this pleasant waterfall plunge 100 feet along Emile Creek. Some have also refered to it as Emile Falls. However, *Emile Falls* USGS Mace Mtn (1985) is actually another cataract farther downstream and was not accessible when this entry was field-truthed. The creek and its namesake falls, plus Shivigny Mountain, are named after Emile Shivigny, who homesteaded nearby in 1875.

Backtrack 9.5 miles from Lake in the Woods Camp or continue 5.3 miles past Wolf Creek Falls along Little River Road #27 (described earlier). Turn north onto Road #2703, drive 4.4 miles, then turn left on Road #2703/150. Follow this gravel route up the mountain 2 miles farther to Grotto Falls Trail #1503, located on the far side of Emile Creek bridge. The trail goes behind the descent in 0.3 mile.

Grotto Falls

9 CAVITT CREEK

SHADOW FALLS ★★★

MAGNITUDE: 42
WATERSHED: med

ELEVATION: 2200 feet
USGS MAP: Red Butte (1989)

This triple waterfall totaling 80 to 100 feet along Cavitt Creek is aptly named. Over time the falls has worked its way upstream through a rock fracture, forming a narrow, natural grotto that always offers some shade. Immediately downstream from the falls, next to the trail, are interesting weathered bedrock formations.

Turn right (south) off Little River Road (described earlier) onto Cavitt Creek Road #25, which is located 6.6 miles from Glide. After 3.3 miles, you can turn into Cavitt Falls Park and visit *Cavitt Falls* ★ USGS Lane Mtn (1987). Take a footbath in the refreshing pool at the base of this 10- to 15-foot descent. The park is administered by the Bureau of Land Management.

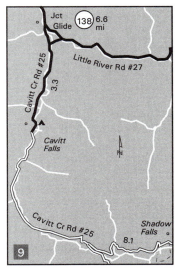

For Shadow Falls, continue along Road #25 for another 8.1 miles, stopping at the signed turnout. Follow Shadow Falls Trail #1504 to the cataract in 0.8 mile.

10 IDLEYLD PARK

Scenic S.R. 138 serves as a convenient corridor between Glide and Crater Lake, making the following waterfalls easily accessible to the traveler.

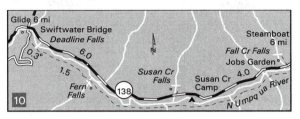

DEADLINE FALLS ★★

MAGNITUDE: 39   ELEVATION: 770 feet
WATERSHED: lg   USGS MAP: Old Fairview (1989 ns)

If you are as fortunate as the author, you will see salmon attempting to jump the 5- to 10-foot height along the 50- to 70-foot breadth of this cataract on the North Umpqua River. Best time of year is May through October. Depart S.R. 138 at the signed parking just south of the Swiftwater Bridge, located 6 miles east of Glide and 16 miles west of Steamboat. A handicap-accessible trail proceeds 0.3 mile to a short spur ending at the viewing area for the falls.

Hikers proceeding onward will also encounter *Fern Falls* ★ USGS Old Fairview (1989 ns), 1.5 miles farther eastward along the North Umpqua Trail. It is a tiered descent, each dropping 5 to 10 feet in segmented fashion along an unnamed tributary. The trail crosses immediately below the falls at a railed footbridge.

SUSAN CREEK FALLS ★★★

MAGNITUDE: 50   ELEVATION: 1060 feet
WATERSHED: med   USGS MAP: Old Fairview (1989)

This 30- to 40-foot cataract along Susan Creek is situated on a Bureau of Land Management parcel. Those hiking beyond the falls can see Indian mounds. Drive east from Swiftwater Bridge (described earlier) along S.R. 138 for 6 miles to Susan Creek Picnic Area. The trailhead is across the road from the parking area. Reach the falls by hiking 1 mile along a relatively gentle path.

Opposite: Shadow Falls

FALL CREEK FALLS ★★★

MAGNITUDE: 57   ELEVATION: 1400 feet
WATERSHED: sm   USGS MAP: Mace Mtn (1989 nl)

Fall Creek tumbles twice, with each tier dropping 35 to 50 feet. It is located within the North Umpqua Ranger District of Umpqua National Forest. Reach this entry by walking around and through slabs of bedrock and past the natural, lush vegetation of Jobs Garden.

Drive 4 miles east from Susan Creek Picnic Area (described earlier) on S.R. 138 to the marked turnout for Fall Creek Falls National Recreation Trail. This beautiful path leads 0.9 mile to the falls.

11 STEAMBOAT

Fishing is prohibited in the entire basin encompassing Steamboat Creek in order to provide undisturbed spawning grounds for the salmon and steelhead of the North Umpqua River drainage. The following waterfalls are all situated within North Umpqua Ranger District, Umpqua National Forest.

STEAMBOAT FALLS ★★★

MAGNITUDE: 47
ELEVATION: 1380 feet
WATERSHED: lg
USGS MAP: Steamboat (1989)

A developed viewpoint showcases this 20- to 30-foot drop along Steamboat Creek. Some fish attempt to jump the falls, while others use the adjacent ladder. Turn northeast off S.R. 138 onto Steamboat Road #38 at Steamboat Junction. After 1.1 miles you can visit more modest *Little Falls* ★ USGS Steamboat (1989), where you have even a better chance of seeing fish jump. Look for an unsigned turnout next to the falls and the adjacent bedrock slabs. Continuing onward for the main display, drive an additional 4.2 miles and turn right (southeast) onto Road #3810. Proceed 0.6 mile to the entrance of Steamboat Falls Campground and the cataract.

JACK FALLS ★★

MAGNITUDE: 32 (l)   ELEVATION: 1460 feet
WATERSHED: sm   USGS MAP: Steamboat (1989)

This set of three falls is closely grouped along Jack Creek. The lower descent slides 20 to 30 feet in two segments. The middle and upper falls are of the horsetail type, descending 25 to 40 feet and 50 to 70 feet, respectively.

Park at an unsigned turnout at mile marker 42, located 3.1 miles southeast of Steamboat junction along S.R. 138. Walk 100 yards farther to Jack Creek. Follow the brushy streambank to the base of the lower falls.

CANTON CREEK FALLS ★★

MAGNITUDE: 41   ELEVATION: 2480 feet
WATERSHED: sm   USGS MAP: Fairview Peak (1986 nl)

Walk to a gorge-rim vista of this 60- to 80-foot slide along Canton Creek. From S.R. 138, turn northeast on Steamboat Road #38, then left in 0.5 mile onto Canton Creek Road. Follow this route for 9.8 miles to Upper Canton Road #26 and turn right. Take Road #26 for 3 miles and turn right (east) on Saddle Camp Road #2300-600. Reach the trailhead in 0.4 mile. Hike 1.5 miles along Canton Creek Falls Trail #1537 to your destination.

12 TOKETEE

The following two waterfalls are among the most impressive in the South Cascades and are not very difficult to access. Both are located within Diamond Lake Ranger District, Umpqua National Forest.

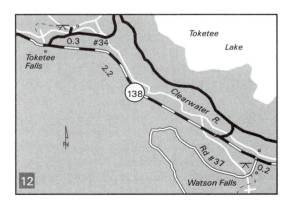

Toketee Falls ★★★★

MAGNITUDE: 61   ELEVATION: 2340 feet
WATERSHED: lg (d)   USGS MAP: Toketee Falls (1986)

These falls are an inspiring sight, as the North Umpqua River drops 30 feet before plunging 90 feet over a sheer wall of basalt. *Toketee* is a Native American word meaning "graceful." The Toketee Pipeline can be seen along the walk to the falls. Pacific Power diverts water from Toketee Lake via its 12-foot redwood-stave pipe. A portion of the North Umpqua River is bypassed for 1,663 feet via a mile-long tunnel. The water then plunges down a steel penstock pipe to the Toketee Powerhouse, where it can generate as much as 210,000 kilowatts of electricity.

Turn north off S.R. 138 on Road #34, heading toward Toketee Lake. Drive 0.3 mile to the left (west) turn marked Toketee Falls Trail #1495. Follow the easily hiked path 0.6 mile to a viewpoint looking into the falls.

Watson Falls ★★★★★

MAGNITUDE: 99 (h)   ELEVATION: 3200 feet
WATERSHED: med   USGS MAP: Fish Creek Desert (1989)

Peer up at Watson Creek plummeting 272 feet from a cliff. The first good vantage is from a footbridge, with the trail continuing more steeply to the base of the waterfall. Drive east 2.2 miles past Toketee Lake along S.R. 138 to Fish Creek Road #37; turn right (south). Proceed 0.2 mile to Watson Falls Picnic Ground. Follow Watson Falls Trail #1495 to the first vista in 0.3 mile.

13 Northeast Umpqua

The cataracts never seem to end in the North Umpqua River watershed. This section describes four more descents within Diamond Lake Ranger District, Umpqua National Forest.

Whitehorse Falls ★★

MAGNITUDE: 37   ELEVATION: 3660 feet
WATERSHED: lg   USGS MAP: Garwood Butte (1985)

Relax at the viewing area overlooking this 10- to 15-foot punchbowl along the course of the Clearwater River. Depart S.R. 138 at the signed turn for Whitehorse Falls Camp, which is located 4.5 miles east of Toketee. Park at the picnic area adjacent to the cataract.

Clearwater Falls ★★

MAGNITUDE: 48   ELEVATION: 4200 feet
WATERSHED: med   USGS MAP: Diamond Lake (1985)

The Clearwater River tumbles 30 feet. Drive 3.5 miles east from Whitehorse Falls (described earlier) along S.R. 138 to the marked turn for Clearwater Falls Camp. Follow the access road 0.2 mile to a picnic area, from which a path quickly leads to the falls.

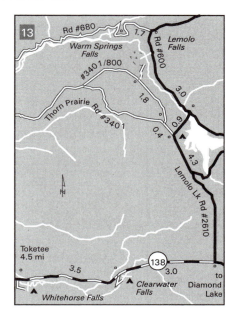

Lemolo Falls ★★★★

MAGNITUDE: 75 (h)   ELEVATION: 3720 feet
WATERSHED: lg (d)   USGS MAP: Lemolo Lake (1986)

While the prior pair of entries is conducive to meditation, this 75- to 100-foot monster along the North Umpqua River won't allow such tranquillity. *Lemolo* is a Chinook word meaning "wild" or "untamed." Depart S.R. 138 by turning north onto Lemolo Lake Road #2610, located 3 miles east of Clearwater Falls (described earlier). Proceed toward Lemolo Lake and bear left (north) after 4.3 miles onto Thorn Prairie Road #3401. Go 0.4 mile, then turn right on Lemolo Falls Road #3401/800. The trailhead is 1.8 miles farther. Lemolo Falls Trail #1468 descends steeply, reaching the base of the thunderous falls in 1 mile.

Warm Springs Falls ★★★

MAGNITUDE: 68   ELEVATION: 3580 feet
WATERSHED: med   USGS MAP: Lemolo Lake (1986 ns)

Warm Springs Creek plummets 50 to 70 feet over cliffs of basalt. Follow the directions to Lemolo Falls (described earlier), but instead of turning at Road #3401, continue 0.9 mile on Lemolo Lake Road #2610 to the far side of Lemolo Dam. Turn left (northwest) on Road #600 and drive 3 miles to Road #680. Bear left here and proceed 1.7 miles to the start of Warm Springs Falls Trail #1499. At the trail's end in 0.3 mile is an unguarded vista above the cataract.

Others: Next to a place called Devils Flat Camp are two historic buildings, providing visitors the opportunity to envision how homesteaders lived. *Cow Creek Falls* ★ USGS Cedar Springs Mtn (1986 ns) is nearby. It drops 25 to 40 feet along a series of rock steps. Across the road from the campground is a short loop trail that passes by the falls. Access the area by departing I-5 at Azalea (Exit 88) and proceed eastward along Cow Creek Road for 17.2 miles. Go online to *The Computer Companion* (described in the Introduction) to see a map for this entry.

14 South Umpqua

The following trio of modestly pleasing waterfalls occurs within the watershed of the South Umpqua River, Tiller Ranger District, Umpqua National Forest. Access the area by driving along S.R. 227 to the hamlet of Tiller.

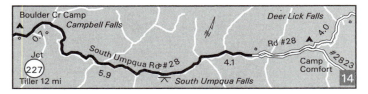

Campbell Falls ★★

MAGNITUDE: 36 (h)   ELEVATION: 1430 feet
WATERSHED: lg   USGS MAP: Dumont Creek (1989)

The South Umpqua River tumbles 10 to 15 feet. The name of the falls honors Robert G. Campbell, a former U.S. Forest Service employee who was killed in action during World War II. Turn off S.R. 227 onto South Umpqua Road #28, located just northwest of the ranger station at Tiller. Proceed 12.7 miles to the signed turnout, 0.7 mile past Boulder Creek Camp. A trail leads quickly to the river in 0.2 mile.

SOUTH UMPQUA FALLS ★★

MAGNITUDE: 25   ELEVATION: 1640 feet
WATERSHED: lg   USGS MAP: Acker Rock (1989)

Water slides 10 to 15 feet over wide slabs of bedrock along the South Umpqua
River. A fish ladder bypasses the falls. Drive southeast on South Umpqua Road
#28, 5.9 miles past Campbell Falls (described earlier) to South Umpqua Falls
Picnic Area and Observation Point.

DEER LICK FALLS ★★

MAGNITUDE: 43   ELEVATION: 2280 feet
WATERSHED: lg   USGS MAP: Twin Lakes Mtn (1989)

Peer from a moderate distance into a series of five blocklike descents ranging from 5 to 20 feet in height along Black Rock Fork. Drive 4.1 miles northeast past South Umpqua Falls (described earlier) along South Umpqua
Road #28. Do not cross the river at the junction, but bear left on Road #28
toward Camp Comfort. Four miles farther find unsigned vantages along
the road.

---

15 UPPER ROGUE RIVER

The following entries are all situated within Prospect Ranger District, Rogue
River National Forest.

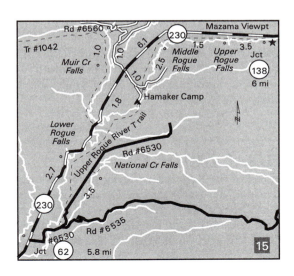

parking area off Mill Creek Road. Follow the main trail 0.2 mile to a trailside view of this entry.

Lower Red Blanket Falls (u) ★★

MAGNITUDE: 75   ELEVATION: 2440 feet
WATERSHED: lg   USGS MAP: Prospect South (1988 nl)

Red Blanket Creek plummets a total of 90 to 140 feet in a secluded setting. The moderately distant cross-canyon vista is recommended for experienced adventurers only. The falls is probably located on private land. Take Red Blanket Road east from Prospect and turn right after 1.3 mile on Butte Falls–Prospect Rd. Continue another 1.7 miles, then bear right (south) toward Butte Falls. After the route switchbacks uphill, look for a jeep trail to the right (west) in another 2.5 miles. It is the first road past a short gravel road ending at a gravel pit. Follow the jeep trail for 1.6 miles as shown on the accompanying map. Park at a short, abandoned jeep trail, which leads toward the canyon rim. Follow the trail for a few hundred yards, then cut through the woods toward the roaring sound of the falls. Pick a route part-way down the moderately steep slope until the falls come into view on the opposite side of the gorge. It will be 0.3 mile to get back to your vehicle.

19 SKY LAKES WILDERNESS

Access to the following waterfalls is via Upper Red Blanket Trail #1090. Reach the trailhead by driving east of Prospect along Red Blanket Road for 15 miles to the road's end. All of the falls are located within Sky Lakes Wilderness, Rogue River National Forest.

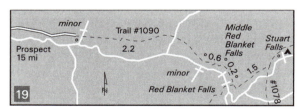

Red Blanket Falls ★★

MAGNITUDE: 50   ELEVATION: 5060 feet
WATERSHED: med   USGS MAP: Union Peak (1985)

Red Blanket Creek takes a double-drop, the upper portion descending 50 to 70 feet. Only the top of the lower tier is visible from the trail. Begin hiking the moderately steep Upper Red Blanket Trail #1090. Just beyond the trailhead and at 2.2 miles you will pass small falls along tributaries. At 2.8 miles, *Middle Red Blanket Falls* (u) ★ USGS Union Peak (1985 ns) drops 20 to 25 feet. Proceed another 0.2 mile to trailside views of the main entry.

STUART FALLS ★★★

MAGNITUDE: 47   ELEVATION: 5460 feet
WATERSHED: med   USGS MAP: Union Peak (1985)

Refresh yourself in the cool mist of water veiling 25 to 40 feet along Red Blanket Creek. Continue 1 mile past Red Blanket Falls (described earlier) to the end of Trail #1090. Follow Stuart Falls Trail #1078 to the left (north) and proceed 0.5 mile to the cataract.

20 BUTTE FALLS

BUTTE FALLS ★★

MAGNITUDE: 54   ELEVATION: 2340 feet
WATERSHED: lg   USGS MAP: Butte Falls (1988)

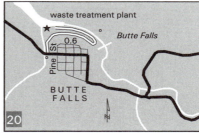

The nearby community is named after this 10- to 15-foot waterfall, which slices diagonally across South Fork Butte Creek. Turn off S.R. 62 at Butte Falls junction, located 5 miles north of Eagle Point. Reach the town of Butte Falls in 16 miles. Upon entering the village, look for Pine Street to the left (north). Backtrack

Butte Falls

1 block to an unmarked gravel road. Take this unpaved route north past a waste treatment plant to an unsigned parking area in 0.6 mile. Well-worn paths quickly lead to the falls.

21 GOLD BAR

DILLON FALLS ★★

MAGNITUDE: 25 (h)   ELEVATION: 1090 feet
WATERSHED: lg   USGS MAP: Gold Hill (1983)

This is one of the lesser known cascades along the extensive Rogue River. Depart I-5 at Gold Hill (Exit 40). Drive north along Upper River Road for 2.3 miles to a dirt road just before a railroad crossing. Navigate around the potholes for 0.2 mile toward road's end and park. Follow the walkway across the sluice, then take the fisherman's path that quickly leads to the base of this 10- to 15-foot challenge to salmon. Also known as Hayes Falls, it is split into two segments by an island.

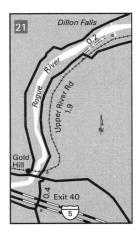

THE COLUMBIA PLATEAU, OREGON

The landscape of eastern Oregon is dominated by a broad region of generally low relief called the Columbia Plateau. This plain, which extends into southeastern Washington, northern Nevada, and southwestern Idaho, is composed of thick layers of basalt which formed from widespread lava flows 30 million years ago. Waterfalls are scarce in the Oregon portion of the plateau. Because of the consistent erosion resistance of the basaltic bedrock, cataracts are lacking along most of the region's major rivers. In addition, low annual precipitation means that few tributary streams flow over the rims of the larger river canyons. Of the region's eighty known waterfalls, twenty-four are listed in this chapter.

Most of the cataracts in this region are found where other geomorphic processes have contributed to waterfall formation. Recent lava flows inundated the course of the Deschutes River 5000 to 6000 years ago. When the

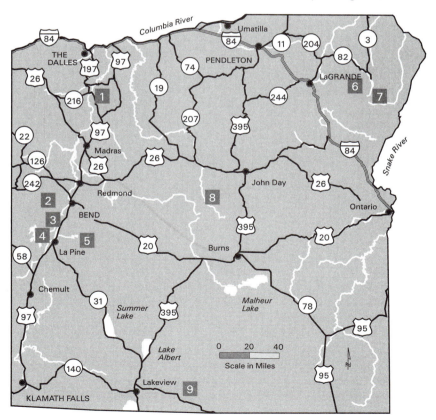

lava cooled, jumbled basaltic rock was formed. The river cuts into and tumbles over these rocky obstructions.

The Strawberry Mountains near the town of John Day were shaped by the accumulation of basalt, rhyolite, and breccia due to volcanic activities 10 million to 13 million years ago. The extreme differences in the erosional resistance of these rock types produce waterfalls in places where streams flow across the contact point between two or more different varieties of rock.

The Wallowa Mountains of northeastern Oregon are one of the few nonvolcanic areas of the region. Here large masses of granite and sedimentary rocks were displaced thousands of feet above the surrounding plain 100 million to 150 million years ago. The range's high relief stopped subsequent lava at its western perimeter. Since the Wallowas rise over 8000 feet above sea level, their climate was sufficiently cold and moist for alpine glaciation to have occurred. The erosive work of these glaciers left vertical breaks for stream courses to plunge over.

1 TYGH VALLEY

Both the Deschutes and White Rivers appear as oases in the dry climate of central Oregon. Scientifically, these are known as exotic streams, because they are fed by the waters of the cooler and moister Cascade Mountains. The following cataracts are sure to quench the thirst of any traveler.

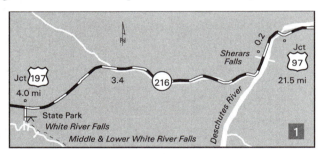

SHERARS FALLS ★★★

MAGNITUDE: 46 (h)   ELEVATION: 680 feet
WATERSHED: lg   USGS MAP: Sherars Bridge (1962 ns)

Watch Native American fishermen net for salmon where the Deschutes River roars 15 to 20 feet in a sagebrush setting. The waterfall is owned by the Warm Springs Tribe. The State Department of Natural Resources and the tribe together regulate fishing on the river.

Drive along S.R. 216 to Sherars Bridge over the Deschutes River. The bridge is located about 7.4 miles east of U.S. 197 and 21.5 miles west of U.S.

97. Stop for views of this entry 0.2 mile south of the bridge. Supervise your children, as the tumultuous river is extremely dangerous.

WHITE RIVER FALLS ★★★

MAGNITUDE: 72   ELEVATION: 1000 feet
WATERSHED: lg   USGS MAP: Maupin (1987 ns)

A viewing platform offers an outstanding vista of rivulets of the White River pouring 70 to 80 feet downward off a 150- to 175-foot-wide escarp-

White River Falls and Middle White River Falls

ment. Also known as Tygh Valley Falls, this waterfall is located within White River Falls State Park. Drive 3.4 miles westward past Sherars Falls (described earlier) along S.R. 216 to the signed turnout for this day-use park. Proceed another 0.2 mile to the parking area and walk 150 feet to the fenced overlook.

MIDDLE WHITE RIVER FALLS (U) ★★★★

MAGNITUDE: 75   ELEVATION: 920 feet
WATERSHED: lg   USGS MAP: Maupin (1987 ns)

This second of a trio of falls is actually a single 25- to 35-foot plunge. The trailside vantage, however, includes the upper falls (described earlier), revealing a dramatic tiered combination. Walk down the paved trail in the downstream direction into the small canyon. The trail quickly turns to dirt, with this entry soon coming into view.

LOWER WHITE RIVER FALLS (U) ★★

MAGNITUDE: 50   ELEVATION: 760 feet
WATERSHED: lg   USGS MAP: Maupin (1987 ns)

The last of the falls in White River State Park tumbles 25 to 35 feet into a large amphitheater. Continue past Middle White River Falls (described earlier), down some wooden steps past an old powerhouse. Follow the trail through the high desert vegetation. Continue on the trail beyond the falls for the best views.

2 TUMALO CREEK

All of the following waterfalls, located within the Bend Ranger District of Deschutes National Forest, can be visited as you head toward the eastern flank of the Cascade Range. Turn off U.S. 97 in Bend onto westbound Franklin Avenue. In 1 mile, at Drake City Park, the street becomes Galveston Avenue. Proceed west 11 miles and turn left (west) on graveled Road #1828. Continue 3 miles to Tumalo Falls Picnic Area.

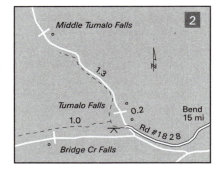

TUMALO FALLS ★★★

MAGNITUDE: 81   ELEVATION: 5080 feet
WATERSHED: lg   USGS MAP: Tumalo Falls (1988)

This 97-foot plummet is framed by stark tree snags—brown remnants of a
forest fire during the summer of 1979. While managed fire is an important
component in modern forestry, this particular case was not planned. The
scarred scene is a reminder of the old adage that "only you can prevent forest
fires."

From the picnic area, look upstream along Tumalo Creek into the falls.
Closer views are also possible from the adjacent trail.

MIDDLE TUMALO FALLS (U) ★★

MAGNITUDE: 52   ELEVATION: 5240 feet
WATERSHED: lg   USGS MAP: Tumalo Falls (1988 nl)

Tumalo Creek tumbles a total of 46
to 65 feet in tiered fashion. Follow the
trail to Tumalo Falls (described earlier), continuing upstream for 1.3
miles until the way deteriorates into
a well-worn path to the creek. Bushwhack streamside for the final 0.2
mile to the base of the cataract.

BRIDGE CREEK FALLS (U) ★★

MAGNITUDE: 46
ELEVATION: 5270 feet
WATERSHED: sm
USGS MAP: Tumalo Falls (1988 nl)

Watch water pouring 25 to 35 feet
from Bridge Creek. From Tumalo
Falls Picnic Area (described earlier),
locate the trailhead to Bridge Creek
Trail. Proceed along this moderately
gentle route for 1 mile to this entry.

Middle Tumalo Falls

Others: Of the five falls that occur along the Deschutes River in the Redmond area, only *Cline Falls* ★ USGS Cline Falls (1962) is readily accessible. The force of this cascade is reduced because a portion of the river has been diverted to a rustic powerhouse nearby. Drive 4.5 miles west of Redmond on S.R. 126. Turn right (north) at the west side of the Deschutes River on Southeast Eagle Road. After 0.3 mile, park at the entrance and look into the canyon at the falls and power facility. Named for Dr. C. A. Cline, who once owned it, the waterfall is now a part of Cline Falls State Park. Go online to *The Computer Companion* (described in the Introduction) to see a map for this entry.

In Bend, it has been reported that *Canal Falls* (u) ★★ USGS Bend (1981 nl) is now surrounded by a residential development. Fed by the irrigation system of the area, this pair of drainageways, actually part of the North Unit Main Canal, drops forcefully 10 to 15 feet over basalt.

In the city of Bend, exit U.S. 97 onto East Greenwood Avenue. Proceed east 0.4 mile and turn left (north) onto 8th Street. Go 1.5 miles, then turn left and parallel the canal 0.4 mile westward to the falls. Go online to *The Computer Companion* (described in the Introduction) to see a map for this entry.

3 LAVA BUTTE GEOLOGICAL AREA

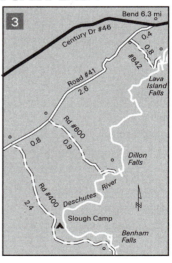

The aptly named Deschutes River (*Deschutes* is French for "of the falls") has ten cataracts along its course from La Pine to the Columbia River. It drops three times along the western fringe of Lava Butte Geological Area, which is located within Fort Rock Ranger District, Deschutes National Forest. From downtown Bend, drive west on Franklin Avenue toward Tumalo Falls (described earlier), but turn left (south) on Cascade Lakes Highway (also known as Century Drive). Continue 6.3 miles and turn left (south) on gravel Road #41 at the sign to Dillon Falls.

LAVA ISLAND FALLS ★★

MAGNITUDE: 24   ELEVATION: 3920 feet
WATERSHED: lg   USGS MAP: Benham Falls (1981)

This entry is simply a set of small cascades, but the jumbled lava rock being split by the Deschutes River makes the site intriguing. Follow Road #41 south for 0.4 mile from Century Drive. Turn left (east) on dirt Road #842 and continue to its end in 0.8 mile.

DILLON FALLS ★★★

MAGNITUDE: 37 (h)   ELEVATION: 4040 feet
WATERSHED: lg   USGS MAP: Benham Falls (1981)

Deschutes River froths 40 to 60 feet within a quarter-mile chasm cut into the basaltic bedrock. The waterfall is named for local homesteader Leander Dillon. Take Road #41 southward 2.6 miles past its junction for Lava Island Falls (described earlier). Turn left (southeast) on dirt Road #600 and drive to its end in

Dillon Falls

0.9 mile. A trail goes from the parking area to views of the gorge and its cascade. The observation points at the rim are unprotected, so be careful.

BENHAM FALLS ★★★

MAGNITUDE: 36 (h)   ELEVATION: 4130 feet
WATERSHED: lg   USGS MAP: Benham Falls (1981)

Deschutes River "chutes" down 40 to 60 feet through a narrow canyon. The cataract is named for J. R. Benham, who unsuccessfully filed a homesteading claim for land nearby in 1885. Continue along Road #41 for 0.8 mile beyond the turn for Dillon Falls (described earlier). Turn left (south) onto Road #400 and drive 2.4 miles, parking where the road meets the river. Benham Falls is immediately downstream. A short pathway leads to secure, but unfenced views.

---

4 LA PINE

FALL RIVER FALLS ★★

MAGNITUDE: 22   ELEVATION: 4120 feet
WATERSHED: lg   USGS MAP: Pistol Butte (1981)

Fall River tumbles 10 to 15 feet next to grassy banks surrounded by pine trees. The falls is located within La Pine State Recreation Area. Leave U.S. 97 at

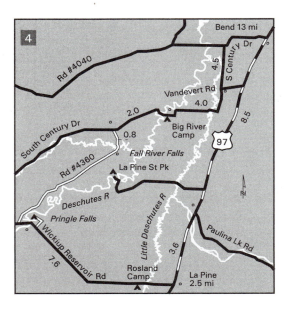

Fall River Falls

South Century Drive 13 miles south of Bend. Drive west 10.5 miles and turn left (south) on dirt Road #4360. Continue 0.8 mile, then park at the wide turn-out preceding the Fall River bridge. Follow the jeep trail 0.2 mile to this pleasant setting.

Others: Although pictured in travel guides and labeled on road maps, the main portion of *Pringle Falls* ★ USGS La Pine (1981) can no longer be seen by the public. A housing development now lines the Deschutes River in the area near the falls and its security system makes it clear that visitors are not welcome. Only uninspiring views remain at the beginning and the end of the falls, which were named for O. M. Pringle, who bought land nearby in 1902. At the junction of U.S. 97 and Wickiup Reservoir Road 2.5 miles north of La Pine turn toward Wickiup Reservoir. The first view of the falls occurs in 7.6 miles at the bridge crossing at the headwaters of the falls. Another view is available at Pringle Falls Camp immediately downstream from the falls. From the bridge follow dirt Road #218 to the campground.

5 NEWBERRY CRATER

A dominant feature of the geology south of Bend is a large, gently sloping shield volcano. Atop this mound is a caldera, the Newberry Crater, where the central portion of the volcano collapsed about 200,000 years ago. Paulina Lake and East Lake currently fill the depression. The erosive power of Paulina Creek as it flows from Paulina Lake has cut through the volcano's layers of basalt at a greater rate than through the more resistant rhyolite layers. Waterfalls occur where these two rock layers meet along the stream's course. The area is now the centerpiece of the Newberry National Volcanic Monument, a part of Deschutes National Forest.

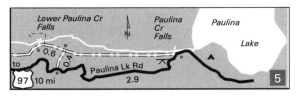

Lower Paulina Creek Falls (u) ★★★

MAGNITUDE: 51   ELEVATION: 5340 feet
WATERSHED: med   USGS MAP: Paulina Peak (1981 nl)

Paulina Creek descends a total of 50 to 80 feet as the creek diverges along its upper portion before fanning out below. The scenic rating decreases during low-water periods in late summer. Turn east off U.S. 97 at Paulina Lake Road, 6 miles north of La Pine. Drive 10 miles to a large, unsigned parking area to the left (north). Hike along an old jeep trail beginning at the far end of the turnout. At a junction in 0.4 mile, bear left (west) and walk 0.6 mile until the falls can be heard. Here an unsigned trail leads across a footbridge over the creek and downstream to views of the falls.

Paulina Creek Falls ★★★★★

MAGNITUDE: 84   ELEVATION: 6200 feet
WATERSHED: med   USGS MAP: Paulina Peak (1981)

This 100-foot dual segmented cataract is best seen in early summer when Paulina Creek has substantial flow. Drive along the paved road for 2.9 miles

Paulina Creek Falls

past the turnout for Lower Paulina Creek Falls (described earlier). Park at the parking lot signed for Paulina Falls. A short trail leads to a developed vista offering superb vantages of the falls. Hikers can also trek to more views below the falls.

6 ENTERPRISE

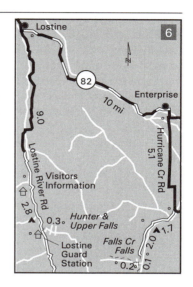

Waterfalls, many officially named, have been mapped in the Wallowa Mountains. Unfortunately, unless you are a back-packer, most are inaccessible since they lie deep within the Eagle Cap Wilderness Area, Wallowa National Forest. The exceptions are the five cataracts on the north end. They are described in this section and the one that follows.

HUNTER FALLS ★★★

MAGNITUDE: 56 (h)
ELEVATION: 5700 feet
WATERSHED: med
USGS MAP: North Minam Meadows (1990)

Lake Creek forcefully squeezes a total of 50 to 60 feet through eroded bedrock. From S.R. 82 at the hamlet of Lostine, turn off the highway and head south along Lostine River Road. The visitors information station is at 9 miles. Continue 2.8 additional miles and park at Lostine Guard Station.

Find the unsigned trailhead by walking back across the creek crossing to a wide spot in the road. The path initially ascends steeply before leveling off over 0.3 mile. A very short spur goes to close-up side views of the lower tier.

UPPER HUNTER FALLS (U) ★★

MAGNITUDE: 28 (h)   ELEVATION: 5780 feet
WATERSHED: med   USGS MAP: North Minam Meadows (1990 ns)

Water stairsteps 40 to 50 feet along Lake Creek. Continue steeply past Hunter Falls (described earlier) along the main path. You will attain a trailside vantage in 0.1 mile.

FALLS CREEK FALLS ★★★★

MAGNITUDE: 53 (h)   ELEVATION: 5420 feet
WATERSHED: med   USGS MAP: Chief Joseph Mtn (1990 nl)

Falls Creek Falls

What a picturesque scene as Falls Creek plummets 60 to 80 feet with usually snow-laden Sawtooth Peak in the background. From S.R. 82 in Enterprise, turn south onto Hurricane Creek Road. Bear right after 5.1 miles, which takes you up Hurricane Creek. Pass a campground in 1.7 additional miles, with road's end and trailhead 2 miles farther.

Embark upon Hurricane Creek Trail #1807. Hike 0.1 mile and turn right on the spur marked as Falls Creek. Go another 0.2 mile to a somewhat distant view of the waterfall. Depending upon stream discharge, you may or may not be able to bushwhack upstream to its base. Others have previously reported a path ascending alongside the stream, but the scoured-out appearance of the place suggests an event such as an avalanche or major flood destroyed it.

Others: *Lookingglass Falls* ★ USGS Rondowa (1983) will probably disappoint, unless you happen to be in this part of Umatilla National Forest with time to visit one more falls. Most of this waterfall has been altered by its namesake fish hatchery. From Palmer Junction, drive north along Lookingglass Creek Road for 2.3 miles to road's end at the visitors parking area at the hatchery. Hike 0.2 mile upstream to the cascades. Go online to *The Computer Companion* (described in the Introduction) to see a map for this entry.

7 WALLOWA LAKE

Wallowa Lake is a stunningly beautiful example of a form of paternoster lake, a body of water formed by a natural dam of deposits blocking part of a glacial valley. Drive 6 miles past the town of Joseph along S.R. 82 to Wallowa Lake State Park, which is located within Wallowa-Whitman National Forest. Turn left (south) toward the picnic area and away from the main boating and camping facilities.

WALLOWA FALLS ★★★

MAGNITUDE: 52 (h)   ELEVATION: 4660 feet
WATERSHED: lg   USGS MAP: Joseph (1990 nl)

Peer down at the West Fork Wallowa River pouring over a 30- to 50-foot escarpment. Not recommended for children or skittish adults. To reach the falls, follow West Fork Trail #1820, which starts at the picnic area, toward Ice Lake. A footbridge crosses the East Fork Wallowa River, then ascends shortly to a rocky outcrop adjacent to the West Fork in 0.1 mile. From this natural vista, follow the ridge a short distance downstream to a well-worn path above the river.

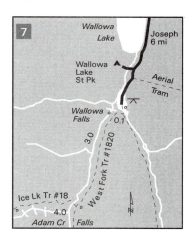

ADAM CREEK FALLS ★★★

MAGNITUDE: 66   ELEVATION: 7200 feet
WATERSHED: sm   USGS MAP: Eagle Cap (1990 ns)
Accessible by aerial tram

This series of falls descends hundreds of feet along Adam Creek and can be seen collectively or individually, depending upon whether you hike to them or take the aerial tram. Hikers should proceed 3 miles along West Fork Trail #1820 (described earlier), then turn right (west) on Ice Lake Trail #18. The tiers of this cataract will be encountered one at a time, as you make the 4-mile trek to its end at Ice Lake. Tourists atop Mount Howard will see this entry as silvery threads along the mountainside. For unforgettable views of Eagle Cap Wilderness, Wallowa Lake, and the Columbia Plateau, take the High Wallowas gondola 3700 feet above the valley. Look for the falls toward the southwest.

8 OCHOCO

SOUTH FORK FALLS ★★

MAGNITUDE: 28   ELEVATION: 3540 feet
WATERSHED: lg   USGS MAP: Suplee Butte (1981)

Water tumbles 75 feet over a 200- to 300-foot reach of the South Fork John Day River. Located on Bureau of Land Management land, the cascades are locally known as Izee Falls. The surrounding steep canyon walls are composed of impressive columns of basalt.

Drive 32 miles west from U.S. 395 on County Road #63, or 32 miles east from Paulina along County Roads #112 and #67, to BLM Road #6207. Proceed north, following the river, for 5.5 miles to Forest Road #58. Bear right, staying on #6207, for 0.8 mile to an unsigned turnout next to the top of the cataract.

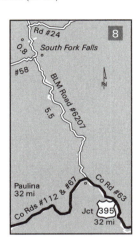

9 ADEL

DEEP CREEK FALLS ★★★

MAGNITUDE: 56   ELEVATION: 4800 feet
WATERSHED: lg   USGS MAP: Adel (1968)

This 30- to 50-foot drop along Deep Creek Canyon is framed by columns of basalt in a sagebrush setting. It is likely situated on either private property

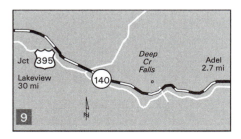

or Bureau of Land Management land. For a roadside view of this entry, drive 2.7 miles west from Adel or 30 miles east from Lakeview along S.R. 140.

Deep Creek Falls

THE PANHANDLE, IDAHO

The Panhandle of northern Idaho separates Washington from Montana. Stretching 170 miles southward from the Canadian border to Lewiston, its width varies from 45 to 125 miles. Although many states have unusual shapes, Idaho's is unique in its historical and political significance. No other state was shaped wholly by boundaries originally set by its neighbors. Idaho is made up of land not annexed by Montana, Wyoming, Utah, Nevada, Oregon, or Washington.

The Panhandle is a region of large lakes and rolling to rugged mountains. Lake Coeur d'Alene, Lake Pend Oreille, Priest Lake, and Dworshak Reservoir cover large areas. All but Dworshak are natural. Mountain ranges such as the Selkirks, the Purcells, the Bitterroots, and the Clearwaters are distributed through the region. The Panhandle has thirty-seven recognized waterfalls, of which twenty-five are described here.

Geomorphologists, scientists who study landforms, classify waterfalls as destructive or constructive. Most cataracts, including almost all of those in the Pacific Northwest, are of the destructive variety. The force of running water slowly erodes the streambeds, usually causing the falls to recede upstream through geologic time. Constructive descents, on the other hand, mostly flow over mineral deposits and migrate downstream as the deposits accumulate. (*Fall Creek Falls,* listed in the Snake River Plain chapter, is a constructive falls.)

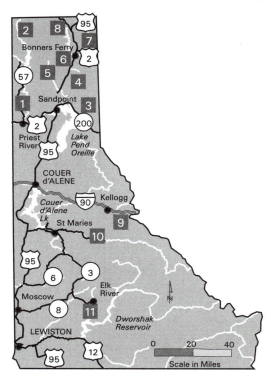

Destructive falls are further classified by how they developed. Consequent falls are located where a preexisting break occurs along the course of a stream. An example is water plunging into a glacier-carved valley, as at *Copper Falls.* When streams erode along rock materials of varying rates of erosional resistance, subsequent falls may form, as at *Lower Snow Creek Falls.*

The waterfalls of the Northwest can be enjoyed

for their beauty alone, but they are even more interesting when one ponders the variety of ways in which they were created.

---

1 PRIEST RIVER

Access this area from the town of Priest River by departing U.S. 2 onto S.R. 57.

TORRELLE FALLS ★★

MAGNITUDE: 32   ELEVATION: 2300 feet
WATERSHED: lg   USGS MAP: Quartz Mtn (1967)

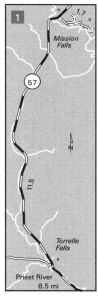

A rustic restaurant spans the West Branch Priest River at the base of this 10- to 15-foot descent. Drive 8.5 miles north from the town of Priest River along S.R. 57. Find this unique site on the left (west) side of the highway.

Continuing northward along S.R. 57, waterfall collectors can also seek out *Mission Falls* ★ USGS Outlet Bay (1967), where water tumbles a total of 5 to 10 feet along a breadth of the Upper West Branch Priest River in Priest Lake Ranger District, Idaho Panhandle National Forest. Proceed 11.5 miles beyond Torrelle Falls. Park at the northeast side of the bridge across the river. Follow a jeep trail next to the bridge for 0.2 mile to a road junction. Take the right fork and follow the dirt route for 1.5 miles farther, bearing right at all junctions. When you near the river, a well-worn trail leads to the falls in a few hundred yards.

---

2 PRIEST LAKE

Recreational activities occur year-round near 26,000-acre Priest Lake. The area's waterfalls are remote, however, and are easiest to visit from early summer through late autumn.

GRANITE FALLS ★★★

MAGNITUDE: 55 (h)   ELEVATION: 3460 feet
WATERSHED: med   USGS MAP: Helmer Mtn (1986)

Granite Creek slides 50 to 75 feet within Priest Lake Ranger District, Idaho Panhandle National Forest. This entry is actually located in Washington, but it is listed in this chapter because the primary access is from Idaho.

Drive 37 miles north of Priest River along S.R. 57 to Nordman. Continue 13 miles and turn onto the entrance road to Stagger Inn Camp and Granite Falls. (Note: S.R. 57 becomes Granite Creek Road #302 about 2 miles past Nordman.) The trailhead is at the south end of the camp. The sign to the falls is misleading. Do not cross the log over the stream to which the arrow points. Instead walk straight past the sign less than 100 yards to the cataract.

UPPER PRIEST FALLS ★★★★

MAGNITUDE: 71 (h)
ELEVATION: 3420 feet
WATERSHED: lg
USGS MAP: Continental Mtn (1968)

The Upper Priest River noisily crashes 100 to 125 feet within the secluded northwest tip of Idaho. Located within Priest Lake Ranger District, Idaho Panhandle National Forest, this falls is also known as American Falls to distinguish it from Canadian Falls, located farther upstream in British Columbia.

Drive 1.7 miles north of Stagger Inn Camp (described earlier) on Road #302 and turn right (northeast) on Road #1013, which eventually turns into Road #637. Proceed approximately 11.5 miles to the Upper Priest River Trailhead #308. This path follows the river for 9 miles, ending at the falls. If your vehicle has good road clearance, continue along Road #637 for another 11 miles to Continental Trail #28. Hike 0.7 mile north on Trail #28 and turn right on Trail #308 for another 1.5 miles to the descent.

---

3 PEND OREILLE

CHAR FALLS ★★★

MAGNITUDE: 61 (h)   ELEVATION: 4140 feet
WATERSHED: med   USGS MAP: Trestle Peak (1989)

Lightning Creek descends powerfully for 50 to 75 feet, with the viewpoint framed by coniferous trees. This falls is located within Sandpoint Ranger District, Idaho Panhandle National Forest. Turn east off U.S. 2/95 onto S.R. 200 and drive 12.2 miles along S.R. 200 to Trestle Creek Road #275. Turn left (east) and proceed 13 miles to Lightning Creek Road #419. Turn right (south) and continue 0.6 mile to a primitive road to the left. Park here and

Char Falls

follow the rocky road 0.5 mile to a wide trail at its end. Take the trail only 20 yards, then find a faint path to the right. It leads to an unfenced overlook of the falls in less than 100 yards.

WELLINGTON CREEK FALLS (U) ★★★

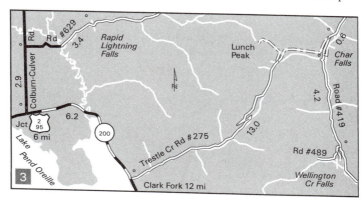

MAGNITUDE: 56   ELEVATION: 3120 feet
WATERSHED: med   USGS MAP: Trestle Peak (1989 ns)

Lush vegetation surrounds this wonderful 50- to 75-foot waterfall along Wellington Creek. Be careful near the edge of the vista's unfenced precipice in this undeveloped area, which is located within Sandpoint Ranger District, Idaho Panhandle National Forest.

Continue 4.2 miles past Char Falls (described earlier) along Lightning Creek Road #419 to Augor Road #489 and turn right (west). Cross Lightning Creek and either drive or hike down the primitive road to the left. Bear right at the fork in 0.4 mile and continue 0.4 mile on this bumpy road to its end. Walk toward the creek and a bit upstream, listening for the falls. Continue toward Wellington Creek for good overviews of this obscure entry.

Others: Water rushes 20 to 30 feet along Rapid Lightning Creek. *Rapid Lightning Falls* (u) ★ USGS Elmire (1989 ns) is probably located on private property. Turn east off U.S. 2/95 onto S.R. 200 and drive 6 miles before turning left (north) on Colburn–Culver Road. In 2.9 miles, turn right (east) at the schoolhouse onto the road marked Rapid Lightning Creek (Road #629). Park at an unsigned turnout 3.4 miles farther. The cataract is accessible from short, well-trod paths.

4 COLBURN

GROUSE CREEK FALLS ★★

MAGNITUDE: 18
WATERSHED: lg

ELEVATION: 2670 feet
USGS MAP: Wylie Knob (1989)

Grouse Creek cuts through bedrock in a small series of descents totaling 15 to 20 feet, situated within Sandpoint Ranger District, Idaho Panhandle National Forest. Turn east off U.S. 2/95 at Colburn onto Colburn–Culver Road. Drive east 4.5 miles and

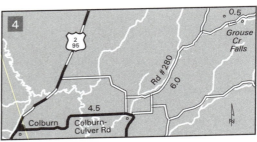

turn left on the gravel Road #280. Continue 6 miles up Grouse Creek Valley to a turnout near a dirt road to the right. Park and follow the road, which becomes a trail in 0.3 miles. The waterfall is 0.2 mile farther.

5 PACK RIVER

JERU CREEK FALLS (U) ★★★

MAGNITUDE: 59
WATERSHED: sm

ELEVATION: 3060 feet
USGS MAP: Dodge Peak (1967 nl)

Jeru Creek slides 100 to 150 feet. The waterfall is probably located on private property. Turn northwest off
U.S. 2/95 at Samuels onto Pack River Road #231. Drive
9 miles to the unsigned turnout on the north side of Jeru
Creek. The 1-mile trek from the road starts on an ob-
solete four-wheel-drive route and eventually turns into
a seldom-used, unmaintained trail. The descent will be
encountered soon after the point at which the path
seems to end.

6 BONNERS FERRY

The following waterfalls occur within a fairly undeveloped area of Bonners Ferry Ranger District, Idaho Panhandle National Forest.

LOWER SNOW CREEK FALLS (U) ★★

MAGNITUDE: 64   ELEVATION: 1900 feet
WATERSHED: lg   USGS MAP: Moravia (1965
                       ns)

Snow Creek splits as it descends 50 to 75 feet over an escarpment. Drive
2.5 miles south of Bonners Ferry on U.S. 2/95. Turn right onto Moravia
Road at the golf course. Bear right in 3 miles on West Side Road #417 and
drive 2 miles to a turnout and informal campsite. The unnamed trail on
the north side of Snow Creek leads shortly to this entry. (Note: The named
trail south of the creek goes up the ridge and does not provide any views of
the falls.)

　　　Farther upstream is *Snow Creek Falls* ★ USGS Moravia (1965 nl).
This 75- to 125-foot drop would be impressive except there are no good
views. A bird's-eye glimpse of the falls can be gained from Snow Creek
Road #402. Drive about 1.5 miles west of its junction with West Side
Road #417.

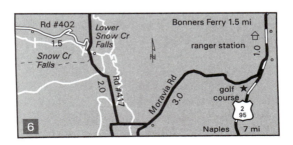

7 MOYIE RIVER

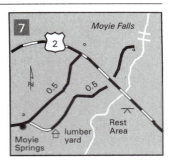

Moyie Falls is purported to be one of Idaho's great scenic attractions. No argument here. But contrary to what most directions imply, you can't get good views from the main highway. The following description, however, will direct you to a picture-perfect vista.

MOYIE FALLS ★★★★★

MAGNITUDE: 71 (h)   ELEVATION: 2020 feet
WATERSHED: lg   USGS MAP: Moyie Springs (1965)

Moyie River absolutely thunders through a small gorge in tiered form. The upper portion crashes 60 to 100 feet beneath an antiquated span crossing the canyon. The lower portion cascades 20 to 40 feet. The falls is probably located on private property.

Turn off U.S. 2 at the Moyie Springs Exit immediately west of the Moyie River bridge. In 0.5 mile, turn left on the street adjacent to a lumber yard. Follow this residential road 0.5 mile to various turnouts offering good views into the canyon.

Moyie Falls

8 BOUNDARY LINE

SMITH FALLS ★★★

MAGNITUDE: 67   ELEVATION: 1800 feet
WATERSHED: lg   USGS MAP: Smith Falls (1968)

A high volume of water plummets 60 feet along Smith Creek. The falls and the viewpoint are situated on private property. Please obey the posted restrictions so others can continue to enjoy this entry.

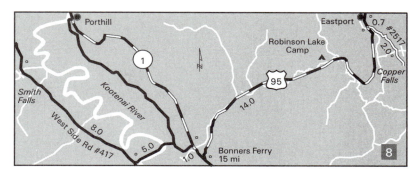

About 15 miles north of Bonners Ferry turn north onto S.R. 1 from U.S. 95. Drive 1 mile, then turn left (west) on an unsigned paved road and continue for 5 miles, crossing the Kootenai River at the halfway point. Turn right (north) onto West Side Road #417 and proceed 8 miles to a marked turnout at the falls.

Smith Falls

Copper Falls ★★★★

MAGNITUDE: 77   ELEVATION: 3400 feet
WATERSHED: sm   USGS MAP: Eastport (1965)

Copper Creek hurtles 160 feet from a cliff within Bonners Ferry Ranger District, Idaho Panhandle National Forest. Turn east off U.S. 95 onto Road #2517 less than 0.7 mile south of the Eastport border crossing or 14 miles northeast of the junction with S.R. 1. Follow this bumpy gravel road for 2 miles to Copper Falls Trail #20. Hike 0.3 mile along the moderately steep trail to the falls.

9 MULLAN

As you travel east from Coeur d'Alene along I-90, you will pass the historic mining towns of Kellogg, Wallace, and Mullan. The following modest waterfalls, accessible from late summer to early autumn, are located near the Bitterroot Divide, which separates Idaho from Montana. Both are situated within Wallace Ranger District, St. Joe National Forest.

Stevens Lake Falls (u) ★★★

MAGNITUDE: 53
ELEVATION: 4420 feet
WATERSHED: sm
USGS MAP: Mullan (1988 ns)

The tiers of this entry can be viewed either collectively or individually. The lower portion plunges 30 to 50 feet along Willow Creek, while the horsetail form of the upper part drops 30 to 50 feet. Leave I-90 at Mullan (Exit 68). Drive through the town and continue east. The route turns right after 1.5 miles and becomes Willow Creek Road. Continue another 1.5 miles, crossing I-90, to the road's end near an old set of railroad tracks. Follow Willow Creek Trail #8008 for 2 miles; after passing *Willow Creek Falls* (u) ★ USGS Mullan (1988 ns), where East Fork Willow Creek cascades 10 to 20 feet downward, the way steepens considerably. In 0.2 mile the lower part of Stevens Lake Falls will be encountered. Hike 0.2 mile farther for a close-up view of the upper tier.

Opposite: Copper Falls

10 ST. JOE RIVER

St. Joe River is particularly known for two things: first, it is navigable to one of the highest elevations of any river in North America. Second, its sport fishing is regarded as excellent, especially along the remote upper reaches where you can practically jump across the "mighty" St. Joe.

FALLS CREEK FALLS ★★

MAGNITUDE: 46 (h)   ELEVATION: 1980 feet
WATERSHED: med   USGS MAP: Saint Joe (1985 ns)

Unsuspecting travelers are likely to miss this 20- to 30-foot drop of Falls Creek into the St. Joe River. It is located on private property surrounded by St. Maries Ranger District, St. Joe National Forest. Turn east off S.R. 3 onto the St. Joe River Road 0.5 mile northeast of St. Maries. The falls is 15 miles up the River Road, or 4.5 miles past Shadowy St. Joe Camp. Park at the turnout closest to the bridge over Falls Creek.

11 ELK CREEK

Many waterfalls are to be found within this portion of Palouse Ranger District, Clearwater National Forest. Drive south from Bovill toward the Elk

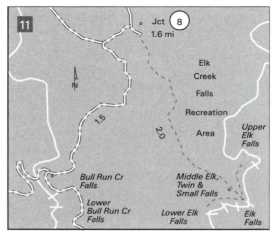

River on S.R. 8. After 16 miles, turn right (south) at the signed access road. Proceed 1.6 miles to a parking area for the Elk Creek Canyon Trailhead, which is next to a fork in the road. The trail system has recently been upgraded and may vary slightly from the following descriptions. Updated maps are available at the trailhead.

Upper Elk Falls (u) ★★

MAGNITUDE: 31   ELEVATION: 2660 feet
WATERSHED: lg   USGS MAP: Elk Creek Falls (1969 nl)

The uppermost descent along Elk Creek drops 30 to 50 feet into a circular basin. Hike along the left fork of the road, which soon becomes a moderately sloped trail. Walk 2 miles to a small open area, then descend quickly to the grassy slopes of the north rim of the canyon. Turn left, following a trail back into the woods and toward the creek for 0.3 mile to the falls.

Elk Falls ★★★★

MAGNITUDE: 72   ELEVATION: 2550 feet
WATERSHED: lg   USGS MAP: Elk Creek Falls (1969)

This 125- to 150-foot cataract, also called Elk Creek Falls, is the highest of the six waterfalls along Elk Creek. Follow the directions to Upper Elk Falls (described earlier), except once at the canyon rim, follow the trail to the right among the grassy slopes. There are many views of the falls over the next 0.2 mile. At this point, look down into the gorge for a path-side view of *Middle Elk Falls* (u) ★ USGS Elk Creek Falls (1969 ns). Water pours 20 to 30 feet from Elk Creek. Avid fishermen and other nimble individuals often bushwhack down to this reach of the stream.

Twin Falls (u) and Small Falls (u) ★★

MAGNITUDE: 45   ELEVATION: 2400 feet
WATERSHED: lg   USGS MAP: Elk Creek Falls (1969 ns)

This pair of waterfalls can be viewed in tandem from the trail. Twin Falls is a 10- to 20-foot segmented descent, while Small Falls drops 10 to 20 feet in a punchbowl form. Proceed along the trail for 0.1 mile downstream from Middle Elk Falls (described earlier).

LOWER ELK FALLS ★★★★

MAGNITUDE: 72   ELEVATION: 2350 feet

WATERSHED: lg   USGS MAP: Elk Creek Falls (1969 nl)

This 75- to 100-foot plunge is the most powerful of the waterfalls along Elk Creek. It is recommended only for adults who are not deterred by some mod-

Lower Elk Falls

est rock climbing. Walk to the end of the well-worn trail about 0.1 mile past Small Falls (described earlier). Carefully follow the faint path to the top of the unfenced basaltic outcrop for an excellent view. It will be a 2.4-mile hike back to the trailhead.

Bull Run Creek Falls ★★★

MAGNITUDE: 60　　　　ELEVATION: 2480 feet
WATERSHED: med　　　USGS MAP: Elk Creek Falls (1969)

Bull Run Creek tumbles a total of 75 to 100 feet. This and the following entry straddle timber company property and an undeveloped portion of Elk Creek Falls Recreation Area. Instead of parking at the trailhead for Elk Creek Canyon (described earlier), continue along the right fork of the unnamed road, turning at the junctions as shown on the accompanying map. Park in 1.5 miles, although part of this route has reportedly been gated, so you may have to walk all or part of this distance. A small, faint path leads shortly to this cataract.

Lower Bull Run Creek Falls (u) ★★

MAGNITUDE: 45　　　　ELEVATION: 2420 feet
WATERSHED: med　　　USGS MAP: Elk Creek Falls (1969 ns)

Water pours 30 to 50 feet along Bull Run Creek. This entry is recommended for determined bushwhackers only. Return to the road from Bull Run Creek Falls (described earlier) and continue walking along the ridge in the downstream direction for 0.1 mile. After passing a small marshy area, scramble down the steep timbered slope to the creek below the base of the falls.

CENTRAL WILDERNESS AREAS, IDAHO

The interior of Idaho is dominated by swift rivers cutting deep canyons through rugged mountains. This sparsely populated region contains the largest tracts—3 million acres—of wilderness in the contiguous United States. Adventurers can explore the Selway-Bitterroot, Frank Church River of No Return, Gospel Hump, and Sawtooth Wildernesses; the Hells Canyon and Sawtooth National Recreation Areas; and the Wild and Scenic Salmon River.

The geology of this region is largely determined by the history of its igneous rocks. During the late Mesozoic era, 75 million to 100 million years ago, extensive masses of magma crystallized in the subsurface of central

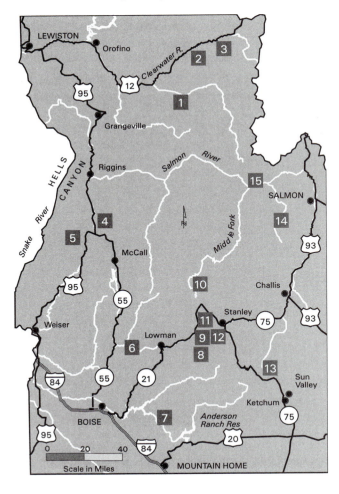

Idaho. Rocks ranging from igneous granite and diorite to metamorphic gneisses were formed. Over the next 50 million years, these masses, collectively called a batholith, were uplifted to form mountains.

The mountainous terrain of the Idaho interior has been shaped mostly by erosion. Alpine glaciers carved the batholith at least four times over the last 2 million years, sharpening peaks and widening valleys. Most waterfalls in the region were created by glaciation. *Warbonnet Falls* descends from a mountainside into a glacial valley. Other streams follow along valleys and encounter obstacles called moraines—linear rock deposits left by glacial activity. *Lady Face Falls,* for instance, breaks through and drops over a moraine.

Stream erosion also contributes to the configuration of the batholith. The Salmon, Snake, Selway, and Lochsa Rivers have carved impressive canyons and gorges. Waterfalls tumble into these powerful waterways from tributaries that erode at a slower rate than the main rivers (*Fountain Creek Falls* and *Tumble Creek Falls* are examples). Cascades such as *Selway Falls* and *Carey Falls* are cases where heterogeneous rock material is eroded unevenly by rivers.

Because of the wild nature of central Idaho, large descents remain to be found, described, and mapped. Many of these cataracts are accessible only by plane, but a good share await discovery by hikers and backpackers. This book describes twenty-eight of the fifty-seven falls known to occur within the central interior.

---

1 SELWAY RIVER

The Selway River begins in the interior of the Selway-Bitterroot Wilderness. As it flows from the wilderness area, its waters become a river of substantial magnitude. Farther downstream at Lowell, the Selway meets the Lochsa River to become the Middle Fork Clearwater River.

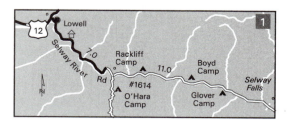

SELWAY FALLS ★★

MAGNITUDE: 39 (h) ELEVATION: 1700 feet
WATERSHED: lg USGS MAP: Selway Falls (1987)

A long reach of the Selway River cascades a total of 50 feet within Moose Creek Ranger District, Nez Perce National Forest. Turn southeast off U.S.

12 at Lowell and drive 18 miles to the end of Selway River Road #1614. The cataract can be seen beside the gravel roadway.

2 LOCHSA RIVER

U.S. 12 faithfully parallels the Lochsa River from its beginning near Lolo Pass to its confluence with the Selway River 78 miles downstream. There are plenty of campsites along this stretch of the highway, but no vehicle service is available from Lolo Hot Springs to Lowell. Be sure your automobile has a full tank of gas before you start. Several waterfalls pour from tributary streams into the Lochsa within a 2-mile stretch 16 to 18 miles northeast of Lowell. The following waterfalls occur within the Middle Fork Clearwater Wild and Scenic River area, Lochsa Ranger District, Clearwater National Forest.

HORSETAIL FALLS ★★

MAGNITUDE: 59   ELEVATION: 2000 feet
WATERSHED: vsm   USGS MAP: McLendon Butte (1966 ns)

Peer across the Lochsa River to Horsetail Falls descending 60 to 100 feet from an unnamed stream. Drive to a marked turnoff along U.S. 12 between mile markers 114 and 115.

SHOESTRING FALLS ★★

MAGNITUDE: 51   ELEVATION: 1920 feet
WATERSHED: vsm   USGS MAP: McLendon Butte (1966)

Water stairsteps 150 to 200 feet in five sections where an unnamed creek drops into the Lochsa River. View this waterfall from across the river at the marked turnout between mile markers 115 and 116.

WILD HORSE CREEK FALLS (U) ★★

MAGNITUDE: 48   ELEVATION: 1880 feet
WATERSHED: sm   USGS MAP: McLendon Butte (1966 ns)

Wild Horse Creek descends in a double-drop totaling 40 to 60 feet. Park at the Shoestring Falls turnout (described earlier) and walk 0.1 mile along U.S. 12 for a close-up view of this entry.

Tumble Creek Falls

Others: *Tumble Creek Falls* (u) ★ USGS McLendon Butte (1966 ns) veils 20 to 30 feet before flowing beneath the highway into the Lochsa River. Look for this entry, which is not signed, along the east side of U.S. 12 between mile markers 113 and 114.

3 WARM SPRINGS CREEK

Warm Springs Creek derives its name from the thermal waters that flow into the stream from Jerry Johnson Hot Springs. Most hikers head for the rustic hot springs, often entering the waters *au naturel*. The area rapidly becomes secluded as you progress upstream past the springs.

JERRY JOHNSON FALLS (U) ★★★

MAGNITUDE: 56 (h)   ELEVATION: 3900 feet
WATERSHED: lg   USGS MAP: Tom Beal Peak (1984 nl)

Warm Springs Creek roars 40 to 70 feet into a large basin. This entry is located within Powell Ranger District, Clearwater National Forest. Drive to the parking area for Warm Springs Creek Trail #49, located along U.S. 12, 1 mile east of Jerry Johnson Campground. A footbridge crosses the Lochsa River before the trail reaches Warm Springs Creek and follows it upstream 1.5 miles to the hot springs. One mile beyond the springs the trail crosses a small tributary creek, then gradually climbs above Warm Springs Creek to trailside views of the falls in another mile.

4 LITTLE SALMON RIVER

Idaho consists of two broadly settled areas—the Panhandle and the Snake River Plain—separated by the Central Wilderness. The existence of this large, mostly uninhabited area helps explain the distinctly different characters, both cultural and physical, of the two populated regions, which are connected by only one paved road, U.S. 95.

All of the cataracts described in this section occur on either private parcels or Bureau of Land Management lands bounded by New Meadows Ranger District, Payette National Forest.

LITTLE SALMON FALLS (U) ★★

MAGNITUDE: 35   ELEVATION: 3640 feet
WATERSHED: lg   USGS MAP: Indian Mtn
                       (1983 ns)

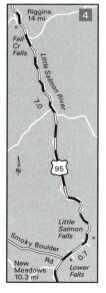

Several small descents occur along the Little Salmon River where it parallels U.S. 95. This 10- to 15-foot drop is the prettiest and easiest to visit. Drive 11 miles north of New Meadows to an unsigned turnout adjacent to this cataract. By backtracking 0.7 mile, waterfall enthusiasts can add *Lower Little Salmon Falls* (u) ★ USGS Bally Mtn (1983 ns) to their collections. Water froths 5 to 10 feet downward along the Little Salmon River. Park at the unsigned turnout, located immediately north of the junction signed Smoky Boulder Road. Be careful of the speeding traffic when walking along the highway.

Fall Creek Falls (u) ★★

MAGNITUDE: 30
WATERSHED: sm

ELEVATION: 2920 feet
USGS MAP: Indian Mtn (1983 ns)

Fall Creek tumbles 15 to 25 feet before continuing beneath the highway and into the Little Salmon River. Drive 7 miles north of Little Salmon Falls (described earlier) to an unsigned turnout along U.S. 95.

Others: Located east of Riggins is *Carey Falls* ★ USGS Carey Dome (1989). This entry, located along the Salmon River, where it serves as a boundary between the Gospel Hump and Frank Church River of No Return Wildernesses, is more like rapids and riffles than a waterfall. Pretty scenery, including several small cascades from tributary streams, will be experienced along the route. Less than 1 mile south of Riggins turn off U.S. 95 onto Big Salmon Road #1614. Wind along the river for 23 miles to Wind River Pack Bridge. Continue 0.4 mile beyond this point to a roadside vantage. Go online to see a map for this entry.

5 Lost Valley

Lost Creek Falls ★★

MAGNITUDE: 15
WATERSHED: lg

ELEVATION: 4380 feet
USGS MAP: Tamarack (1986)

Lost Creek drops serenely 5 to 10 feet in a wooded setting. This falls is situated within Council Ranger District, Payette National Forest. Depart U.S. 95 about 1 mile south of Tamarack, and turn right (west) onto Lost Valley Reservoir Road #089. Drive 5.3 miles to the dam, then proceed south on Road #154 for 2.7 miles to the cataract. It can be seen from the road with close-up views via fishermen's paths.

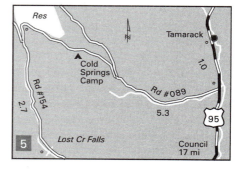

6 GARDEN VALLEY

At the town of Banks, turn off S.R. 55 onto South Fork Road, heading toward Lowman. The road is now paved its entire route to the town of Lowman. Along the way you will pass many hot springs adjacent to the South Fork Payette River. The following cataracts are located within Lowman Ranger District, Boise National Forest.

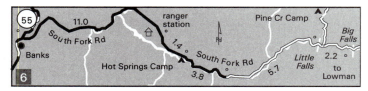

LITTLE FALLS ★★

MAGNITUDE: 40   ELEVATION: 3350 feet
WATERSHED: lg   USGS MAP: Grimes Pass (1988)

This 5- to 10-foot drop along the breadth of South Fork Payette River is aptly named. There was once an abandoned mine shaft across the road from the falls, but it has been obliterated by construction of the improved highway. Drive 9.5 miles eastward past Hot Springs Camp along South Fork Road.

BIG FALLS ★★

MAGNITUDE: 42   ELEVATION: 3480 feet
WATERSHED: lg   USGS MAP: Pine Flat (1972)

This 25- to 40-foot waterfall is "big" only in contrast to its downstream counterpart. The best roadside views are from a moderate distance. Continue 2.2 miles past Little Falls (described earlier). Look upstream; the falls is visible at the bottom of the canyon floor 100 to 150 feet below.

7 SOUTH FORK BOISE RIVER

Travel through rangeland, prairie, and wooded tracts into South Fork Canyon. The 300- to 400-foot-deep gorge is seldom visited. Leave I-84 at Mountain Home and drive 20 miles north on U.S. 20 to Road #134, signed Anderson Ranch Dam/Prairie. Proceed 5 miles to the dam. After crossing the dam, turn left (west) on Road #113 and drive 2 miles to the hamlet of Prairie. At the junction, turn left (west). The following falls are located within Mountain Home Ranger District, Boise National Forest.

SMITH CREEK FALLS (U) ★★★

MAGNITUDE: 76
WATERSHED: lg

ELEVATION: 3700 feet
USGS MAP: Long Gulch (1964 nl)

The waters of this 80- to 120-foot plummet roar into an impressive grotto carved by Smith Creek. This entry is appropriate for nimble adults only. Drive westward from Prairie for 2.4 miles to the junction with Road #189. Bear left onto #189 and proceed 3.7 miles toward South Fork Canyon. About 0.1 mile before entering the canyon you will encounter a cattle guard in the road. About 200 feet or so past this guard, there is a wide spot in the road. Park here. Cross a 5- to 10-foot-wide irrigation canal, in which the water may be from knee to waist deep and walk carefully through the sagebrush toward Smith Creek. In about 100 feet you will come to the canyon rim and its cliffs. Be careful!

Smith Creek Falls

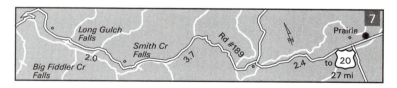

BIG FIDDLER CREEK FALLS ★★

MAGNITUDE: 35 (l)
WATERSHED: vsm

ELEVATION: 4000 feet
USGS MAP: Long Gulch (1964 ns)

This 252-foot drop is the highest officially measured waterfall in Idaho. Unfortunately, the creek is seasonal and thus usually dry during summer. From the cattle guard on Road #189 (described earlier), drive 2 miles into South Fork Canyon and look across the canyon to the falls. In summer look for evidence of water flow along the canyon's upper tier of cliffs. Immediately upstream, on seasonal Big Fiddler Creek, another small cataract may be seen pouring 60 to 80 feet from the lower canyon tier into the South Fork Boise River.

LONG GULCH FALLS (U) ★★

MAGNITUDE: 24 (l)   ELEVATION: 3600 feet
WATERSHED: med   USGS MAP: Long Gulch (1964 ns)

Long Gulch plunges 100 to 125 feet into the South Fork Boise River. The creek is seasonal, but often maintains some flow during summer. From the same location described in the Big Fiddler Creek Falls entry (see above), look toward the near side of the canyon to see this entry.

8. SAWTOOTHS WEST

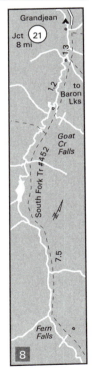

The rugged Sawtooth Mountains are a tribute to the strength of glacial sculpturing during the Ice Age. The following four sections all describe waterfalls within the Sawtooth Wilderness portion of Sawtooth National Recreation Area. Reach the following pair of cataracts on the western flank of the mountains by turning off S.R. 21 at the marked access road to Grandjean Camp. Drive 8 miles to the trailheads at the end of the gravel road.

GOAT CREEK FALLS (U) ★★

MAGNITUDE: 39   ELEVATION: 5260 feet
WATERSHED: med   USGS MAP: Edaho Mtn
                          (1972 ns)

Goat Creek tumbles a total of 50 feet over a series of cascades. Start on South Fork Trail #452, which parallels the South Fork Payette River. Reach the junction of Baron Creek Trail #101 in 1.3 miles; continue on Trail #452 to Goat Creek a moderate 1.2 miles farther. Scramble a short distance upstream to a vantage of this descent.

FERN FALLS ★★

MAGNITUDE: 44   ELEVATION: 6380 feet
WATERSHED: lg   USGS MAP: Warbonnet Peak (1972)

South Fork Payette River tumbles twice in an attractive 30-foot display. Continue 7.5 miles past Goat Creek Falls (described earlier) on South Fork Trail #452. From the falls, it is 10 miles back to the trailhead.

9 BARON CREEK

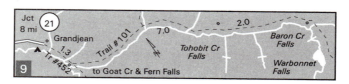

TOHOBIT CREEK FALLS (U) ★★

MAGNITUDE: 42   ELEVATION: 6960 feet
WATERSHED: vsm   USGS MAP: Warbonnet Peak (1972 ns)

This is the first of several ribbon falls dropping from tributaries into the glacial valley currently occupied by Baron Creek. Drive to the trailheads near Grandjean Camp as described in the Sawtooths West section. Hike 1.2 miles along South Fork Trail #452 to Baron Creek Trail #101. Turn left and follow this trail 7 miles to a cross-canyon trailside view.

WARBONNET FALLS (U) ★★

MAGNITUDE: 42   ELEVATION: 7120 feet
WATERSHED: vsm   USGS MAP: Warbonnet Peak (1972 ns)

An unnamed stream hurtles from the lip of a hanging valley. Continue 1 mile past Tohobit Creek Falls (described earlier) along Baron Creek Trail #101. Look across the canyon to see the cataract.

BARON CREEK FALLS ★★★

MAGNITUDE: 56   ELEVATION: 7500 feet
WATERSHED: sm   USGS MAP: Warbonnet Peak (1972)

Baron Creek pours 50 feet downward as the stream breaks through a glacial moraine of rock debris. Hike along Baron Creek Trail #101 for 1 mile past the view of Warbonnet Falls (described earlier) to this waterfall, located 10.2 miles from the trailhead. The route continues up to Baron Lakes.

10 MIDDLE FORK SALMON RIVER

Aptly nicknamed "The River of No Return," the Salmon River and its major tributaries are famous whitewater rafting destinations. Hundreds of river miles flow through the Frank Church Wilderness Area, which is so large it intersects with five national forests. The following descent is fortuitously accessible to all, because it happens to be located next to a major "put-in" point along the Middle Fork.

DAGGER FALLS ★★

MAGNITUDE: 26 (h)
ELEVATION: 5680 feet
WATERSHED: lg
USGS MAP: Big Soldier Mtn (1990)

The rafting put-in point for the Middle Fork Salmon River is just below this falls. Don't be deceived by the 10- to 15-foot drop that may look like a negotiable obstacle; it is rated for experts only. When visiting this falls, the author was told that two experienced rivermen had perished within the past week attempting to run the falls.

Depart S.R. 21 at the sign for Bruce Meadows/Boundary Creek. Pass the meadows after 9.4 miles, where there is a junction. Turn right for Forest Road #568/Dagger Falls Camp. After another 9.5 miles, turn right at the T, and continue 0.7 mile along Forest Road #553 to the campground and the falls. Walk a short distance to the observation deck. If you see salmon jumping, consider how many hundreds of miles they have traveled from the Pacific Ocean to make it this far to spawn.

Dagger Falls

11 STANLEY LAKE CREEK

To reach the following two waterfalls, enter the Sawtooths from the north by driving 5 miles northwest of Stanley along S.R. 21. Turn left at Stanley Lake Road #455 and drive 3.5 miles to Inlet Camp. The trailhead for Stanley Lake Creek Trail #640 is near Area B of the campground.

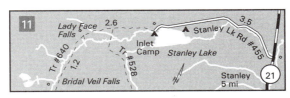

LADY FACE FALLS ★★

MAGNITUDE: 57   ELEVATION: 6680 feet
WATERSHED: med   USGS MAP: Stanley Lake (1972)

Stanley Lake Creek breaks through a moraine and plunges 50 to 75 feet into a basin. Follow Stanley Lake Trail #640 for 2.6 miles. The first 2 miles are easy hiking, then the trail steepens. After another 0.5 mile look for a sign marking the falls (for some reason it faces hikers walking in the opposite direction),

Lady Face Falls

where a spur path leads 0.1 mile farther to a partially obscured gorge-rim view of the cataract. If you cross the creek, you've gone too far.

BRIDAL VEIL FALLS ★★

MAGNITUDE: 62   ELEVATION: 7320 feet
WATERSHED: sm   USGS MAP: Stanley Lake (1972)

The outlet from Hanson Lakes cascades steeply 120 to 160 feet in two distinct drops. Hike 1.2 miles past Lady Face Falls (described earlier) along Stanley Lake Trail #640 to a sign announcing the waterfall. Nearby is an open area offering a distant view up the side of the valley.

---

12 SAWTOOTHS EAST

Grizzly bears are among the inhabitants of the Sawtooth Mountains. Don't let this fact intimidate you and prevent you from visiting this magnificent area. However, do remain alert and follow the guidelines posted at the campground and various trailheads.

GOAT FALLS ★★★★★

MAGNITUDE: 70
ELEVATION: 8100 feet
WATERSHED: sm
USGS MAP: Stanley Lake (1972)

This is the best waterfall of the Sawtooths, as Goat Creek veils 250 to 300 feet down the mountainside. Drive 2.3 miles west of Stanley on S.R. 21 to Iron Creek Road #619. Drive 4 miles to the end of the gravel road and the beginning of Alpine Lake/Sawtooth Lake Trail #640. Hike 1 mile, then turn left (east) at the junction with Alpine Trail #528. Continue 2.5 miles to full views of the falls. Distant views of this cataract are also possible a couple of miles south of Stanley along S.R. 21.

Opposite: Goat Falls (photo by Bill Rember)

FOUNTAIN CREEK FALLS ★★

MAGNITUDE: 15 (l)   ELEVATION: 3200 feet
WATERSHED: sm   USGS MAP: Butts Creek Point (1962 ns)

Fountain Creek descends from a canyon wall in a stairstep display totaling 35 to 50 feet. It is located within North Fork Ranger District, Salmon National Forest. Turn west off U.S. 93 at North Fork and follow Salmon River Road westward. Reach Shoup in 18 miles and Cache Bar Camp after another 22.2 miles. Look for the falls 0.5 mile past the campground. The road ends 4 miles beyond the falls.

THE SNAKE RIVER PLAIN, IDAHO

Southern Idaho presents the traveler interested in waterfalls with a dilemma. There is no best time of the year to visit its cataracts. The prime viewing time for individual falls varies more dramatically here than in any other region of the Pacific Northwest.

The least temperamental are streams originating from springs, since they flow continuously. Jump Creek and the Thousand Springs area offer examples. Some flows fluctuate with the demand for hydroelectric power. The falls near Hagerman and Clear Lakes are altered by the amount of water being diverted to the nearby power stations. The waterfalls along the Snake River near Twin Falls actually stop flowing most summers because Milner Dam, located farther upstream, impounds water for irrigation of agricultural lands.

Some hydro projects along the Snake have destroyed waterfalls. American Falls Dam and Swan Falls Dam have replaced the original descents, and the waters of C. J. Strike Reservoir cover *Crane Falls*. The highland waterfalls northeast of Rexburg flow perennially but are easily accessible only during summer. Cross-country skis or snowmobiles are required to reach them from November to May.

The Snake River Plain has sixty-nine recognized falls, of which twenty-eight are described here. The majority of these were created by stream courses eroding across heterogeneous bedrock at varying rates. The falls along the Snake River formed because bedrock such as rhyolite resists stream erosion

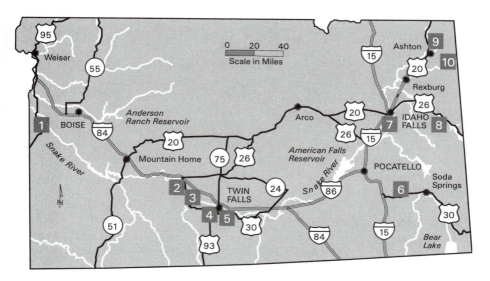

more effectively than basalt, its igneous counterpart. Most of the falls in the eastern highland areas were shaped in the same way.

Waterfalls descend from the canyon rims of the Snake River for two reasons. Runoff from irrigation finds its way into channels, which in some locales empty over solidified lava flows into the Snake. Along other reaches of the river, waterfalls descend from springs issuing forth from the canyon walls. Details of this latter phenomenon are provided later in the chapter.

1 JUMP CREEK CANYON

This small canyon is one of Idaho's hidden gems. Follow U.S. 95 to Poison Creek Road, located 2.5 miles south of the junction of 95 with S.R. 55. In 3.5 miles, where the paved road takes a sharp right, turn left (south) on an unnamed gravel road. Follow it for 0.5 mile, then turn right (west) onto a dirt road. Do not get discouraged if you see a "No Trespassing" sign. This

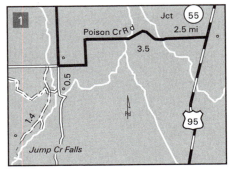

route is the correct public access to the canyon. In 0.4 mile, the road forks. The low road leads to a private homestead and the high road to the right ends at the mouth of the canyon in 1 additional mile. The land is administered by the Bureau of Land Management.

JUMP CREEK FALLS ★★★★

MAGNITUDE: 55   ELEVATION: 2640 feet
WATERSHED: lg   USGS MAP: Jump Creek Canyon (1989)

Water splashes 40 to 60 feet from Jump Creek into a small canyon. Interesting rock formations frame the cataract. Follow the pathway that begins at the end of the road into the canyon. Proceed along the canyon floor, hopping from stone to stone across the creek and climbing over, around, and under large boulders that have fallen into the gorge. The destination is at the end of the trail in 0.2 mile.

2 HAGERMAN

There are dams and power plants next to each of the falls along this section of the Snake River, which means that their scenic quality varies depending

Opposite: Jump Creek Falls

on the amount of water allowed to flow over their natural courses, which in turn is determined by the region's electrical demand. The area is accessible via U.S. 30, which is also called Thousand Springs Scenic Route.

LOWER SALMON FALLS ★★

MAGNITUDE: 50
ELEVATION: 2790 feet
WATERSHED: lg
USGS MAP: Hagerman (1992)

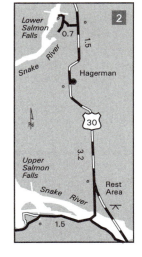

A portion of the Snake River tumbles 10 to 15 feet downward. Turn off U.S. 30 at the marked entrance to Lower Salmon Power Plant, located 6.8 miles south of I-84 at the Gooding–Hagerman Exit 141 and 1.5 miles north of downtown Hagerman. Drive 0.7 mile to the best vantage. Look for the descent along the far side of the river below the power plant substation.

UPPER SALMON FALLS ★★★

MAGNITUDE: 70   ELEVATION: 2880 feet
WATERSHED: lg   USGS MAP: Hagerman (1992)

The water in this entry diverges into four main blocks, each descending 15 to 25 feet along the Snake River. Drive 3.2 miles south of Hagerman on U.S. 30 and turn right (west) at the Upper Salmon Falls access sign. If you pass the rest area, you have missed the turnoff. Follow this secondary road 1.5 miles to the power plant. There is an obscured vista of the falls from the gravel road. For closer views, park at the east end of the road and cross an unmarked catwalk to an island halfway across the Snake, then proceed down the cement walkway to the falls. *Warning:* Periodically, the walkway area is flooded by Idaho Power, and the company is not liable if unwary visitors become trapped on the island.

Others: It has been reported that *Indian Bathtub Falls* (u) ★ USGS Hot Springs (1992 nl) is periodically dry. Even when flowing, it's only a 7- to 12-foot trickle. Although the waterfall is unimpressive, the thermal springs below it justify a visit. Drive along S.R. 51 to Bruneau, then continue southeast for 7.2 miles along Hot Springs Road. Turn right on the road marked Indian Bathtub, then left in 0.7 mile on the road marked Sugar Creek. After another 2.9 miles, turn left (east) on a dirt road that leads 0.9 mile to the parking area adjacent to the hot springs. This site is on land administered by the

Bureau of Land Management. Go online to *The Computer Companion* (described in the Introduction) to see a map for this entry.

South of Glenns Ferry is Deadman Canyon, a gaping gorge slowly carved by the erosive powers of seasonal Deadman Creek. Within it is the 125- to 175-foot escarpment for *Deadman Falls* ★ USGS Glenns Ferry (1992). It would be a great display if only water were flowing, but a small Bureau of Land Management dam prevents the creek from plunging into the canyon the majority of the year. Perhaps a good show can be seen after an intense storm. Exit I-84 at Glenns Ferry. Drive 1.7 miles west of town along Frontage Road and turn left (south) onto Sailor Creek Road. Cross the bridge over the Snake River and continue 5.8 miles to the canyon rim. Go online to *The Computer Companion* to see a map for this entry.

3 SNAKE PLAINS AQUIFER

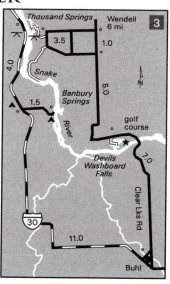

The Snake River Plain northeast of Hagerman harbors one of the world's greatest groundwater resources. The mountain ranges in the southeastern part of central Idaho receive large amounts of precipitation, particularly during the winter. But the streams flowing south from these mountains fail to reach the Snake River because they sink into lava formations on the plain. Water collects in the pores of the subsurface bedrock, and since these rock layers gently dip southwestward, gravity pushes the groundwater toward Hagerman.

The course of the Snake River has been eroded to such an extent that it intersects with the aquifer. As a result, numerous springs gush from the river canyon's north wall. Most of these springs are high above the floor of the canyon, so are seen as waterfalls descending into the river.

FALLS OF THOUSAND SPRINGS (U) ★★★

MAGNITUDE: 73   ELEVATION: 3000 feet
WATERSHED: lg (s)   USGS MAP: Thousand Springs (1992 ns)

There are eight major falls and many minor falls descending 40 to 100 feet from springs along the north wall on this 1-mile stretch of the Snake River Canyon located between 15 and 16 miles northwest of Buhl. The springs increase the river's volume by up to tenfold along this reach of the river.

All the horsetail forms of these cataracts can be seen from across the Snake River along U.S. 30/Thousand Springs Scenic Route. For a close-up view of the easternmost descent, turn off Clear Lakes Road (described later) at the sign to Thousand Springs Picnic Area.

Others: Some of the 30- to 80-foot drop of *Falls of Banbury Springs* (u) ★ USGS Thousand Springs (1992 ns) can be seen from across the river, but most of it is obscured by the surrounding vegetation. Turn off U.S. 30 and drive to the marked access road for Banbury Hot Springs Resort, located 4 miles south of Thousand Springs. The resort is 1.5 miles off the main highway.

Devils Washboard Falls ★ USGS Thousand Springs (1992) is a pretty 15- to 30-foot cascade when the adjacent powerhouse isn't diverting most of the water flow from spring-fed Clear Lakes. Nearby is the Clear Lakes Trout Company, reputed to be the largest trout farm in the world. Drive along Clear Lakes Road to the Buhl Country Club, located 7 miles north of Buhl and 12 miles south of Wendell. Find the falls by walking a short distance westward from the country club parking area.

4 SNAKE RIVER CANYON WEST

The Snake River has carved sharply through basaltic rock layers to create a narrow, 400- to 500-foot canyon near Twin Falls. The area has several waterfalls, many of which are seasonal.

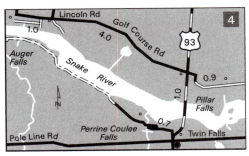

PILLAR FALLS ★★★

MAGNITUDE: 53   ELEVATION: 3200 feet
WATERSHED: lg (d)   USGS MAP: Twin Falls (1992)

Towers of 30- to 70-foot rhyolitic rock rise between 10- to 20-foot cascades along the Snake River. From the canyon rim, there is also a distant but stunning view of Shoshone Falls (see entry below). You may wonder about the huge sand pile located along the south rim halfway between the two falls. It was the launch site for Evel Knievel's ill-fated attempt to jump the canyon on a "rocket-cycle" during the early 1970s.

From the city of Twin Falls, drive north along U.S. 93 for 1 mile to Golf Course Road and turn east. Continue along this dusty route for 0.9 mile, then stop. Walk through the old dumping grounds for about 0.3 mile to the abrupt, unguarded canyon rim. Pillar Falls is directly below with Shoshone Falls farther upstream.

PERRINE COULEE FALLS ★★★★

MAGNITUDE: 90 (h)   ELEVATION: 3500 feet
WATERSHED: med   USGS MAP: Twin Falls (1992)

Agricultural activities allow this otherwise seasonal waterfall to flow year-round. In fact, its discharge actually increases during the dry summer. This occurs because the coulee collects the water that overflows from the irrigated uplands. A natural pathway goes behind the 197-foot plunge.

Drive north from the city of Twin Falls on U.S. 93; just beyond Pole Line Road, turn west onto Canyon Springs Road. Park at the unsigned turnout in 0.7 mile. The view is inspiring.

Others: Water churns in strange convolutions for 25 to 50 feet over rocky obstructions along the Snake River's *Auger Falls* ★ USGS Jerome (1992). Public views from the north rim are rapidly dwindling as rangeland is converted into housing developments. Turn left (west) off U.S. 93 at Golf Course Road (described earlier) and proceed 5 miles to the subdivision area. With luck, there will still be an undeveloped lot offering a vista. Be careful near the rim. For closer views, try driving about 5 miles west of U.S. 93 along Canyon Springs Road (described earlier).

Perrine Coulee Falls

5 SNAKE RIVER CANYON EAST

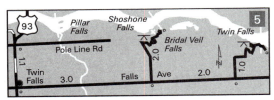

TWIN FALLS ★★★★

MAGNITUDE: 96 (h)   ELEVATION: 3400 feet
WATERSHED: lg (d)   USGS MAP: Kimberly (1992)

Only one of this pair of cataracts still flows. The larger portion has been dammed. A torrent of water hurtles down 125 feet during early spring, but is reduced to a trickle in summer months as Milner Dam farther upstream draws off a large part of the Snake River for irrigation during the mid-year growing season.

From the city of Twin Falls follow Falls Avenue 5 miles east, passing the junction to Shoshone Falls (described later). Turn left (north) at the marked road; after 1 mile it meets with a picnic area adjacent to the falls.

BRIDAL VEIL FALLS ★★

MAGNITUDE: 30   ELEVATION: 3200 feet
WATERSHED: sm   USGS MAP: Twin Falls (1992 ns)

Water tumbles 25 to 40 feet from spring-fed Dierkes Lake. The stream nearly sprays onto the road before reaching a culvert that directs the water into a pond below. Backtrack from Twin Falls (described earlier) for 3 miles along Falls Avenue to the marked turn for Shoshone Falls Park. This and the following entry are 2 miles from the junction.

SHOSHONE FALLS ★★★★★

MAGNITUDE: 120   ELEVATION: 3200 feet
WATERSHED: lg (d)   USGS MAP: Twin Falls (1992)

This is the most famous waterfall in Idaho. It measures over 1000 feet across and plunges 212 feet. The awesome display is best viewed during spring-time. Later in the year, when the water is diverted upstream for agricultural

Shoshone Falls in summer

uses, the river dries up and only large ledges of rhyolite can be seen. To reach the falls, located in Shoshone Falls Park, follow the directions in the previous entry.

In pioneer days a Shoshoni Indian named Quish-in-demi told the following tale to J. S. Harrington. The story is recorded in *Idaho: A Guide in Words and Pictures,* published in 1937 as part of the Federal Writers' Project:

> In the gloomy gorge above the falls there was, long ago, the trysting place of a deep-chested Shoshoni [warrior] and the slender wild girl whom he loved. Their last meeting was here on a pile of rocks which overlooked the plunging waters. He went away to scalp with deft incisions and then to lift the shaggy mane of white men with a triumphant shout; and she came daily to stand by the thundering avalanche and remember him. That he would return unharmed she did not, with the ageless resourcefulness of women, ever allow herself to doubt. But time passed, and the moons that came and ripened were many, and she still came nightly to stand on the brink and watch the changeless journeying of the water. And it was here that she stood one black night above the roar of the flood when a warrior stepped out of shadow and whispered to her and then disappeared. As quiet as the flat stone under her feet, she stood for a long while, looking down into the vault where the waters boiled up like seething white hills to fill the sky with dazzling curtains and roll away in convulsed tides. For an hour she gazed down there 200 feet to a mad pouring of motion and sound into

a black graveyard of the dead. And then, slowly, she lifted her arms above her, listed her head to the fullest curve of her throat, and stood tiptoe for a moment, poised and beautiful, and then dived in a long swift arc against the falling white background... And the river at this point and since that hour has never been the same.

Others: It's not particularly scenic but it *is* unusual. *Big Drops* ★ USGS Shoshone (1992) was artificially created to help channel water through the Milner-Gooding Canal. Drive 1.6 miles north of the junction of U.S. 93/26 in Shoshone along S.R. 75. Turn right (east) onto East Huyser Drive and go 0.6 mile. Turn left and continue 0.1 mile down a dirt road to the canal. When the author visited one hot day, people were using the falls as a water slide! Go online to *The Computer Companion* (described in the Introduction) to see a map for this entry.

6 LAVA HOT SPRINGS

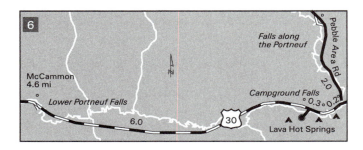

LOWER PORTNEUF FALLS (U) ★★

MAGNITUDE: 37   ELEVATION: 4840 feet
WATERSHED: lg   USGS MAP: McCammon (1968 nl)

Portneuf River diverges into a pair of 15- to 25-foot cataracts. One appears in the form of a plunge, the other a cascade. From the town of Lava Hot Springs drive 6 miles west along U.S. 30. Park at an old jeep trail and walk down to the stream and its modest display.

CAMPGROUND FALLS (U) ★★

MAGNITUDE: 37   ELEVATION: 5000 feet
WATERSHED: lg   USGS MAP: Lava Hot Springs (1968 ns)

This 10- to 15-foot drop along Portneuf River is located within a private campground, hence its unofficial name. Drive 0.3 mile past the east end of Lava Hot Springs along U.S. 30.

Waterfall collectors may also wish to explore several small cataracts comprising the *Falls Along the Portneuf* (u) ★ USGS Haystack Mtn (1968 nl). Drive 0.2 mile past Campground Falls and turn off U.S. 30 onto Pebble Area Road. Proceed 2 miles north to an unsigned loop road. Bushwhack a short distance to the stream and its northernmost descent. The ground tends to be marshy in this area, so appropriate footwear is recommended on your cross-country trek.

7 CITY OF IDAHO FALLS

A low, turbulent descent on the Snake River shares its name with this community of 40,000. Stop and enjoy the falls from the adjacent city park.

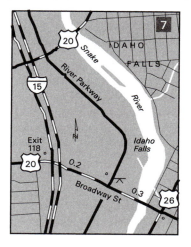

IDAHO FALLS OF THE SNAKE RIVER ★★★

MAGNITUDE: 71   ELEVATION: 4670 feet
WATERSHED: lg (d)   USGS MAP: Idaho Falls South (1979 ns)

This 15- to 25-foot falls is over 1200 feet wide and has the distinction of being man-made. In pioneer days there were only rapids at this location. A concrete dam was first built on the river in 1909 to channel some of the water to the Eagle Rock power plant for generating electricity. By the 1970s, the dam had deteriorated severely. In order to assure reliable streamflow for newer turbines, the old dam was replaced in 1981. The artificial falls was constructed as a part of the project.

Turn off I-15 at Broadway Street (Exit 118) and drive toward the city center. Immediately before the bridge crossing the Snake, turn left (north) on River Parkway and find an available parking spot.

8 SWAN VALLEY

FALL CREEK FALLS ★★★★

MAGNITUDE: 78
WATERSHED: lg

ELEVATION: 5280 feet
USGS MAP: Conant Valley (1966)

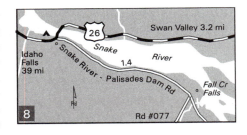

Fall Creek plunges 60 feet over travertine deposits into the Snake River. On either side of the central falls the water plumes to form a natural fountain that all waterfall collectors should include on their "must-see" list. Drive 39 miles east of Idaho Falls or 3.2 miles west of Swan Valley along U.S. 26 to Snake River–Palisades Dam Road. Turn south and follow this gravel route 1.4 miles; park where the road widens. The best views of this cataract are a short walk farther along the roadway.

9 HENRYS FORK

Henrys Fork is a wild and scenic river in all but official federal designation. As it winds through the Ashton Ranger District of Targhee National Forest, the following waterfalls roar throughout its gorge.

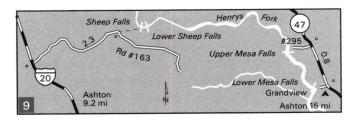

LOWER MESA FALLS ★★★

MAGNITUDE: 78
WATERSHED: lg

ELEVATION: 5420 feet
USGS MAP: Snake River Butte (1965)

The rushing waters of Henrys Fork tumble 65 chaotic feet in this waterfall some 400 feet below an overlook. Drive 15 miles northeast of Ashton on Mesa Falls Scenic Byway (S.R. 47) to the signed turnout, appropriately named Grandview.

Lower Mesa Falls

Upper Mesa Falls ★★★★

MAGNITUDE: 95   ELEVATION: 5600 feet
WATERSHED: lg   USGS MAP: Snake River Butte (1965)

Henrys Fork plummets 114 feet from a sheer wall of rhyolitic bedrock. It is also known as Big Falls. In 1986, Targhee National Forest acquired the property and more recently Big Falls Inn has been restored, housing an interpretive center and gift shop.

About 0.8 mile past Grandview (described earlier) depart S.R. 47 by turning left (west) onto Upper Mesa Falls Road #295. Drive to the road's end in less than 1 mile. A view at the brink of the falls is just a short walk away along a new pathway and boardwalk. Be careful at the canyon rim!

Upper Mesa Falls

Sheep Falls ★★★

MAGNITUDE: 50   ELEVATION: 5820 feet
WATERSHED: lg   USGS MAP: Lookout Butte (1965)

Henrys Fork tumbles 15 to 25 feet within Ashton Ranger District, Targhee National Forest. Drive 9.2 miles north of Ashton along U.S. 20 to signed Sheep Falls Road #163. Turn right (east) and follow the route 2.3 miles to the trailhead. Sheep Falls Trail #760, built in 1986 by Challenger Group YSC, goes down to the river and reaches the falls in 1 mile.

Lower Sheep Falls (u) ★★

MAGNITUDE: 47   ELEVATION: 5800 feet
WATERSHED: lg   USGS MAP: Lookout Butte (1965 ns)

Water drops 15 to 25 feet along Henrys Fork within Ashton Ranger District, Targhee National Forest. Walk fewer than 100 yards downstream from Sheep Falls (described earlier).

10 YELLOWSTONE

Although two of the following falls are actually in Wyoming, they have been included here because they can be most easily reached from just across the border in Idaho. The Falls River, which flows out of the southwestern corner of Yellowstone National Park, is aptly named. A total of 27 cataracts are known to occur in its drainage basin. Four of these are described here.

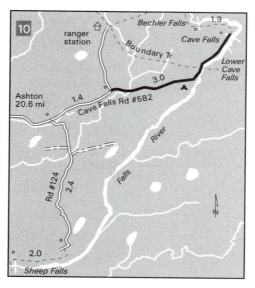

SHEEP FALLS ★★★

MAGNITUDE: 51
WATERSHED: lg

ELEVATION: 5890 feet
USGS MAP: Sheep Falls (1989)

The name of this 35-foot waterfall comes from the sheep drives that once occurred in the vicinity. It is situated within Ashton Ranger District, Targhee National Forest. Drive 6 miles east from Ashton on S.R. 47 to the Cave Falls Road #582. Bear right, follow Road #582 for 14.6 miles, then turn right (south) at Wyoming Creek Road #124. Drive down this gravel road for 2.4 miles to a junction with an unsigned jeep trail on the left. (Note: The gravel road ends 0.3 mile farther on.) Hike down the jeep trail for 2 miles to the top of the falls. Nimble adults can follow a faint path that leads to the best views.

CAVE FALLS ★★★★

MAGNITUDE: 73
WATERSHED: lg

ELEVATION: 6260 feet
USGS MAP: Cave Falls (1989)

This picturesque block waterfall descends 35 feet along the Falls River within Yellowstone National Park. It is named after a large recess beneath the stream's west bank. Follow the directions to Sheep Falls (described earlier), but stay on Cave Falls Road #582 to its end at the falls, 25 miles from Ashton.

LOWER CAVE FALLS (U) ★★

MAGNITUDE: 40   ELEVATION: 6220 feet
WATERSHED: lg   USGS MAP: Cave Falls (1989 nl)

Falls River descends 5 to 10 feet within Yellowstone National Park. Look for this cataract about 0.1 mile downstream from Cave Falls (described earlier).

BECHLER FALLS ★★

MAGNITUDE: 31   ELEVATION: 6340 feet
WATERSHED: lg   USGS MAP: Bechler Falls (1989)

Water tumbles 15 to 25 feet along a wide reach of the Bechler River in Yellowstone National Park. Follow the Bechler River Trail 1.3 miles beyond Cave Falls (described earlier) to this cataract.

SELECTED READINGS

Adams, Kevin. *North Carolina Waterfalls: Where to Find Them, How to Photograph Them.* Winston-Salem, North Carolina: John F. Blair, 1994.

———. *Waterfalls of Virginia and West Virginia.* Birmingham, Alabama: Menasha Ridge Press, 2002.

Bloom, Barbara L. and Garry W. Cohen. *Romance of Waterfalls.* Portland, Oregon: Outdoor Romance Publishing, 1998.

Blouin, Nicole, Steve Bordonaro, and Marylou Wier Bordonaro. *Waterfalls of the Blue Ridge: A Guide to the Blue Ridge Parkway and Great Smoky Mountains National Park,* 2nd ed. Birmingham, Alabama: Menasha Ridge Press, 1996.

Bolnick, Bruce, and Doreen Bolnick. *Waterfalls of the White Mountains: 30 Hikes to 100 Waterfalls,* 2nd ed. Woodstock, Vermont: Countryman Press, 2003.

Boyd, Brian A. *Waterfalls of the Southern Appalachians,* 3rd ed. Clayton, Georgia: Fern Creek Press, 1997.

Brooks, Benjamin and Tim Cook. *The Waterfalls of South Carolina,* 2nd ed. Spartanburg, South Carolina: Palmetto Conservation Foundation, 2001.

Brown, Ann Marie. *California Waterfalls,* 2nd ed. Emeryville, California: Avalon Travel Publishing, 2000.

Conly, Marc. *Waterfalls of Colorado.* Boulder, Colorado: Pruett Publishing, 1993.

Doeffinger, Derek. *Waterfalls and Gorges of the Finger Lakes.* Ithaca, New York: McBooks Press, 1997.

Doeffinger, Derek and Keith Boas. *Waterfalls of the Adirondacks and Catskills.* Ithaca, New York: McBooks Press, 2000.

Dow, Charles Mason. *Anthology and Bibliography of Niagara Falls.* Albany, New York: State of New York, 1921.

Fielder, John. *Colorado Waterfalls.* Englewood, Colorado: Westcliffe Publishers, 1996.

Freeman, Rich, Sue Freeeman, and Sue J. Freeman. *200 Waterfalls in Central and Western New York: A Finders Guide.* Fishers, New York: Footprint Press, 2002.

Harris, Mark and George Fisher. *Waterfalls of Ontario.* Toronto, Ontario: Firefly Books, 2003.

Hubbs, Hal, Charles Maynard, and David Morris. *Waterfalls & Cascades of the Great Smoky Mountains.* Seymour, Tennessee: Panther Press, 1992.

Lawton, Jerry and Mikal Lawton. *Waterfalls: The Niagara Escarpment.* Erin, Ontario: Boston Mills Press, 2000.

Lisi, Patrick. *Wisconsin Waterfalls: A Touring Guide.* Madison, Wisconsin: Prairie Oak Press, 1998.

Maynard, Charles. *Waterfalls of Grand Teton National Park*. Seymour, Tennessee: Panther Press, 1996.

————. *Waterfalls of Yellowstone National Park*. Seymour, Tennessee: Panther Press, 1996.

Mitchell, Sam. *Pura Vida: Waterfalls and Hot Springs of Costa Rica,* 2nd ed. Birmingham, Alabama: Menasha Ridge Press, 1995.

Morrision, Mark. *Waterfall Walks and Drives in Georgia, Alabama, and Tennessee*. Douglasville, Georgia: H.F. Publishing, 1995.

————. *Waterfall Walks and Drives in the Western Carolinas*. Douglasville, Georgia: H. F. Publishing, 1994.

Osborne, Michael. *Granite Water and Light: Waterfalls of Yosemite Valley*. El Portal, California: Yosemite Natural History Association, 1989.

Parsons, Greg and Kate B. Watson. *New England Waterfalls: A Guide to more than 200 Cascades and Waterfalls*. Woodstock, Vermont: Countryman Press, 2003

Penrose, Laurie, Bill Penrose, and Ruth Penrose. *A Guide to 199 Michigan Waterfalls,* 2nd ed. Davison, Michigan: Friede Publications, 2000.

Plumb, Gregory A. "A Scale for Comparing the Visual Magnitude of Waterfalls." *Earth-Science Reviews* 34 (1993): 261–270.

————. *Waterfalls of Tennessee*. Johnson City, Tennessee: Overmountain Press, 1996.

————. *The Computer Companion to Waterfall Lover's Guide to the Pacific Northwest*. Website at *www.mymaps.com/nwfalls/toc.htm*.

Rubinstein, Paul, Lee H. Whittlesey, and Mike Stevens. *The Guide to Yellowstone Waterfalls and Their Discovery*. Englewood, Colorado: Westcliffe Publishers, 2000.

Shaffer, Chris. *The Definitive Guide to the Waterfalls of Southern and Central California*. Westlake Village California: Shafdog Publications, 2003.

Swan, Bryan. *Waterfalls of the Pacific Northwest*. Website at *www.waterfallsnorthwest.com*.

Wunder, Dick. *100 Utah Waterfalls*. Thompson Springs, Utah: Arch Hunter Books, 1999.

APPENDIX

This appendix lists 777 additional waterfalls known to occur within the Pacific Northwest. It is organized into the same fourteen geographic regions used in this guidebook. The name of each waterfall is accompanied by the name of the USGS topographic map that illustrates where it is located.

The North Cascades, Washington

Agnes Falls, Mount Lyall (1987 ns)
Anderson Falls (u), Lawrence (1994 nl)
Angeline Falls (u), Big Snow Mtn (1965 nl)
Arbuthnet Lake Falls, Shuksan Arm (1989 nl)
Asbestos Falls, Helena Ridge (1989)
Bear Creek Falls, Monte Cristo (1982 ns)
Boulder Creek Falls (u), Welker Peak (1989 nl)
Boulder Falls, Meadow Mtn (1989)
Burnboot Creek Falls (u), Snoqualmie Pass (1989 nl)
Calligan Creek Falls (u), Mount Si (1989 nl)
Cherry Creek Falls, Monroe (1993 ns)
Colchuck Falls (u), Enchantment Lakes (1989 nl)
Cole Creek Falls (u), Easton (1989 nl)
Copper Creek Falls (u), Holden (1988 nl)
Crack-in-the-Ground Falls (u), Scenic (1982 ns)
Crown Point Falls, Suiattle Pass (1988)
Deer Falls, Blanca Lake (1982 ns)
Dingford Creek Falls, Snoqualmie Lake (1982 ns)
East Fork Falls (u), Lester (1989 nl)
East Picket Falls (u), Mount Blum (1989 nl)
Elk Falls (u), Mount Stickney (1989 nl)
Elliott Creek Falls (u), Sloan Peak (1982 nl)
Eureka Creek Falls (u), McLeod Mtn (1991 ns)
Falls Creek Falls (u), Enchantment Lakes (1989 nl)
Falls of Bessemer Mountain, Mount Si (1989 ns)
Fifteenmile Falls, Hobart (1993 ns)
Findley Creek Falls (u), Findley Lake (1989 nl)
Florence Falls, Snoqualmie Lake (1982 ns)
Fontal Falls, Monroe (1993 ns)
Friday Creek Falls (u), Lester (1989 nl)
Goat Creek Falls (u), Snoqualmie Pass (1989 nl)

Gold Creek Falls (u), Chikamin Peak (1989 nl)
Goodell Basin Falls (u), Mount Challenger (1989 nl)
Great Falls (u), Grotto (1982 ns)
Green Mountain Falls (u), Lake Philippa (1989 nl)
Greider Creek Falls (u), Mount Stickney (1989 nl)
Greider Lake Falls (u), Mount Stickney (1989 nl)
Hard Scrabble Falls, Deming (1994)
Hardscrabble Creek Falls (u), Enchantment Lakes (1989 nl)
Hart Lake Falls (u), Holden (1988 nl)
Hilt Creek Falls (u), Rockport (1982 nl)
Iceberg Lake Falls (u), Chikamin Peak (1989 nl)
Icy Peak Falls (u), Mount Shuksan (1989 nl)
Indian Valley Falls 1-2 (u), Mount Redoubt (1989 nl)
Jasper Pass Falls (u), Mount Blum (1989 nl)
Kelly Creek Falls (u), Verlot (1989 ns)
Lake Isabel Falls (u), Index (1989 nl)
Lemah Creek Falls (u), Chikamin Peak (1989 nl)
Lemah Valley Falls (u), Chikamin Peak (1989 nl)
Little Beaver Falls 1-5 (u), Mount Challenger (1989 nl)
Little Beaver Falls 6-9 (u), Mount Redoubt (1989 nl)
Lower Bald Eagle Falls (u), Mount Blum (1989 nl)
Lower Canyon Creek Falls (u), Granite Falls (1989 nl)
Lower Copper Creek Falls (u), Big Snow Mtn (1965 ns)
Lower Icy Peak Falls (u), Mount Blum (1989 nl)
Lower North Baker Falls (u), Mount Blum (1989 nl)
Lower Pass Valley Falls (u), Mount Blum (1989 nl)

Lower Wallace Falls (u), Gold Bar (1989 nl)

Luna Basin Falls 1-2 (u), Mount Challenger (1989 nl)

Lyman Lake Falls (u), Suiattle Pass (1988 nl)

Marsh Creek Falls (u), Lake Chaplain (1989 nl)

Mazama Falls, Shuksan Arm (1989)

McCauley Falls, Monroe (1993)

Middle Canyon Creek Falls (u), Granite Falls (1989 nl)

Middle Lemah Creek Falls (u), Chikamin Peak (1989 nl)

Middle Pass Valley Falls (u), Mount Blum (1989 nl)

Middle Picket Falls (u), Mount Blum (1989 nl)

Middle Wells Creek Falls 1-3 (u), Bearpaw Mtn (1989 nl)

Mineral Creek Falls (u), Mount Blum (1989 nl)

Mineral Mountain Falls (u), Mount Blum (1989 nl)

Monkey Case Falls (u), Scenic (1982 ns)

Mount Index Falls (u), Index (1989 nl)

Mount Thomson Falls (u), Chikamin Peak (1989 nl)

North Bald Eagle Falls (u), Mount Blum (1989 nl)

North Fork Cedar Falls (u), Findley Lake (1989 nl)

Olney Falls, Wallace Lake (1989)

Park Creek Falls (u), Shuksan Arm (1989 nl)

Perfection Lake Falls (u), Enchantment Lakes (1989 nl)

Perry Creek Falls (u), Bedal (1982 nl)

Phantom Pass Falls (u), Mount Blum (1989 nl)

Picket Basin Falls (u), Mount Challenger (1989 nl)

Pioneer Ridge Falls (u), Mount Blum (1989 nl)

Ptarmigan Basin Falls (u), Shuksan Arm (1989 nl)

Redoubt Valley Falls (u), Mount Redoubt (1989 nl)

Ruth Mountain Falls (u), Mount Shuksan (1989 nl)

Salmon Creek Falls (u), Mount Stickney (1989 nl)

San Juan Falls, Blanca Lake (1982 ns)

Scramble Creek Falls (u), Mount Blum (1989 nl)

Scramble Valley Falls (u), Mount Blum (1989 nl)

Seahpo Peak Falls (u), Mount Shuksan (1989 nl)

Seattle Creek Falls (u), Findley Lake (1989 nl)

Sholes Creek Falls (u), Mount Baker (1989 nl)

Shuksan Creek Falls (u), Shuksan Arm (1989 nl)

Shuksan Valley Falls 1-3 (u), Shuksan Arm (1989 nl)

Snow Creek Falls (u), Leavenworth (1989 nl)

South Baker Falls (u), Mount Blum (1989 nl)

Stehekin Falls (u), McGregor Mtn (1987 nl)

Sulphide Basin Falls (u5), Mount Shuksan (1989 nl)

Sunday Falls, Monte Cristo (1982 ns)

Swift Valley Falls 1-4 (u), Shuksan Arm (1989 nl)

Sygitowicz Creek Falls (u), Deming (1994 nl)

Teanaway Falls, Mount Stuart (1989 ns)

Tinling Creek Falls (u), Deming (1994 nl)

Twin Camp Falls (u), Lester (1989 nl)

Upper Bald Eagle Falls (u), Mount Blum (1989 nl)Upper Canyon Creek Falls (u), Granite Falls (1989 nl)

Upper Green Mountain Falls (u), Lake Philippa (1989 nl)

Upper Lemah Creek Falls (u), Chikamin Peak (1989 nl)

Upper North Baker Falls (u), Mount Blum (1989 nl)

Upper Pass Creek Falls (u), Mount Blum (1989 nl)

Upper Pass Valley Falls (u), Mount Blum (1989 nl)

Upper Rainbow Falls (u), Shuksan Arm (1989 nl)

Upper Snow Creek Falls (u), Enchantment Lakes (1989 nl)

Upper Twin Camp Falls (u), Lester (1989 nl)

Upper Wallace Falls (u), Wallace Lake (1989 nl)

Upper Whatcom Falls (u), Bellingham North (1994 ns)

Viola Creek Falls (u), Findley Lake (1989 nl)

West Picket Falls (u), Mount Blum (1989 nl)

Winchester Creek Falls (u), Mount Sefrit (1989 nl)

The Olympics and Vicinity, Washington

All-in Creek Falls (u), Hunger Mtn (1990 nl)

Bear Creek Falls, Ellis Mtn (1984 ns)

Bridge Creek Falls (u), Mount Carrie (1950 nl)

Cedar Creek Falls, Eden Valley (1993)

Dean Creek Falls (u), Dean Creek (1986 nl)

Deschutes Falls, Bald Hill (1990)

Elwha Valley Falls #1–3 (u), Mount Queets (1990 nl)

Fisk Falls, Pe Ell (1986)

Glacier Creek Falls (u), Mount Olympus (1990 nl)

Godkin Falls (u), Chimney Peak (1990 nl)

Goodman Falls (u), Toleak Point (1982 nl)

Graves Creek Falls (u), Mount Hoquiam (1990 nl)

Hamma Hamma Falls (u), Mount Skokomish (1990 nl)

Hatana Falls, Wellesley Peak (1990)

Heather Creek Falls (u), Mount Deception (1990 nl)

Herman Falls, Ellis Mtn (1984 ns)

Hoh Lake Falls (u), Bogachiel Peak (1950 nl)

Home Sweet Home Falls (u), Mount Steel (1990 nl)

Honeymoon Meadows Falls 1-3 (u), Mount Steel (1990 nl)

LaCrosse Falls (u), Mount Steel (1990 nl)

Lilliwaup Falls, Lilliwaup (1985)

Lower Hamma Hamma Falls (u), Mount Washington (1985 nl)

Martin Creek Falls (u), Mount Olympus (1990 nl)

Martins Falls (u), Mount Christie (1990 nl)

Marys Falls, Mount Angeles (1990 nl)

McKenna Falls, Wildcat Lake (1968)

Middle Martin Creek Falls (u), Mount Olympus (1990 nl)

Mineral Creek Falls (u), Owl Mtn (1990 nl)

Morse Creek Falls (u), Morse Creek (1985 nl)

Mount Skokomish Falls (u), Mount Skokomish (1990 nl)

Murphy Creek Falls (u), Quillayute Prairie (1982 nl)

Naselle Falls (u), Sweigiler Creek (1986 nl)

Pluvius Falls (u), Pluvius (1986 nl)

Rock Creek Falls, Malone (1986 ns)

Royal Creek Falls (u), Mount Deception (1990 nl)

Seattle Creek Falls (u), Mount Christie (1990 nl)

Service Falls, Mount Olympus (1990)

Skokomish Falls (u), Mount Tebo (1990 nl)

Upper Martin Creek Falls (u), Mount Olympus (1990 nl)

Upper Service Falls (u), Mount Olympus (1990 nl)

Upper Willapa Falls (u), Pluvius (1986 nl)

Vincent Creek Falls (u), Vance Creek (1990 nl)

Warkum Creek Falls (u), Hunger Mtn (1990 nl)

Wet Weather Falls (u), Mount Townsend (1990 nl)

White Creek Falls (u), Mount Steel (1990 nl)

Whitehorse Creek Falls (u), Mount Skokomish (1990 nl)

Willapa Falls, Pluvius (1986)

Mount Rainier Region, Washington

Affi Falls, Sunrise (1971)

Alice Falls, Mowich Lake (1971)

American Valley Falls (u), Cougar Lake (1988 nl)

Baker Point Falls (u), Sunrise (1971 nl)

Basaltic Falls, Mt Rainier East (1971)

Boulder Creek Falls (u), Chinook Pass (1987 nl)

Bumping River Falls (u), Bumping Lake (1988 nl)

Butter Creek Falls (u), Mt Rainier West (1971 nl)

Chimneys Falls (u), Chinook Pass (1987 nl)

Clear Fork Falls (u), Old Snowy Mtn (1988 nl)

Colonnade Falls (u), Mt Rainier West (1971 nl)

Crag Lake Falls (u), Cougar Lake (1988 nl)

Crescent Creek Falls (u), Mowich Lake (1971 nl)

Cress Falls, Mowich Lake (1971)

Denman Falls, Mount Wow (1971)

Devil Creek Falls, Cliffdell (1987)

Eagle Creek Falls (u), The Rockies (1993 nl)

East Basaltic Falls (u), Mt Rainier East (1971 nl)

East Canyon Creek Falls (u), Bearhead Mtn (1986 nl)

East Nickel Creek Falls (u), Mt Rainier East (1971 nl)

East Van Trump Falls (u), Mt Rainier West (1971 nl)

Ethania Falls, Mount Wow (1971)

Falls Creek Falls (u), Bearhead Mtn (1986 nl)

Fryingpan Creek Falls (u), Chinook Pass (1987 nl)

Garda Falls, Sunrise (1971)

Giant Falls, Mowich Lake (1971)

Goat Mountain Falls (u), Sunrise (1971 nl)

Helen Falls (u), Mount Wow (1971 nl)

Huckleberry Creek Falls (u), Sunrise (1971 nl)

Indian Creek Falls, Spiral Butte (1988 nl)

Jennings Falls, Packwood (1989 ns)

Jordan Basin Falls (u), Packwood Lake (1989 nl)

Kan Falls (u), Purcell Mtn (1989 nl)

Kautz Creek Falls (u), Mt Rainier West (1971 nl)

Larrupin Falls, Mount Wow (1971)

Laughingwater Creek Falls (u), Chinook Pass (1987 nl)

Lower Nickel Creek Falls (u), Mt Rainier East (1971 nl)

Lower Sunbeam Falls (u), Mt Rainier East (1971 nl)

Lower Van Trump Falls (u), Mt Rainier West (1971 nl)

Lower Williwakas Falls (u), Mt Rainier East (1971 nl)

Maple Falls, Mt Rainier East (1971)

Margaret Falls, Mt Rainier East (1971)

Marie Falls, Mt Rainier East (1971)

Mary Belle Falls, Mt Rainier East (1971)

Middle Boulder Creek Falls (u), Chinook Pass (1987 nl)

Middle Fork Lake Falls (u), Packwood Lake (1989 nl)

Middle Ohanapecosh Falls (u), Chinook Pass (1987 nl)

Middle Ohanapecosh Falls (u), Mt Rainier East (1971 nl)

Needle Creek Falls (u), Chinook Pass (1987 nl)

Nisqually Valley Falls (u), Mt Rainier West (1971 nl)

Ohanapecosh Park Falls 1-6 (u), Mt Rainier East (1971 nl)

Pearl Falls, Mt Rainier West (1971)

Saint Johns Falls, Chinook Pass (1987)

Skate Valley Falls (u), Wahpenayo Peak (1989 nl)

South Ohanapecosh Falls (u), Chinook Pass (1987 nl)

St Andrews Falls (u), Mount Wow (1971 nl)

Stevens Valley Falls (u), Mt Rainier East (1971 nl)

Sunbeam Falls, Mt Rainier East (1971)

Sunrise Falls (u), White River Park (1971 nl)

Tilton River Falls (u), The Rockies (1993 nl)

Trixie Falls, Mt Rainier East (1971)

Twin Falls, Mt Rainier East (1971)

Upper Boulder Creek Falls (u), Chinook Pass (1987 nl)

Upper Chimneys Falls (u), Chinook Pass (1987 nl)

Upper Clear Fork Falls (u), Old Snowy Mtn (1988 nl)

Upper Davis Creek Falls (u), Purcell Mtn (1989 nl)

Upper Eagle Creek Falls (u), The Rockies (1993 nl)

Upper Falls Creek Falls (u), Bearhead Mtn (1986 nl)

Upper Mesatchee Falls, Sawtooth Ridge (1989 nl)

Upper Middle Fork Falls (u), Packwood Lake (1989 nl)

Upper Ohanapechosh Falls (u), Mt Rainier East (1971 nl)

Upper Olallie Falls (u), Chinook Pass (1987 nl)

Upper South Fork Falls (u), Spiral Butte (1988 nl)

Upper St Andrews Falls (u), Mt Rainier West (1971 nl)

Upper Sunbeam Falls (u), Mt Rainier East (1971 nl)

Upper Van Horn Falls (u), Sunrise (1971 (nl)

Upper Voight Creek Falls (u), Wilkeson (1956 nl)

Upper Williwakas Falls (u), Mt Rainier East (1971 nl)

Vernal Park Falls (u), Sunrise (1971 nl)

Victor Falls, Sumner (1993)

Voight Creek Falls (u), Wilkeson (1956 nl)

Wauhaukaupauken Falls, Mt Rainier East (1971)

Wenas Creek Falls (u), Manastash Lake (1971 nl)

West Canyon Creek Falls (u), Bearhead Mtn (1986 nl)

West Nickel Creek Falls (u), Mt Rainier East (1971 nl)

West Ohanapecosh Falls (u), Chinook Pass (1987 nl)

West Van Trump Falls (u), Mt Rainier West (1971 nl)

Wildcat Falls, Lake Kapowsin (1987)

Gifford Pinchot Country, Washington

Bear Creek Falls (u), Elk Mtn (1983 nl)

Big Rock Falls (u), Siouxon Peak (1993 nl)

Big Spring Falls (u), Steamboat Mtn (1970 nl)

Canyon Valley Falls 1-3 (u), Siouxon Peak (1993 nl)

Cape Horn Creek Falls (u), Ariel (1994 nl)

Castile Falls, Castile Falls (1970)

Dry Creek Falls, Camas Patch (1965)

Hidden Falls, Dole (1986 nl)

Hidden Falls, Fairview Ridge (1987 nl)

Huckleberry Creek Falls (u), Walupt Lake (1970 nl)

Jakes Creek Falls (u), Siouxon Peak (1993 nl)

Klickitat Falls (u), Signal Peak (1970 nl)

Lake Corral Falls, Walupt Lake (1970 nl)

Little Niagara Falls, Quartz Creek Butte (1965)

Logy Creek Falls, Logy Creek Falls (1965)

Loowit Falls, Mount St Helens (1983 ns)

Lower Hellroaring Falls (u), Mount Adams East (1970 nl)

Lower Klickitat Falls (u), Signal Peak (1970 nl)

Lower Rattlesnake Falls (u), Camas Prairie (1983 nl)

McCall Basin Falls (u), Old Snowy Mtn (1988 nl)

North Fork Kalama Falls (u), Elk Mtn (1983 nl)

Paradise Falls, Smith Creek Butte (1983)

Rattlesnake Falls (u), Camas Prairie (1983 nl)

Rusk Creek Falls (u), Mount Adams East (1970 nl)

Salmon Falls, Yacolt (1990)

Smith Creek Falls (u), Smith Creek Butte (1983 nl)

Snagtooth Creek Falls (u), Quartz Creek Butte (1965 nl)

Trapper Creek Falls, Bare Mtn (1993 ns)

Upper Big Tree Creek Falls (u), Yale Dam (1986 ns)

Upper Lava Canyon Falls (u), Smith Creek Butte (1983 ns)

Upper Rusk Creek Falls (u), Mount Adams East (1970 nl)

Washboard Falls, Wolf Point (1984)

West Fork Falls (u), Windy Point (1970 nl)

West Smith Creek Falls (u), Smith Creek Butte (1983 nl)

The Inland Empire, Washington

Albeni Falls, Newport (1986 ns)

Buckeye Creek Falls (u), Chapman Lake (1980 nl)

Calispell Creek Falls (u), Sacheen Lake (1986 nl)

Crater Coulee Falls (u), Babcock Ridge (1966 nl)

Delzer Falls, Sullivan Lake (1968)

Flume Creek Falls (u), Boundary Dam (1986 nl)

Hompegg Falls, Eckler Mtn (1983)

Kettle Falls, Marcus (1969 ns)

Little Chamokane Falls, Wellpinit (1973)

Little Nespelem Falls (u), Armstrong Creek (1989 nl)

Martin Falls, Steamboat Rock SE (1968)

McLoughlin Falls, Keystone (1980)

Nine Mile Falls, Nine Mile Falls (1986 ns)

Ninemile Falls, Ninemile Flat (1985)

Reiser Falls, Sullivan Lake (1968)

Rickey Rapids, Bangs Mtn (1982 ns)

Sheep Creek Falls (u), Stentz Spring (1983 nl)

Towell Falls, Honn Lakes (1981)

Tucannon River Falls (u), Tucannon (1967 nl)

Weimer Creek Falls (u), Falling Springs (1981 nl)

Wilmont Creek Falls (u), Miller Mtn (1985 ns)

Wilson Creek Falls, Almira (1969)

The Columbia Gorge, Washington/ Oregon

Celilo Falls, Stacker Butte (1965 ns)

Divers Creek Falls (u), Dee (1994 nl)

Eagle Tanner Falls (u), Wahtum Lake (1979 nl)

East Fork Falls (u), Wahtum Lake (1979 nl)

Falls Creek Falls (u), Tanner Butte (1994 nl)

Four Mile Falls (u), Tanner Butte (1994 nl)

Greenleaf Falls (u), Bonneville Dam (1994 nl)

Greenleaf Peak Falls (u), Bonneville Dam (1994 nl)

Lindsey Creek Falls (u), Mount Defiance (1994 nl)

Middle Four Mile Falls (u), Wahtum Lake (1979 nl)

Middle Ruckel Creek Falls (u), Bonneville Dam (1994 nl)

Middle Tanner Creek Falls (u), Tanner Butte (1994 nl)

Mile Five Falls (u), Dee (1994 nl)

Mill Creek Falls, Brown Creek (1994)

Moffett Falls, Tanner Butte (1994 nl)

North Benson Falls (u), Wahtum Lake (1979 nl)

North Fork Falls (u), Lookout Mtn (1986 nl)

Opal Creek Falls (u), Tanner Butte (1994 nl)

Rock Falls (u), White Salmon (1978 nl)

Slide Creek Falls (u), Carson (1994 nl)

Sorenson Creek Falls (u), Bonneville Dam (1994 nl)

Summit Creek Falls (u), Mount Defiance (1994 nl)

The Dalles, The Dalles South (1994 ns)

Tish Creek Falls (u), Tanner Butte (1994 nl)

Upper Bridal Veil Falls (u), Bridal Veil (1994 nl)

Upper Dog Creek Falls (u), Mount Defiance (1994 nl)

Upper Falls Creek Falls (u), Tanner Butte (1994 nl)

Upper Four Mile Falls (u), Wahtum Lake (1979 nl)

Upper Greenleaf Falls (u), Bonneville Dam (1994 nl)

Upper Moffett Falls (u), Tanner Butte (1994 nl)

Upper Opal Creek Falls (u), Tanner Butte (1994 nl)

Upper Ruckel Creek Falls (u), Bonneville Dam (1994 nl)

Upper Tanner Creek Falls (u), Tanner Butte (1994 nl)

Upper Tenas Falls (u), Tanner Butte (1994 nl)

Upper Wauna Falls (u), Tanner Butte (1994 nl)

Upper West Branch Falls (u), Tanner Butte (1994 nl)

Wahe Falls, Tanner Butte (1994)

Waucoma North Falls (u), Wahtum Lake (1979 nl)

Waucoma South Falls (u), Wahtum Lake (1979 nl)

West Branch Falls (u), Tanner Butte (1994 nl)

West Fork Falls (u), Husum (1994 nl)

Woodward Falls (u), Beacon Rock (1994 nl)

Northern Coast Range, Oregon

Baker Creek Falls, Fairdale (1979)

Barth Falls, Green Mtn (1977)

Berry Creek Falls, Falls City (1974)

Boulder Creek Falls (u), Warnicke Creek (1974 nl)

Burton Creek Falls (u), Springer Mtn (1979 nl)

Camp Creek Falls (u), Laurel Mtn (1974 nl)

Carcus Creek Falls (u), Baker Point (1979 nl)

Central Line Creek Falls (u), Warnicke Creek (1974 nl)

Chitwood Falls, Neskowin (1985 ns)

Clatskanie Falls (u), Delena (1985 nl)

Crowley Mine Falls (u), Warnicke Creek (1974 nl)

Cruiser Creek Falls (u), Gobblers Knob (1979 nl)

East Crowley Forks Falls (u), Warnicke Creek (1974 nl)

East Rock Valley Falls (u), Warnicke Creek (1974 nl)

Echo Falls, Devils Lake (1984)

Euchre Falls, Euchre Mtn (1984)

Far Rock Creek Falls (u), Warnicke Creek (1974 nl)

Gilbert Creek Falls (u), Springer Mtn (1979 nl)

Gnat Creek Falls, Nicolai Mtn (1985)

Haines Falls, Turner Creek (1979)

Jackson Falls, Hillsboro (1990)

Kilchis Falls, Cedar Butte (1984)

Lava Creek Falls (u), Baker Point (1979 nl)

Lee Creek Falls (u), Turner Creek (1979 nl)

Little Boulder Creek Falls (u), Warnicke Creek (1974 nl)

Little Luckiamute Falls (u), Fanno Ridge (1974 nl)

Lower Rock Creek Falls (u), Midway (1979 nl)

Maple Valley Falls (u), Gobblers Knob (1979 nl)

Martin Falls, Newport North (1984 ns)

Middle Rock Creek Falls (u), Warnicke Creek (1974 nl)

Mill Creek Falls (u), Laurel Mtn (1974 nl)

Nenamusa Falls, Springer Mtn (1979 ns)

North Fork Falls, Hamlet (1984 nl)

Rock Creek Falls (u), Midway (1979 nl)

Silver Falls, Laurel Mtn (1974)

Slide Mountain Falls (u), Fairdale (1979 nl)
Upper Lee Creek Falls (u), Turner Creek (1979 nl)
Upper Rock Creek Falls (u), Warnicke Creek (1974 nl)
Valsetz Falls, Valsetz (1974 ns)
Warnicke Creek Falls (u), Warnicke Creek (1974 nl)
Warnicke Valley Falls (u), Warnicke Creek (1974 nl)
West Crowley Forks Falls (u), Warnicke Creek (1974 nl)
West Rock Valley Falls (u), Warnicke Creek (1974 nl)
Wheelock Creek Falls (u), Tidewater (1984 nl)
Wilson Falls, Jordan Creek (1984 ns)

Southern Coast Range, Oregon
Beulah Creek Falls (u), Ivers Peak (1990 nl)
Bone Mountain Falls (u), Rasler Creek (1990 nl)
Brewster Canyon Falls (u), Mount Gurney (1990 nl)
Briggs Creek Falls (u), Chrome Ridge (1989 nl)
Brummit Valley Falls (u), Sitkum (1990 nl)
Camas Creek Falls (u), Kenyon Mtn (1990 nl)
Camp Creek Falls (u), Old Blue (1990 nl)
Cascade Falls, Five Rivers (1984 ns)
Cedar Valley Falls (u), Callahan (1990 nl)
Coal Creek Falls (u), Eden Valley (1990 nl)
Coal Valley Falls 1-4 (u), Eden Valley (1990 nl)
Cole Creek Falls (u), Rasler Creek (1990 nl)
Coos Valley Falls (u), Coos Mtn (1990 nl)
Darius Creek Falls (u), Golden Falls (1990 nl)
Dulog Falls, Kelsey Peak (1989 ns)
East Indigo Creek Falls (u), Hobson Horn (1989 nl)
East Millicoma Falls (u), Ivers Peak (1990 nl)
Elk Creek Falls (u), Eden Valley (1990 nl)
Elk Creek Falls (u), Ivers Peak (1990 nl)
Estell Falls, Allegany (1971 ns)
Fall Creek Falls (u), Biscuit Hill (1989 nl)
Fall Creek Falls (u), Cedar Creek (1990 nl)
Fall Creek Falls (u), Rasler Creek (1990 nl)
Fish Hatchery Falls (u), Alsea (1985 nl)
Hamilton Falls (u), Sitkum (1990 nl)
Henrys Falls, Allegany (1971)
Hewett Falls, Golden Falls (1990)

Hubbard Creek Falls (u), Callahan (1990 nl)
Kelsey Falls, Kelsey Peak (1989 ns)
Little Dixie Creek Falls (u), Barklow Mtn (1986 nl)
Little Matson Falls (u), Golden Falls (1990 nl)
Lost Creek Falls, Mount Gurney (1990)
Lost Valley Falls (u), Mount Gurney (1990 nl)
Lower Black Bar Falls, Bunker Creek (1989)
Lower Elk Creek Falls (u), Ivers Peak (1990 nl)
Matson Creek Falls (u), Golden Falls (1990 nl)
Middle Creek Falls, McKinley (1971 ns)
Millicoma Falls (u), Ivers Peak (1990 nl)
Myrtle Creek Falls (u), Rasler Creek (1990 nl)
North Fork Elk Falls (u), Eden Valley (1990 nl)
North Silver Creek Falls (u), Hobson Horn (1989 nl)
Pidgeon Falls, Allegany (1971)
Rock Creek Falls (u), Kenyon Mtn (1990 nl)
Rock Valley Falls (u), Rasler Creek (1990 nl)
Schoolmarm Creek Falls (u), Galice (1989 nl)
Scottsburg Falls (u), Scottsburg (1985)
Secret Creek Falls (u), Onion Mtn (1989 nl)
Silver Falls, York Butte (1989)
Stulls Falls, Elk Peak (1985)
Surprise Creek Falls (u), Loon Lake (1985 nl)
Taylor Creek Falls, Onion Mtn (1989)
Upper Black Bar Falls, Bunker Creek (1989)
Upper Brummit Valley Falls (u), Sitkum (1990 nl)
Upper Elk Creek Falls (u), Eden Valley (1990 nl)
Upper Fall Creek Falls (u), Cedar Creek (1990 nl)
Upper Fall Creek Falls (u), Rasler Creek (1990 nl)
Upper Little Matson Falls (u), Golden Falls (1990 nl)
Upper Matson Falls (u), Golden Falls (1990 nl)
Upper Rock Creek Falls (u), Camas Valley (1990 nl)

Upper Rock Valley Falls (u), Rasler Creek (1990 nl)

West Millicoma Falls (u), Ivers Peak (1990 nl)

The Middle Cascades, Oregon

Abiqua Falls, Elk Prairie (1985)

Ayers Falls, Lyons (1985)

Bald Peter Creek Falls (u), Keel Mtn (1984 nl)

Battle Ax Creek Falls (u), Battle Ax (1985 nl)

Bear Valley Falls (u), Upper Soda (1985 nl)

Bonnie Creek Falls (u), Keel Mtn (1984 nl)

Boundary Creek Falls (u), Swamp Mtn (1989 nl)

Cascade Falls, Farmers Butte (1988 nl)

Cascade Falls, Yellowstone Mtn (1985)

Cedar Creek Falls (u), Sweet Home (1984 nl)

Compass Creek Falls (u), Mount Hood South (1980 nl)

Cougar Creek Falls (u), Upper Soda (1985 nl)

Crabtree Creek Falls (u), Yellowstone Mtn (1985 nl)

Crabtree Valley Falls (u), Keel Mtn (1984 nl)

Dan Falls (u), Elkhorn (1985 ns)

Dave Falls (u), Elkhorn (1985 ns)

Deadman Creek Falls (u), Keel Mtn (1984 nl)

Deanna's Slide (u), Elkhorn (1985 ns)

Drift Creek Falls, Drake Crossing (1985)

East Coe Branch Falls (u), Mount Hood South (1980 nl)

Evans Creek Falls (u), Elkhorn (1985 ns)

Fall Creek Falls, Elk Prairie (1985)

Falls Creek Falls (u), Upper Soda (1985 nl)

Final Falls, High Rock (1985)

French Basin Falls 1-4 (u), Battle Ax (1985 nl)

Frustration Falls, High Rock (1985)

Gatch Falls, Marion Lake (1993 ns)

Hall Creek Falls (u), Mill City South (1985 nl)

Hamilton Creek Falls (u), Lacomb (1984 nl)

Hideaway Falls, High Rock (1985)

Homestead Creek Falls (u), Elk Prairie (1985 nl)

Horseshoe Falls, Lyons (1985)

Husky Creek Falls (u), Upper Soda (1985 nl)

Indian Prairie Falls (u), Snow Peak (1985 nl)

Jackie Falls (u), Elkhorn (1985 ns)

Jerry Falls (u), Elkhorn (1985 ns)

Little Niagara Falls, High Rock (1985 ns)

Lower Falls Creek Falls (u), Upper Soda (1985 nl)

Lower Gooch Falls (u), Marion Forks (1988 nl)

Lower Rock Creek Falls (u), Keel Mtn (1984 nl)

Mark Falls (u), Elkhorn (1985 ns)

McDowell Creek Falls (u), Sweet Home (1984 nl)

McNabb Falls, Chimney Peak (1984)

Middle Falls Creek Falls (u), Upper Soda (1985 nl)

Middle Moose Mtn Falls (u), Upper Soda (1985 nl)

Middle Rock Creek Falls (u), Keel Mtn (1984 nl)

Moose Creek Falls, Cascadia (1985 ns)

Moose Lake Falls (u), Upper Soda (1985 nl)

Moose Mountain Falls (u), Upper Soda (1985 nl)

Moose Valley Falls (u), Yellowstone Mtn (1985 nl)

Neal Creek Falls (u), Snow Peak (1985 nl)

Panther Creek Falls (u), Yellowstone Mtn (1985 nl)

Pencil Falls, Mount Hood South (1980 nl)

Polallie Creek Falls (u), Mount Hood South (1980 nl)

Pup Creek Falls, Three Lynx (1985 ns)

Puzzle Creek Falls (u), Marion Forks (1988 nl)

Ron Falls (u), Elkhorn (1985 ns)

Sandy River Falls (u), Government Camp (1980 nl)

Sardine Creek Falls (u), Elkhorn (1985 nl)

Scott Creek Falls (u), Lacomb (1984 nl)

Shot Pouch Creek Falls (u), Green Peter (1984 nl)

Shower Creek Falls, Bagby Hot Springs (1985 ns)

Split Falls, Wolf Peak (1985)

Stein Falls, Wolf Peak (1985)

Steve Falls (u), Elkhorn (1985 ns)

Stout Creek Falls, Lyons (1985 nl)

Tally Creek Falls (u), Upper Soda (1985 nl)

Trinity Falls, Elk Prairie (1985 ns)

Trout Creek Falls (u), Upper Soda (1985 nl)

Upper Battle Ax Cr Falls (u), Battle Ax (1985 nl)

Upper Compass Creek Falls (u), Mount Hood South (1980 nl)

Upper Downing Creek Falls (u), Marion Forks (1988 nl)

Upper Eagle Creek Falls, Cherryville (1985 ns)

Upper Falls Creek Falls (u), Upper Soda (1985 nl)

Upper Husky Creek Falls (u), Upper Soda (1985 nl)

Upper Moose Creek Falls (u), Upper Soda (1985 nl)

Upper Moose Lake Falls (u), Upper Soda (1985 nl)

Upper Moose Mtn Falls (u), Upper Soda (1985 nl)

Upper Rock Creek Falls (u), Keel Mtn (1984 nl)

Upper Soda Falls, Cascadia (1985)

Upper Tally Creek Falls (u), Upper Soda (1985 nl)

Upper West Fork Falls (u), Keel Mtn (1984 nl)

Vanishing Falls, High Rock (1985)

West Coe Branch Falls (u), Mount Hood South (1980 nl)

West Fork Falls (u), Keel Mtn (1984 nl)

West Fork Falls (u), Snow Peak (1985 nl)

West Fork Valley Falls (u), Yellowstone Mtn (1985 nl)

Whitcomb Creek Falls (u), Keel Mtn (1984 nl)

Wiley Creek Falls (u), Swamp Mtn (1989 nl)

Wiley Valley Falls (u), Swamp Mtn (1989 nl)

Wizard Falls, Candle Creek (1988)

The South Cascades, Oregon

Button Creek Falls (u), Sugarpine (1989 nl)

Cascade Creek Falls (u), Hamaker Butte (1985 nl)

Chocolate Falls, Mount Ashland (1983)

Coal Valley Falls (u), Staley Ridge (1986 nl)

Duwee Falls, Union Peak (1985)

Emigrant Creek Falls (u), Siskiyou Pass (1983 nl)

Emile Falls, Mace Mtn (1989)

Fall Creek Falls (u), Sinker Mtn (1986 nl)

Far Upper Falls (u), Hamaker Butte (1985 nl)

Fir Creek Falls (u), Warner Mtn (1986 nl)

Flat Creek Falls (u), Sugarpine (1989 nl)

Gold Basin Falls (u), Sinker Mtn (1986 nl)

Grouse Mountain Falls, Bearbones Mtn (1986)

Honey Creek Falls, Substitute Point (1988)

Indian Holes Falls, South Sister (1988)

Linton Falls, Linton Lake (1988)

Logan Creek Falls (u), Sinker Mtn (1986 nl)

Lower South Fork Falls (u), Trout Creek Butte (1988 nl)

Lower Squaw Creek Falls (u), Trout Creek Butte (1988 nl)

Mesa Creek Falls (u), South Sister (1988 nl)

Middle Fork Falls (u), Waldo Mtn (1986 nl)

Mile 44 Falls (u), Old Fairview (1989 nl)

Mosquito Valley Falls (u), French Mtn (1989 nl)

Obsidian Falls, North Sister (1988)

Park Creek Falls (u), Trout Creek Butte (1988 nl)

PK Creek Falls (u), Sinker Mtn (1986 nl)

Separation Creek Falls (u), South Sister (1988 nl)

Shadow Creek Falls (u), Linton Lake (1988 nl)

Squaw Creek Falls, Trout Creek Butte (1988)

Upper Fir Creek Falls (u), Warner Mtn (1986 nl)

Upper Fork Falls (u), Waldo Mtn (1986 nl)

Upper Mesa Creek Falls (u), South Sister (1988 nl)

Upper Separation Cr Falls (u), South Sister (1988 nl)

Upper South Fork Falls (u), Trout Creek Butte (1988 nl)

Upper Susan Creek Falls (u), Old Fairview (1989 nl)

Verdun Rock Falls 1-3 (u), Mt David Douglas (1986 nl)

Youngs Creek Falls (u), Warner Mtn (1986 nl)

The Columbia Plateau, Oregon

Awbrey Falls, Tumalo (1962)

Big Falls, Cline Falls (1962)

Bogus Creek Falls (u), Lambert Rocks (1972 nl)

Buck Falls, Chapin Creek (1983)

Chapman Hollow Falls (u), Macken Canyon (1970 nl)

Chloride Falls (u), Bourne (1984 nl)

Copper Creek Falls, Bennet Peak (1990)

Deep Creek Falls (u), Fingerboard Saddle (1990 nl)

East Fork Falls, Cornucopia (1990)

Fall Creek Falls (u), Dog Lake (1980 nl)

Fall Creek Falls (u), Mount Vernon (1983 nl)

Falls of Sycan River 1-6 (u), Spodue Mtn (1988 nl)

Far Tumalo Falls (u), Tumalo Falls (1988 nl)

Glutton Falls, Hardman (1969)

Groundhog Falls, Whitehorse Butte (1980)

Horseshoe Falls, Harmony (1971)

Imnaha Falls, Deadman Point (1990)

John Henry Falls (u), North Minam Meadows (1990 nl)

Kettle Creek Falls, Krag Peak (1990 nl)

Klamath Falls, Klamath Falls (1985)

Lilyville Falls (u), North Minam Meadows (1990 ns)

Little Willow Creek Falls (u), Ladycomb Peak (1981 nl)

Loveless Creek Falls (u), Crooked Creek Valley (1964 nl)

Lower Falls, Committee Creek (1983)

Lower Falls Little Minam River, Mount Fanny (1993 ns)

Meadow Brooks Falls, Dale (1990)

Middle Sycan River Falls (u), Spodue Mtn (1988 nl)

Minam Falls, Jim White Ridge (1993 ns)

Murray Creek Falls (u), Chief Joseph Mtn (1990 nl)

North Fork Falls (u), Bourne (1984 nl)

North Fork Wolf Falls (u), Tucker Flat (1984 nl)

Odin Falls, Cline Falls (1962)

Pine Hollow Falls (u), Macken Canyon (1970 nl)

Pine Lakes Falls (u), Cornucopia (1990 nl)

Rock Creek Falls (u), Bourne (1984 nl)

Silver Creek Falls (u), Chief Joseph Mtn (1990 nl)

Slide Falls, Strawberry Mtn (1988 nl)

Squaw Falls, Elbow Creek (1983)

Steelhead Falls, Steelhead Falls (1985)

Strawberry Falls, Strawberry Mtn (1988)

The Water Fall, Hoppin Springs (1982 nl)

Thompson Falls, Thompson Flat (1983)

Tumwater Falls, Quinton (1971 ns)

Upper Falls, Keys Creek (1985)

Upper Falls Deschutes River, Benham Falls (1981 ns)

Upper Rock Creek Falls (u), Bourne (1984 nl)

Upper Sycan River Falls (u), Spodue Mtn (1988 nl)

Waterfalls Hollow Falls (u), Wolf Hollow Falls (1970 nl)

West Fork Falls (u), Cornucopia (1990 nl)

Wolf Hollow Falls, Wolf Hollow Falls (1970)

The Panhandle, Idaho

Caribou Falls, Caribou Creek (1969)

Chute Creek Falls (u), Gleason Mtn (1986 nl)

Cooper Gulch Falls (u), Thompson Pass (1988 nl)

Fern Falls, Pond Peak (1966 ns)

Hellroaring Creek Falls (u), Colburn (1968 nl)

Johnson Creek Falls (u), Clark Fork (1989 nl)

Kalispell Falls, Gleason Mtn (1986)

LaSota Falls, Helmer Mtn (1986)

McAbee Falls, Prater Mtn (1967)

Rambiker Falls, Illinois Peak (1988)

Shadow Falls, Pond Peak (1966 ns)

Snow Creek Falls, Moravia (1965 nl)

Tumbledown Falls, Conrad Peak (1988 ns)

Central Wilderness Areas, Idaho

Bear Creek Falls, Rocky Comfort Flat (1986)

Benton Creek Falls (u), Sturgill Creek (1987 nl)

Bimerick Falls, McLendon Butte (1966 nl)

Boulder Falls (u), Galena Peak (1970 nl)Bridal Veil Falls, Stanley Lake (1972)

Dead Elk Creek Falls (u), Jeanette Mtn (1966 nl)

Devlin Falls, Leesburg (1989)

East Pass Creek Falls (u), Meridian Peak (1967 nl)

Falls Creek Falls (u), House Mtn (1973 nl)

Forge Creek Falls (u), Yellowjacket (1963 nl)

Gold Fork Falls (u), Sloans Point 1988 nl)

Hazard Falls, Indian Mtn (1963)

Hoodoo Creek Falls (u), Big Cedar (1966 nl)

Lower Rush Falls (u), Rush Peak (1986 nl)

Mallard Creek Falls, Whitewater Ranch (1987)

Patsy Ann Falls, Tin Cup Lake (1991)

Rush Falls, Rush Peak (1986)

Salmon Falls, Devils Teeth Rapids (1978)
Scenic Creek Falls (u), Nahneke Mtn (1972 nl)
Sixmile Creek Falls (u), Boiling Springs (1988 nl)
Slippy Creek Falls (u), McKinzie Creek (1963 nl)
Smith Falls, Warbonnet Peak (1972)
Tappen Falls, Bear Creek Point (1962 ns)
Trail Creek Falls, Rock Roll Canyon (1967 nl)
Upper Goat Creek Falls (u), Warbonnet Peak (1972 nl)
Upper Sixmile Creek Falls (u), Sixmile Point (1988 nl)
Veil Falls, Puddin Mtn (1962 ns)
Velvet Falls, Big Soldier Mtn (1990)
Wildhorse Falls, Cuddy Mtn (1987)

The Snake River Plain, Idaho
Albright Falls, Trischman Knob (1986 ns)
Austin Butte Falls (u), Austin Butte (1980 nl)
Boundary Creek Falls (u), Buffalo Lake (1986 nl)
Boundary Valley Falls (u), Buffalo Lake (1986 nl)
Camel Falls, Wagon Box Basin (1973)
Cascade Acres, Grassy Lake Reservoir (1989)
Clover Creek Falls (u), King Hill (1986 nl)
Colonnade Falls, Cave Falls (1989)
Crane Falls (historical), Bruneau (1992 ns)
Dunanda Falls, Bechler Falls (1989)
Falls River Falls (u), Cave Falls (1989 nl)

Gwinna Falls, Trischman Knob (1986)
Houtz Creek Falls (u), Stump Peak (1980 nl)
Iris Falls, Cave Falls (1989)
Lower Boundary Creek Falls (u), Bechler Falls (1989 nl)
Lower Cave Falls (u), Cave Falls (1989 nl)
Morning Falls (u), Cave Falls (1989 nl)
Ouzel Falls, Cave Falls (1989)
Phantom Falls, Mahogany Butte (1977 nl)
Quiver Cascade, Trischman Knob (1986)
Ragged Falls, Trischman Knob (1986)
Rainbow Falls, Cave Falls (1989)
Rainbow Falls, Palisades Peak (1966 ns)
Robinson Creek Falls, Bechler Falls (1989 nl)
Ross Falls, Pike Mtn (1978 ns)
Silver Scarf Falls, Bechler Falls (1989)
Sinking Canyon Falls (u), Balanced Rock (1992 nl)
Sluiceway Falls, Trischman Knob (1986)
Swan Falls, Sinker Butte (1992 ns)
Tendoy Falls, Trischman Knob (1986)
Terraced Falls, Grassy Lake Reservoir (1989)
The Falls, Auburn (1980)
The Falls, Sugarloaf (1972)
Union Falls, Grassy Lake Reservoir (1989)
Upper Morning Falls (u), Cave Falls (1989 nl)
Wahhi Falls, Trischman Knob (1986)
Winter Camp Falls (u), Austin Butte (1980 nl)
Zeno Falls (u), Hill Pasture (1972 ns)

INDEX

Page numbers in *italics* indicate photographs.

ABOUT THE AUTHOR

Greg Plumb is a geographer who has spent over twenty years driving and hiking tens of thousands of spray-soaked miles to document waterfalls throughout the United States. Currently an Oklahoma resident, he continues to take expeditions to the Pacific Northwest to update his database and seek out the seemingly never-ending number of cataracts in the region. Greg is an Associate Professor and Chair of the Department of Cartography and Geography at East Central University *(www.ecok.edu/)* and does statistical mapping and analysis as owner of Personalized Map Company *(www.mymaps.com)*. He is also the author of *Waterfalls of Tennessee*.

Author at Big Creek Falls, Taylor River, North Cascades
(photo by Corey Gillum)

THE MOUNTAINEERS, founded in 1906, is a nonprofit outdoor activity and conservation club, whose mission is "to explore, study, preserve, and enjoy the natural beauty of the outdoors. . . . " Based in Seattle, Washington, the club is now one of the largest such organizations in the United States, with seven branches throughout Washington State.

The Mountaineers sponsors both classes and year-round outdoor activities in the Pacific Northwest, which include hiking, mountain climbing, ski-touring, snowshoeing, bicycling, camping, kayaking, nature study, sailing, and adventure travel. The club's conservation division supports environmental causes through educational activities, sponsoring legislation, and presenting informational programs.

All club activities are led by skilled, experienced instructors, who are dedicated to promoting safe and responsible enjoyment and preservation of the outdoors.

If you would like to participate in these organized outdoor activities or the club's programs, consider a membership in The Mountaineers. For information and an application, write The Mountaineers, Club Headquarters, 7700 Sandpoint Way NE, Seattle, WA 98115. You can also visit the club's website at www.mountaineers.org or contact The Mountaineers via email at clubmail@mountaineers.org.

The Mountaineers Books, an active, nonprofit publishing program of the club, produces guidebooks, instructional texts, historical works, natural history guides, and works on environmental conservation. All books produced by The Mountaineers Books fulfill the club's mission.

Send or call for our catalog of more than 500 outdoor titles:

The Mountaineers Books
1001 SW Klickitat Way, Suite 201
Seattle, WA 98134
800-553-4453

mbooks@mountaineersbooks.org
www.mountaineersbooks.org

The Mountaineers Books is proud to be a corporate sponsor of The Leave No Trace Center for Outdoor Ethics, whose mission is to promote and inspire responsible outdoor recreation through education, research, and partnerships. The Leave No Trace program is focused specifically on human-powered (nonmotorized) recreation.

Leave No Trace strives to educate visitors about the nature of their recreational impacts, as well as offer techniques to prevent and minimize such impacts. Leave No Trace is best understood as an educational and ethical program, not as a set of rules and regulations.

For more information, visit www.lnt.org, or call 800-332-4100.

OTHER TITLES YOU MIGHT ENJOY FROM
THE MOUNTAINEERS BOOKS

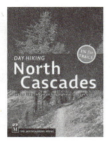

Day Hiking North Cascades
Craig Romano
Discover the beauty of the North Cascades on a short day hike or an extended trip!

Day Hiking Central Cascades
Craig Romano; photography by Alan L. Bauer
"Romano is one of the better guidebook writers around . . . "
—*Seattle P-I*

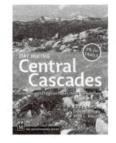

Day Hiking South Cascades
Dan A. Nelson; photography by Alan L. Bauer
Remote, pristine trails in rugged volcano country

Day Hiking Snoqualmie Region
Dan A. Nelson; photography by Alan L. Bauer
Great hikes—done in a day!

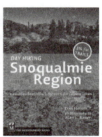
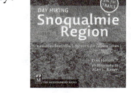

Day Hiking Olympic Peninsula
Craig Romano
" . . . covers a lot of territory that other guidebooks have passed up"
—*Seattle P-I*

Day Hiking Mount Rainier
Dan A. Nelson; photography by Alan L. Bauer
"A marvelous new guide to day hikes around the great Northwest mountain; detailed maps, elevation charts, and photos add to the guide's essential character."
—*Seattle P-I*

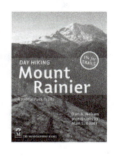

Day Hiking Oregon Coast
Bonnie Henderson
"It makes sense to pack *Day Hiking Oregon Coast* if you are planning a trip to the ocean."
—*The Bend Bulletin*

The Mountaineers Books has more than 500 outdoor recreation titles in print.
Receive a free catalog at
www.mountaineersbooks.org.